METROPOLITAN PHOENIX

METROPOLITAN PORTRAITS

Metropolitan Portraits explores the contemporary metropolis in its

diverse blend of past and present. Each volume describes a North

American urban region in terms of historic experience, spatial con-

figuration, culture, and contemporary issues. Books in the series

are intended to promote discussion and understanding of metro-

politan North America at the start of the twenty-first century.

JUDITH A. MARTIN, SERIES EDITOR

METROPOLITAN

PHOENIX

Place Making and Community Building in the Desert

PATRICIA GOBER

Maps by Barbara Trapido-Lurie

University of Pennsylvania Press | Philadelphia

10 9 8 7 6 5 4 3 2 1

Published by

University of Pennsylvania Press

Philadelphia, Pennsylvania 19104–4112

Library of Congress Cataloging-in-Publication Data

Gober, Patricia.

Metropolitan Phoenix : place making and community building in the desert /
Patricia Gober ; maps by Barbara Trapido-Lurie.

    p.   cm.— (Metropolitan portraits)

    Includes bibliographical references and index.

    ISBN-13 : 978-0-8122-3899-0 (cloth : alk. paper)

    ISBN-10 : 0-8122-3899-0 (cloth : alk. paper)

    ISBN-13 : 978-0-8122-1927-2 (paper : alk. paper)

    ISBN-10 : 0-8122-1927-2 (paper : alk. paper)

    1. Phoenix Metropolitan Area (Ariz.)—Social conditions.   2. Phoenix
Metropolitan Area (Ariz.)—Economic conditions.   3. Phoenix (Ariz.)—History.
I. Trapido-Lurie, Barbara. II. Title. III. Series

HN80.P53 G63 2005

979.1'73—dc22   2005047161

CONTENTS

Foreword, Judith A. Martin   ix

1   Desert Urbanization   1

2   Building a Desert City   11

3   An Ever-Changing Social Dynamic   53

4   You Can Never Get Hurt in Dirt   101

5   Not Another LA!   139

6   Downtown Redevelopment: A Tale of Two Cities   169

7   Thinking Small and Living Big   201

Notes   209

Index   225

Acknowledgments   233

F O R E W O R D
Judith A. Martin

Pat Gober's *Metropolitan Phoenix: Place Making and Community Building in the Desert*, the fourth volume in the Metropolitan Portraits Series, is one book I've really been waiting for. Like the three companion volumes on Portland, Boston, and San Diego, *Metropolitan Phoenix* seeks to portray the *entire* metropolitan region in a compact and vibrant fashion. Having first "met" Phoenix in 1977, I found it superficially dissimilar from most other cities—except for its great big street grid, which comfortably mimicked Chicago's. I've returned many times, and now know that, despite cacti and lizards, Phoenix shares many common metropolitan challenges. Still, despite increasing familiarity, I've been waiting a very long time for a "good read" about the Phoenix region. Pat Gober's careful attention to her long-time home offers that and more.

Gober here illuminates contemporary Phoenix through a historical, spatial, and environmental lens. She shares with the reader an informed sense of the region's diverse population, its vast ambitions, and its ongoing accommodation to its desert surroundings, with Frank Lloyd Wright, Carl Hayden, and Barry Goldwater in supporting roles. From its ancient Hohokam origins, to Del Webb's Fourth Sun City, to the international airport on the Salt River floodplain, the story of creating Phoenix incorporates gems of urban ingenuity and folly in equal measure. A dedicated car city now building several major light rail spines; potentially more than six million residents by 2050; New Urbanist projects on the desert fringe—in describing these, Gober asks: is the form of contemporary Phoenix sustainable without shifts in behavior *and* attitude?

Gober portrays a maturing Phoenix region dramatically transformed over the past four decades, spreading throughout the Valley of the Sun in all directions. It has taken in well over a million migrants from the rest of the country and from Mexico, plus hundreds of thousands of seasonal snowbirds, all the while humming "we are not LA." It has exchanged cotton fields for high tech manufacturing. Parts of greater Phoenix display creative methods to address intermittent flash floods, creating significant recreational possibilities at Indian Bend Wash and along the canals. It might surprise outsiders to recognize that "new" Phoenix is generally denser than the older neighborhoods of single-family homes surrounded by grass—or to recognize that desert landscaping is increasingly the norm everywhere. As elsewhere, downtown vitality has challenged Phoenix. Gober highlights the sports stadia-convention center path toward renewal chosen by Phoenix and contrasts it with Tempe's chosen residential-entertainment-lifestyle path. She also transports the reader to Scottsdale, Chandler, Gilbert, and Mesa, each with its own character amid the ever present sprawling desert landscape.

Finally, *Metropolitan Phoenix* questions the region's future, positing an imminent need to really discover how to coexist in a dry and fragile ecosystem while continuing to grow. This book will frame public debate, and will surely become a necessary resource for Valley newcomers. And with a chapter called "You Can Never Get Hurt in Dirt," how can anyone honestly not be intrigued?

C H A P T E R O N E

Desert Urbanization

The mythical phoenix fire bird rising from the ashes of a previous civilization is an apt metaphor for modern Phoenix. The spiritual core of Phoenix is about starting over, wiping the slate clean, freedom from the familiar, and the excitement and challenge of migration. The collective identity eschews the past and looks to the future. Asked to describe Phoenix to the people he grew up with in Pittsburgh, local columnist E. J. Montini noted that Phoenix is a place you move to; Pittsburgh is a place you bring with you. It's easy to be a stranger in Phoenix because everyone is from someplace else.[1] Established traditions are few and the larger sense of community is weak, but in Phoenix there is the opportunity to put aside the bonds of convention, conforming expectations and obligations, and fashion a new life.

This sense of beginning again and building anew has been deeply embedded in wave after wave of human migration to the region. The first settlers were prehistoric Hohokam farmers who constructed more than 1,000 miles of irrigation canals to support a complex civilization estimated to have peaked at 40,000 people. The Hohokam disappeared after A.D. 1450, and the region was largely unoccupied until Euro-American farmers transformed a desolate, isolated, dryland river valley into an agricultural paradise at the end of the nineteenth century. Asthmatics and arthritis and tuberculosis sufferers—so-called health seekers—arrived early in the twentieth century in the hopes of leading more vigorous and productive lives in the warm, desert climate of central Arizona. World War II veterans, many of whom trained at the region's military camps and flight-training facilities, returned after the war with their families to work in emerging electronics and defense industries, go to college, and start new lives. The postwar period also drew a new generation of the elderly who came to see retirement, not as slow decline, but as a new, liberating phase of life by escaping to retirement communities on the perimeter of Phoenix. The concept later was popularized and delivered to a mass market in Sun City. Critical to this process, and far more important than a sunny climate and affordable housing, was the opportunity to participate in a radical social experiment called "active retirement." The idea of Phoenix as a new kind of place and a place to start over continues to draw migrants. Tens of thousands of domestic migrants and Mexican immigrants—both legal and illegal—vote with their feet annually and move to Phoenix in search of work, a place to retire, the beauty of the desert, affordable housing, an outdoor lifestyle, and a better future for themselves and their families.

Few people embody this wipe-the-slate-clean, futurist ethic more than Del Webb, founder of Sun City. Born in Fresno, California, in 1899, Delbert Eugene Webb dropped out of school to work in construction and play minor-league baseball. He contracted typhoid fever and, after being confined to bed for more than a year, gave up baseball and moved to Phoenix for his health. After a long career in construction, including large jobs related to the war effort, he purchased the New York Yankees in 1945. Widely recognized and respected for his business acumen and baseball savvy, Webb is perhaps best known and remembered for developing Sun City and popularizing what *Time* magazine in 1962 called "a new way of life for the old."[2] Webb surrounded himself with subordinates who understood both the local housing market and the larger changes taking place in society. People were living longer. Older people had more wealth, and many were eager to discover new pursuits and live with age peers on their own terms away from traditional expectations of what being old means. People who moved to the original Sun City called themselves pioneers; the deeds for the first homes were inscribed "New Life Number One."[3] Del Webb's original Sun City was the forerunner for myriad lifestyle communities in Phoenix and elsewhere, based not only on retirement but also on an affinity for golf, interest in the environment, food and diet, multigenerational ties, college affiliations, and religion.

Deeply embedded in this search for something new was the relentless push toward new land at the urban fringe, a push that continues today. Despite periodic efforts to reinvigorate its downtown, Phoenix has the least developed urban core of any large city in America. Municipal and economic leaders pay lip service to the importance of downtown redevelopment, but their hearts, until recently, have been in annexing and developing new peripheral land. The metropolis now stretches some fifty miles from the eastern reaches of Apache Junction to the western borders of Buckeye, from Cave Creek and Carefree on the north to Queen Creek on the southeast (Figure 1). Within the built-up area are a patchwork of cities, native American reservations, and the largest municipal park in the nation. Dairies, cotton fields, and truck farms, remnants of the region's agricultural past, are interwoven with new housing subdivisions and shopping centers at the urban fringe. Urbanized Phoenix[4] is roughly half the size of urbanized Los Angeles (800 versus 1,700 square miles), but Los Angeles contains a population four times larger than that of Phoenix (12 versus 3 million) (Figure 2). With limited land for new development and large immigrant families doubling up in inner-city housing, Los Angeles—the urban region whose sprawling urban form

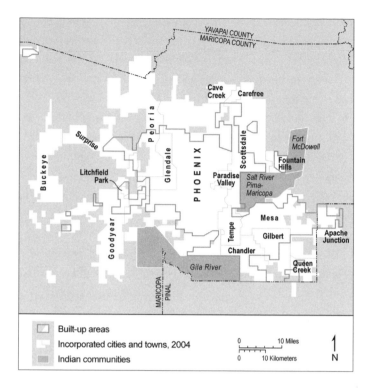

Figure 1. The major cities of Greater Phoenix.

Phoenix has tried so hard not to mimic—is now the nation's most densely populated large urbanized area.

Always with its eye toward the future, Phoenix has casually bulldozed its historical buildings and neighborhoods to make way for future progress. In a revealing recent incident, Mary Rose Wilcox, a member of the Maricopa County Board of Supervisors, and her husband illegally demolished the E. S. Turner home at the corner of First Avenue and Grant Street, a 105-year-old central Phoenix home protected by historical designation. The couple expressed remorse, but the supervisor noted that: "In my eyes, it [the house] was like rubble. We thought we were helping. Crackheads were sleeping there at night. Everybody in the neighborhood was very much afraid of it."[5] The supervisor's observation is the quintessential Phoenician reaction to the old and the past: tear it down, build something new, and move on.

The landlocked suburb of Tempe, more than any other Phoenix-area community, has made the difficult choices to redevelop its downtown, emphasize vertical over horizontal growth, embrace mass transit, integrate historical preservation into future plans, and reclaim its section of the Salt River, in part, because it has not had the option of growth at the fringe for the past twenty years. Current efforts to redevelop the metropolis's inner core reveal inherent tensions between a region traditionally focused on new land development at the fringe and one coming to terms with the limits of such development. Increasingly, Phoenicians acknowledge that mobile, talented, and creative people and entrepreneurial companies—the engines of today's economic growth and prosperity—demand places that provide rich and supportive environments for their endeavors: the kind of environments found in vibrant urban centers, not in humdrum suburban communities.

In addition to a love of newness and rapid growth, Phoenix is defined by its Sonoran Desert geographic setting. New York has its skyline, San Francisco its bridge and bay, Seattle its Space Needle, St. Louis its Arch, and Chicago its shoreline; Phoenix has

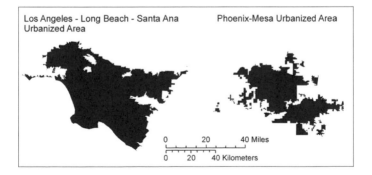

Figure 2. Urbanized Phoenix contains half of Los Angeles's land area but a quarter of its population.

jagged mountain peaks, majestic saguaro cacti, and sweeping desert vistas. Within the urbanized area itself, and visible to most urban residents on a daily basis, are prominent desert landmarks such as Camelback Mountain, South Mountain Park, Piestewa Peak (formerly known as Squaw Peak), the Dreamy Draw, and Papago Park's popular Hole in the Rock. It is significant that Phoenix uses natural rather than human landmarks as a way of presenting itself to the outside world and defining a collective identity. Each day, thousands of hikers prowl the trails of these beloved desert spaces. Local writers wax poetic about breathing the sweet smells of creosote bush after the rain and encountering cottontail rabbits, coyotes, and owls on their daily jogs around the spur of South Mountain. Ordinary people fondly recount seeing all varieties of Arizona cacti, including the saguaro, barrel, hedgehog, pincushion, jumping cholla, and prickly pear, and observing desert animals like gila monsters, jackrabbits, ground squirrels, coyotes, turkey vultures, cactus wrens, and Gamble's quail on their daily hikes. Few other metropolises can claim such a sublime natural landscape within the built environment itself. Luckily, Phoenicians have been mindful to protect these precious places from urban encroachment, although the true test of the region's commitment to its desert legacy lies ahead with the fate of state-owned desert open spaces at the urban fringe. Desert and mountain landscapes play a crucial role in the community's outdoor lifestyle and in its identity as the nation's premier desert city and as a tourist attraction.

If Del Webb epitomizes Phoenix's quality of renewal, another Midwestern transplant, Frank Lloyd Wright, embodies its connection to the desert. Wright was born in Wisconsin in 1867 of Welsh ancestry, which explains his use of the name Taliesin, the Welsh word for "shining brow," for his successive homes.[6] After an early career designing houses for well-to-do Chicago industrialists, Wright gained a reputation as an architect of national and international significance creating office buildings, apartment towers, and resorts and hotels in addition to his signature residences. He first visited the desert when hired by Albert McArthur, a former student, to advise on the construction of the Arizona Biltmore Hotel, the "Jewel of the Desert," which opened in 1929. When, at age seventy, he contracted pneumonia, Wright's doctor advised him to abandon winters in the damp cold of Wisconsin. In 1937, Wright purchased 800 acres in the desert northeast of Phoenix, where he established Taliesin West, the winter headquarters of his architectural practice and school. Drawing on his theories of organic architecture, Wright designed buildings compatible with surrounding mountains and the desert. He invented "desert masonry" in which native boulders—red, yellow, and gray—were laid in rough wood forms and cement poured over them. He used the colors and shapes of the desert in interior decoration. Glass was unnecessary, as canvas-covered roof flaps admitted soft diffused light to studios and living quarters. Taliesin West, now the winter campus for the Frank Lloyd Wright School of Architecture, is physical testament to Wright's view of the way humans might best live in harmony with the desert.

Despite its spectacular beauty and spiritual allure, the desert is, by its very nature, a fragile, demanding, and uncertain place marked by huge extremes in temperature and precipitation. Human efforts to moderate these extremes define the history of central Arizona: first, through the construction of one of the most extensive water storage and delivery systems on the planet; then through the introduction and widespread acceptance of evaporative cooling and refrigeration technology; and, more recently, through flood control and innovative water policy. Success in managing water and taming the desert's heat enabled Greater Phoenix to grow from a network of small mercantile centers at the beginning of the twentieth century into the nation's fastest growing, large metropolitan area 100 years later. The City of Phoenix with

1.4 million residents now ranks as America's sixth-largest city, and Greater Phoenix is the nation's fourteenth largest metropolitan area, with a population of 3.6 million in 2003.[7] With projections of the metropolitan population growing to seven million before mid-century, and in the throes of a persistent and intensive drought, there is growing uneasiness about the capacity to sustain growth. People are asking: Will there be enough water to support the future population in the face of growing climatic uncertainty? Will the expanding urban heat island detract from the livability of the desert and impede summer tourism? Will urban sprawl make the natural desert less accessible to people and thus less important to their lives? Will new jobs be created in places where middle-class people can afford to live? Will population growth exacerbate congestion on freeways and city streets, inhibit mobility, and transform Phoenix into "LA 2"? Will growth erode air quality? And does the prevailing culture of migration and tendency for affluent whites to withdraw into self-contained communities threaten the common purpose needed for regional problem solving?

Related to the capacity for regional decision making is an essential tension between the increasingly small scale at which Phoenicians define community and the increasingly large scale at which important decisions must be made. Phoenicians define their sense of place—the sensation of rootedness, feelings of community and belonging, and faith in something larger than themselves—not as the desert oasis of central Arizona or the Greater Phoenix metroplex, but as the tiny slice of territory that includes their homes and neighborhoods. They consume and relate to the urban desert in fragmented pieces. Unfortunately, neither the desert as a natural feature nor the city as a product of human endeavor works that way. The desert's vastness is part of its essence. Its vistas reveal its complexity and grandeur. Desert animals need lots of territory to roam, and fragmentation reduces biological diversity. The city functions not as an accumulation of

residential districts and employment nodes, but as an intercon-
nected system held together by flows of energy, water, people,
ideas, and materials. While Phoenicians think in ever smaller
terms about what is best for their individual needs and immediate
neighborhoods, the region's future challenges lie at larger scales,
in the issues of transportation, employment, air quality, water
supply and quality, the urban heat island, open-space preservation, downtown redevelopment, and urban growth.

At its heart, this book is about growth, the desert, and community. The central question is how to build a cosmopolitan, multicultural, and cohesive community capable of sustaining large-scale
growth in a fragile and uncertain desert environment. The three
themes of growth, desert, and community are woven throughout
subsequent discussions of the region's environmental history and
the clever and audacious decisions that created a metropolis of
3.6 million residents in the seemingly inhospitable Sonoran Desert (Chapter 2); the cultural history and modern forces that breed
social fragmentation, residential segregation, and a weak regional
perspective in the face of growing diversity (Chapter 3); the
growth machine that is doing away with the desert at an unparal-
leled rate (Chapter 4); systems of transportation and the built
environment they create (Chapter 5); prospects for downtown redevelopment in the region's historic cores (Chapter 6); and the
fundamental geographical dilemma of living large but thinking
small (Chapter 7). Phoenix is at a pivotal moment when its leaders
and residents must decide whether to continue the orgy of new
home construction on pristine desert or to turn to more mature
forms of growth that make use of vacant land within the built-up
area, preserve what is left of the city's historic neighborhoods
and buildings, create authentic and distinctive places that provide
meaning, pleasure, and a sense of belonging in people's lives,
promote a spatial structure where people can live near their workplaces, and forge a sense of common purpose and destiny for a
city based on its desert setting and Southwestern culture.

Building a Desert City

DESERT OASIS

Like all large and successful cities, Phoenix enjoys a splendid natural location that allows it to grow and prosper (Figure 3). It sits at the northern edge of the Sonoran Desert in the Basin and Range Physiographic Province of the western United States. Approximately 100 miles to the northeast is the Colorado Plateau, a mile-high feature cut by deep canyons and punctuated by high mountains. Although Phoenix receives an average of slightly less than eight inches of rainfall annually, its dryland rivers, the Salt and Verde, are fed by the more humid mountain watersheds of the Colorado Plateau and by a transitional zone separating the two regions. The ability to draw life-sustaining water from large upland watersheds allowed prehistoric and modern civilizations to develop. Between 1973 and 1993, Phoenix's hydraulic reach expanded further through construction of the Central Arizona Project, a 336-mile canal to deliver water from the Colorado River at Lake Havasu City to the desert cities of Phoenix and Tucson. Phoenix's location at the edge of desert lowlands and more humid uplands allows it to draw water not only from watersheds of the Salt and Verde Rivers in central Arizona, but also from the vast Colorado River Basin.

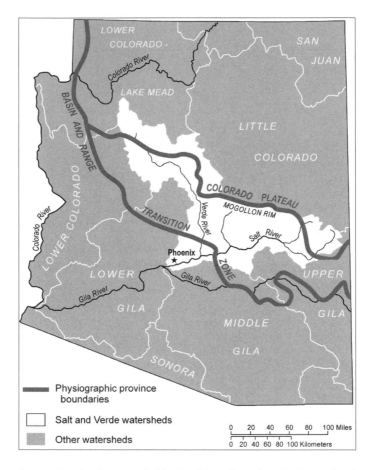

Figure 3. Phoenix enjoys an excellent location at the northern edge of the Sonoran Desert and at the base of large, more humid upland watersheds.

Large tracts of flat land and the presence of underground aquifers in the Phoenix Basin encouraged early agricultural and later urban development. The basin itself is a connected series of depressions filled by water-deposited sediments from the Salt and Verde watersheds, unloaded where the river's gradient flattened. These low-lying sediments were an especially important medium for the prehistoric Hohokam cultivation and later Anglo-European

CHAPTER 2

crop production. In addition, these huge sedimentary deposits, with their breadth, depth, and good transmissivity, came to represent an enormous, but poorly replenished, underground water supply. Water in storage in these alluvial aquifers provides an important reserve during arid periods for a valley faced with a highly variable surface supply and distinguishes Phoenix from Albuquerque, El Paso, and Las Vegas with much poorer groundwater reserves. The Phoenix area has been fortunate to be able to draw upon these banks of underground water when the climate was especially dry from the 1940s through the mid-1960s, and it pumps from these sources now as the western United States is gripped in a persistent and intensive drought.

Emerging from this alluvial sea are mountain ranges: the White Tank Mountains to the west, the Bradshaw Mountains to the northwest, the Superstition and Mazatzal Mountains to the east and northeast, the San Tan Mountains to the southeast, and the Sierra Estrella Mountains to the southwest (Figure 4). Streams issuing from these mountains have deposited cobbles and sands in fan-shaped features called alluvial fans. Exposed bedrock throughout the valley appears as rugged and striking features, including many of the region's natural icons such as Piestewa Peak, Camelback Mountain, the southern end of the White Tank Mountains, the northern end of the Sierra Estrellas, and Usury Mountains. The geological distinction between stream-deposited fans and bedrock pediments is crucial for new home construction as alluvial fans are depositional and thus suffer from occasional dramatic and destructive flooding while bedrock pediments are erosional and highly stable.

PREHISTORIC HOHOKAM

The story of human habitation of this strategic desert site begins more than 2,000 years ago when an ancient people, the Hohokam

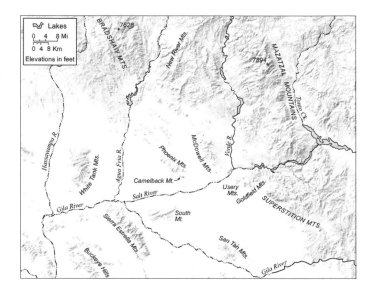

Figure 4. The Salt River Valley is surrounded by mountain ranges.

(a Pima Indian word meaning "those who have disappeared"), established a civilization based on irrigation agriculture in the valleys of the Salt and Gila rivers. They initially farmed the flood plains of the valley floor, but later diverted water to faraway fields through a complex and extensive canal network (Figure 5). Archaeologists believe that such a network would have required a large and sophisticated social organization, initially to build the canals and later to maintain them and allocate water.[1] In the beginning, channeling relatively small quantities of water over short distances would have required only a moderate level of cooperation among households. But later, as the system grew in size and complexity, many households in multiple villages would have been needed to organize labor to construct and maintain the hydraulic infrastructure, schedule water deliveries, and settle disputes among competing users. At the height of Hohokam civilization (around A.D. 1000), an estimated 110,000 acres were under culti-

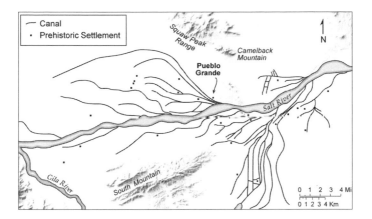

Figure 5. The prehistoric Hohokam built a sophisticated civilization based on irrigation canals and agriculture.

vation, supporting a population of around 40,000.[2] The regional cooperation needed to harness and deliver water to a large population under uncertain conditions was an important model for later water policy and economic development.

Ruins of Pueblo Grande, at the apex of the Hohokam settlement system, are situated less than one mile from the north bank of the Salt River, at the point where water was diverted into several of the largest canals (Figure 5). Residents of Pueblo Grande would have controlled water diversions to thousands of downstream farmers' fields. They would have stood at the pinnacle of their platform mounds and laid eyes on more than ten canals that delivered water to faraway fields and villages. Other aspects of Hohokam settlement are revealed in the arrangement of public architecture in the form of ball courts and platform mounds erected in the middle of large villages. Between A.D. 950 and 1150, games were played on at least 225 ball courts. By 1200, the use of ball courts ended and, with their demise, came a reorganization of the region's settlement system. Increasing environmental stress led to the decline in marginal upland habitations and concentration in more productive and dependable riverine communities.[3]

Hohokam civilization ultimately collapsed as climatic fluctuations and the human response undermined the land's ability to support the population.[4] Hohokam were not, in the end, able to manage the extremes of their natural environment. Between 800 and 1075 when, according to tree-ring data, the Salt and Gila Rivers were relatively stable, the area under cultivation was vast. After 1250, increased climatic variability triggered a series of environmental feedbacks that lowered the land's carrying capacity. Archaeologists surmise that agricultural output diminished and the Hohokam overplanted their good fields, expanded onto marginal fields, and cut back on fallow periods—all strategies destined to undermine long-term soil productivity and future output. Alternatively, they might have enlarged canal intakes, making them more prone to destructive flooding, or allowed fields to become oversalinized through excessive use. Whatever the reason, the Hohokam outgrew their capacity to sustain life in the desert during periods of severe environmental stress, and all but vanished by 1450. Modern members of the Tohono O'odham, Papago, and Pima Nations are thought to be descendants of the Hohokam. Many reside on the Gila River and Salt River Indian reservations, adjacent to modern Phoenix.

RISING FROM THE ASHES

The valleys of the Salt and Gila Rivers were rediscovered some 400 years after the disappearance of the Hohokam by Euro-American settlers looking for ways to supply farm products to the gold and silver mines of the Bradshaw Mountains to the north and west of what is now Phoenix, and to Fort McDowell. The fort was a cavalry post founded in 1865 on the Verde River near its confluence with the Salt, to protect mining towns from raiding Apache

Indians. In need of feed for the fort's horses, Fort McDowell's sut-
ler, John Y. T. (Yours Truly) Smith set up a hay camp west of Tempe
along the Salt River in 1866. While visiting the camp in November
1867, Jack Swilling, a former Confederate officer and man of dubious character, noticed ruins of the prehistoric Hohokam canal
system and opined correctly that the region had considerable agricultural potential. Swilling convinced backers in Wickenburg, a
mining community to the north, to bankroll the Swilling Irrigating
and Canal Company, and the rest, as they say, is history. Swilling
returned to Phoenix with supplies and 16 unemployed miners,
excavated some of the Hohokam canals, constructed new ones,
and negotiated contracts with the mines and the military. The
community of "Pumpkinville" was born with Swilling as its first
citizen, postmaster, and justice of the peace. Two thousand acres
were under cultivation by 1879. One of Swilling's shareholders,
Englishman "Lord" Darrell Duppa, a classical scholar, adventurer,
and inebriate, recognized the symbolism of a new agricultural civilization rising from the dusty, silt-laden Hohokam canals. He
said: "A city will rise phoenix-like, new and beautiful, from these
ashes of the past," and renamed the new community Phoenix.[5]

The original town site, centered on Central Avenue and Washington Street, was chosen in 1870 for its location near the valley's
geographic center, for the lack of Hohokam canals, and for its flat
terrain. In addition, it was erroneously believed to be above the
Salt River's flood plain, a notion later disproved during a catastrophic flood in 1891. William A. Hancock laid out the 320-acre
town site in the spring of 1871. The city plat was one mile wide
and a half-mile deep and was divided into 98 blocks and 1,200
lots. Street naming followed the Southern convention with the
main street, Washington, recognizing the first president, and all
east-west running streets named after U.S. presidents in chrono-
logical order. North-south streets originally recognized the original native American residents: Second, Third, Fourth, Fifth, Sixth,

and Seventh Streets were formerly Maricopa, Pima, Pinal, Arivaipai, Tonto, and Apache, and Second, Third, Fourth, Fifth, Sixth, and Seventh Avenues were formerly Mojave, Papago, Yuma, Cocopah, and Hualapia Streets. These street names later were changed to reflect the growing Anglo-European orientation of the city.[6]

At that time, the Salt River would have flowed year round. There would have been slow-flowing lakes and swamps along the river course. Flows would have been highly variable with many years of low flow interrupted by sudden, massive, turbulent floods. Crossing the river would have been dicey during these high-flow periods. In the 1860s, just such an occasion inspired another Arizona pioneer, Charles Trumbell Hayden, to establish a new settlement along the riverbank in the Tempe area. Hayden was a trader and owner of a freight-hauling business in Tucson. Upon making his way from Tucson to Fort Whipple near Prescott, Hayden attempted to cross the Salt River at its narrowest point in what is now Tempe, but was stopped by the angry, chocolate-colored Salt River, which was in high flood. The "Judge," or "Don Carlos" as he was called at the time, parked his freight wagon below the nearby fish-shaped butte, made camp, and in the morning hiked to the top. In later years, he often told the story of lounging there at the summit daydreaming about the future. Gazing down upon the green ribbon of high grasses growing on either side of the river, willow and cottonwood trees, and Pima Indian grain fields, he saw water uselessly flowing past. If only that water could be harnessed and put to use, you could forget about gold mines and dryland ranching and the importation of foodstuffs and create an agricultural center in the desert.[7] Judge Hayden is known to have exclaimed: "This valley could become an agricultural empire."[8] At nightfall, Hayden hiked down from the butte and cooked his lonely supper. The next day, the river calmed somewhat and he was able to continue his journey to

Prescott, but he made inquiries there about the land below the butte in Tempe.

Charles Trumbell Hayden was born in Windsor, Connecticut, in 1825 of a well-educated and cultured New England family. As a youth, he taught school in Connecticut, but the West beckoned. He traveled first to Indiana to teach and then to St. Louis, the edge of the frontier where the first wagon trains and river steamers were leaving for the West. Soon, the twenty-three year old Hayden quit teaching; made his way to Independence, Missouri, the eastern terminus of the Santa Fe Trail; bought a team, wagon, and load of goods; and set out for Santa Fe. Eventually, he moved to Tucson and established a trading and freight business. He was there when the Civil War broke out and when the Arizona Territory was created in 1863. Hayden competed with the "Tucson Ring," a band of traders who charged the army exorbitant prices on supplies, and this was thought to be one reason he was open to the possibility of starting over in the less developed Salt River Valley to the north.[9]

Judge Hayden learned that Jack Swilling's canal crew was excavating north of the river in Phoenix, downstream from his original crossing in Tempe. He returned to the valley in November 1870 and quickly began a branch canal of his own to drive a grist mill that he intended to build at the base of the Tempe butte. Eventually, he settled his affairs in Tucson, moved to Tempe, and opened a blacksmith shop and general store. By 1874, his grist mill had opened and he had established a cable-ferry operation to regularize river crossings. Hayden sold goods to the occasional traveler and to the ditch diggers working on his canal and others in the area. The main road from the ferry crossing to the grist mill and commercial district became known as Mill Avenue. A meat industry, shops, barns, homes, farms, and a school eventually would follow, realizing Hayden's dream of a new settlement reclaimed from the desert using water from the Salt River. In 1876, he brought his bride, Sallie Calvert Davis, a lady of New England culture who had taught school at Visalia, California, to the rustic little community. During her first year in the desert, Sallie gave birth to Carl Hayden, who became the lone representative from Arizona when it became a state in 1912. He later would be elected to the U.S. Senate and become a leading booster of Phoenix growth. The name, Tempe, is credited to Lord Duppa who named Phoenix. The small agrarian community surrounding the butte south of the river evoked an image of the Vale of Tempe in Greek mythology.

Thus began an era of large-scale agricultural development and canal construction. Canal companies were formed by investors from California and the East, who saw the potential to profit from controlling and selling land and water. "Swilling's Ditch" was later renamed the Salt River Valley Canal. The Maricopa Canal was built in 1873; and the Grand Canal was added in 1878, with extensions from 1880 to 1882. The Arizona Canal, begun in 1883 and finished in 1885, was the first to deviate from the Hohokam pattern. Some 47 miles in length, it was the longest of the Phoenix-area canals.[10] Limited technology at the time meant that canal construction and later deepening relied heavily on human labor. By 1900, ten privately owned and operated canals irrigated 113,000 acres.[11] Consequently, the area's population grew from 5,700 in 1880, to 11,000 in 1890 and 20,500 in 1900.[12]

Canal construction and agricultural development transformed the local vegetation. In its natural state, low shrubs, primarily creosote bush and white bur sage, two of the most drought-tolerant plants in North America, would have dominated the area. A second native vegetation community, the paloverde-saguaro, included the paloverde tree, saguaro cactus, cholla and barrel cactus, prickly pear and hedgehog cactus, along with some creosote bush and bur sage.[13] Mesquite trees would have grown along the larger washes, and the Salt River would have been lined with cottonwoods, willows, mesquite, and an occasional marshy swamp. The river bottom itself would have been covered with wild grasses.[14] With the arrival of Euro-American farmers at the end of the nineteenth century, agricultural fields, fruit orchards, and citrus groves replaced the native vegetation. In 1895 a young girl named Janie Michaels described the landscape and plant life she encountered on a trip from Tempe around Phoenix to Papago Park's Hole in the Rock.

The eight girls composing the party were up betimes and had met at the Tempe Road by seven o'clock. All were well mounted and good riders. Four abreast, they kept a steady, even lope; passing the happy homes of ranchers set within fields of alfalfa; pausing awhile at Arizona Fall (a waterfall along the Arizona Canal) to admire the flashing, foaming water that plunges down with rush and roar; looking with loving eyes upon the "orange orchard" turned by the sun's rays into gardens of golden glow. Presently, they ascended a little rise, bristling with mesquite and sage-brush, and the shadow of "the Rock" appeared.[15]

Canal construction further altered the landscape as water was moved from its natural riparian setting and spread more evenly across the valley's landscape. Tree planting was encouraged along canals, laterals, and ditches, creating a vast network of lush, shady places protected from the hot desert sun by cottonwood, eucalyptus, ash, and mesquite trees. At the turn of the century, canal banks were popular public spaces for swimming, bathing, picnicking, laundering, canoeing, fishing, and even water skiing. Weddings, baptisms, and local dances took place along the canals (Figure 6). Before the advent of air conditioning, canals were popular sleeping places, especially in rural areas. They were used as reference points, and many farmers used the roads that lined canals to move equipment from one field to another.[16]

Figure 6. Early Phoenicians lived near water along irrigation canals. Courtesy of the Salt River Project Research Archives.

The arrival of the transcontinental railroads reinforced the region's agricultural potential, canal construction, and environmental transformation. In 1887, the Maricopa and Phoenix line connected Phoenix to the Southern Pacific 26 miles to the south, and in 1895 Phoenix established a link to a second intercontinental railroad, the Atchinson, Topeka, and Santa Fe, at Ash Fork to the north. Railroads enabled local farmers to move beyond military and mining markets and develop a large and diverse economy based on commercial agriculture. Larger markets in the Midwest and West supported new agricultural specializations in citrus, dairying, cattle ranching, feedlots, and fruits and vegetables. With this transformation, Los Angeles, the western terminus of both intercontinental railroads, replaced San Francisco as the principal wholesaling center for the Salt River Valley.[17] Railroad service also allowed desert dwellers to import building materials and to transform the appearance of their rugged frontier outpost into a modern American town.

BUILDING A MODERN WATERWORKS

As the nineteenth century came to an end, local boosters recognized that a more stable water supply would be needed for continued population and economic growth. Flows in the Salt River were highly variable, with many years of low flow interrupted by large floods. In 1891, flood waters raged through the heart of the agricultural valley, destroying irrigation headgates and canals. In the words of one local resident: "Chocolate in color, hideous in its roaring fury, the torrent spared nothing in its path."[18] Typical of the fickle nature of desert rainfall, the flood was followed by a severe drought between 1898 and 1904, resulting in the loss of thousands of crop acres. Many people moved away. Men patrolled the canals, rifles in hand, to ensure that people did not take more than their rightful share of precious water.[19] But from this environmental near-disaster came a successful regional movement to build an upstream dam to stabilize the water supply and protect the area from flooding. The immediate effect was to create a prosperous agricultural economy, but the long-term effect was to develop the water infrastructure, flood-control capacity, and human institutions needed to support large-scale urbanization.

As early as 1889, there was talk of the need for a large upstream dam to solve the valley's water problem. A special committee, appointed by the Maricopa County Board of Supervisors, identified an excellent site 80 miles east of Phoenix on the Salt River at Tonto Basin. The venture languished for several years but gained support after the flooding and drought of the 1890s. Local efforts were reinforced by President Theodore Roosevelt, who pushed for passage of the 1902 National Reclamation Act, to finance reclamation projects in western states with funds secured from the sale of public lands.[20] Anxious to put the act into practice quickly, George H. Maxwell, president of the National Reclamation Association, and Arthur P. Davis of the Geological Survey came to Phoenix and convinced local leaders that the National Reclamation Act was the answer to their water woes. A Water Storage Conference Committee was formed in the fall of 1902, and articles of incorporation for a water users' association were crafted. Crucial to the Salt River Valley Water Users Association were local landowners whose lands would be collateral for the federal loan to build a dam. In exchange, they received water rights based on the amount of acreage they had under production. The project was a tough sell to these feisty and independent landowners, who feared an attempt by those with inferior water rights to snatch their water rights. Moreover, they objected to the 160-acre limit of land eligible for reclamation specified in the National Reclamation Act.

Despite these reservations, enough landowners signed on by the summer of 1903 to secure the loan, and dam planning and construction got underway. Named for the champion of the 1902 federal legislation, Roosevelt Dam was completed in February 1911, creating the largest artificial lake in the world at the time. President Roosevelt himself attended the official dedication ceremony on March 18, 1911 and declared that the central Arizona oasis had a "glorious future."[21] The dam and irrigation system, operated by the Reclamation Service, eventually was turned over to the Salt River Valley Water Users Association, now known as the Salt River Project. The water storage and flood-control capacity of Roosevelt Dam was augmented by the construction of three more dams on the Salt River and two on the Verde. The Salt River Project's current service area was established some 100 years ago as the land used as collateral for the loans needed to build Roosevelt Dam. Owners of these lands committed to making decades worth of annual payments to the federal government to reimburse it for dam-construction costs.

Canals continued to serve as public gathering places and reminders of the importance of water for human livelihood and comfort in the desert. One particularly memorable site was the Arizona Falls, a 20-foot drop in the Arizona Canal at Indian School Road between Fifty-Sixth and Fifty-Seventh Streets. When building the Arizona Canal in 1884, crews encountered a ridge of hard limestone rock, called caliche, south of Camelback Mountain. Instead of trying to remove it, they allowed the water to flow over it, creating a 15- to 20-foot waterfall. The falls became a popular local attraction for picnics, swimming, fishing, and sightseeing. A hydroelectric power plant was built over it in 1902 and replaced by a larger plant in 1911.[22] At about the same time, William John Murphy built the Ingleside Inn along the Arizona Canal adjacent to the falls, and guests at the Inn were known to have danced near the falling water on the power platform. This entire scene of canal development, water in the desert, and tourism was recreated in 2003 by the Phoenix Arts Commission, in cooperation with the Salt River Project. The former generator is now an outdoor water room lined with desert stone and surrounded by falling water. The dance floor covers the location of falling water where one of the previous generators was located.

The stable water supply created by construction of Roosevelt Dam stimulated agricultural development, reinforced agricultural specializations like citrus and cotton, and sparked other forms of development based on the region's physical attributes. World War I brought an economic boom, as long-staple cotton was essential for tires and airplane fabric. Deprived of foreign supplies, defense contractors sought domestic sources, and the Salt River Valley proved an ideal location for cotton cultivation. The Goodyear Tire Company from Akron, Ohio, bought cotton from local growers and purchased land in what was to become Goodyear and Litchfield Park (Paul W. Litchfield was a Goodyear executive) in the West Valley. Land prices soared, and with grandiose predictions that the price of cotton would reach $1.50 per pound, a majority of farmers switched to cotton. Unfortunately, the boom in cotton was short lived, and after the war, bankruptcy and depression ensued. Local farmers eventually adapted to uncertain agricultural markets by producing a more diverse array of crops, and prosperity was restored.[23]

Conventional wisdom and medical practice at the time held that dryness was a cure for tuberculosis. These beliefs drew some of the region's most prominent early entrepreneurs and residents. Del Webb, Frank Lloyd Wright, and Dwight Heard were all advised by doctors to move to Phoenix for their health. Phoenix gained a national reputation as a "lungers' mecca." The wealthy stayed in hospitals and private residences while the poor were relegated to tents and shacks, just north of the Arizona Canal along the southern slopes of the Phoenix mountains in an area called Sunnyslope. Retired architect W. R. Norton named the subdivision Sunnyslope after his daughter remarked upon seeing the morning sun: "What a pretty sunny slope." Micro-climatic conditions favored these sites, as elevation increases gently from the valley floor into the surrounding mountains and has a cooling effect. Winds generally are from west to east in the daytime (upslope and up the channel of the Salt River) and east to west in the evening and early morning hours (downslope and down valley). During the day, warming air moves upslope, carrying along moisture. In the evening, air at higher elevations cools faster than air in the valley, and the cooler and denser air slides downslope. As early as 1921, a *Monthly Weather Review* study concluded that "there is no question that some of the hillside exposures will give a growing season fully a month longer than Phoenix" and beckoned "health seekers and elderly people" to locate on the hillsides, where

temperature will average from six to ten degrees less than on the floor of the valley and this decrease in range comes mostly at the cold end of the day.

The chill of the early morning is missing and with it the objectionable high humidity. Few places in the world can offer a more nearly ideal winter climate than these hillsides with abundant, healing sunshine and warm days of the desert, but without its great temperature ranges and chilly mornings.[24]

By the 1920s, Sunnyslope had grown into a small community of prospectors, homesteaders, beekeepers, writers, and musicians, as well as health seekers. Elizabeth Beatty, a retired stenographer, and her sister Marguerite Colley raised money to provide health care and social services for the sick and indigent of Sunnyslope. A local women's group provided turkey dinners to bedridden residents of Sunnyslope's health camps, and at Christmastime provided brightly colored shoeboxes filled with homemade candles, candies, and popcorn balls to the needy. In 1927, the Reverend Joseph Hillhouse established the Desert Mission at Sunnyslope to meet the needs of the sick. Through countless letters to friends and acquaintances across the nation, Hillhouse raised money for a permanent chapel and medical clinic. In 1931, John C. Lincoln, millionaire and philanthropist, and his wife Helen spent the winter in the Phoenix area because of Helen's poor health, and several years later, contributed $2,000 for the purchase of land in an area that would eventually become the site of John C. Lincoln Hospital.

City boosters began to worry about attracting too many sick people and changed the spin on their proclamations about Phoenix from a place to cure the sick to a playground for the healthy and wealthy. By 1913, an estimated 3,000 winter tourists visited the area annually.[25] Between Phoenix and Scottsdale, the stylish Ingleside Inn opened in 1910, followed by the new Adams Hotel in downtown Phoenix and the San Marcos in Chandler, both in 1913. Tourism declined during the early years of the Depression, but picked up later as World War II prevented wealthy easterners from traveling to their usual European holiday haunts and inspired them to take advantage of domestic destinations, such as Phoenix.

Increasing reliance on air travel made Phoenix less isolated than previously. After World War I, the army and local boosters encouraged development of an airfield to serve the airmail route between San Antonio and San Diego.[26] In 1925, Phoenix Municipal Airport was built six miles northwest of the city. In 1928, Scenic Airways, a venture backed by Chicago and Phoenix investors to promote tourism from the Midwest, purchased land two miles east of the downtown for an airfield, and Sky Harbor was opened on Labor Day 1929. It was named Sky Harbor to convey Phoenix's futuristic outlook and the significance of air travel to the isolated desert oasis. Phoenix would never have a seaport like the great coastal cities of the time but, in the words of a later observer, would have "a Sky Harbor with all the facilities for receiving the ships of the air."[27] With the stock market crash of 1929 and subsequent repercussions, Scenic Airways sold the airfield to Acme Investment in 1930, and the company soon looked to the city to unload its investment. The City of Phoenix acquired Sky Harbor in 1935. New Deal funding from the Works Projects Administration (WPA) paid for a new 4,500-foot runway in 1936, the construction of a new administration building, a weather observation tower, new hangers, and roads within and around the airport.[28] It was clear that air travel would be critical to the future development of Phoenix, and Sky Harbor would be instrumental in this process.

It was also during this period that the area's social geography was solidified. The most expensive and prestigious homes were built north of the downtown in areas favored by fragrant citrus groves, beautiful views of the Phoenix and Camelback Mountains, and cooling breezes coming off the mountains during the summertime months. Growth was discouraged in less attractive areas east of Phoenix by the presence of the "insane asylum," now the Arizona State Hospital at Twenty-Fourth Street and Van Buren, and to the west by manufacturing plants and warehouses. The area south of the Salt River was the least desirable site for residential expansion because of its low elevation and tendency to flood.[29] Not coincidentally, the city's African American and Hispanic neighborhoods were concentrated there.

During the 1920s, the Salt River Project (SRP) built three more dams on the Salt River to store water and generate hydroelectric power, but the low crop prices during the Depression hurt local farmers, and many had difficulty paying what they owed to the Salt River Project and federal government, even with water subsidies from hydroelectric power sales. As the Depression wore on, SRP had a hard time meeting its payments on the local bonds that financed the additional dams and was forced to change itself from a not-for-profit private association into a political subdivision of the state in order to refinance its bonds, reclassifying them as tax-free and lowering their interest rates and debt service.

Also significant was the development of technology to tame the city's blistering summertime heat. The dry, clear air of the desert heats quickly during the day, reaching high temperatures that average 105° Fahrenheit during June, July, and August. Although desert surfaces cool quickly at night, it is still hot as the typical low in July is 81°. Early settlers slept outside under the open sky or hung wet sheets across sleeping porches to create evaporation and gain relief from the heat. By the mid-1930s, this basic concept had evolved into a somewhat more sophisticated system of evaporative cooling that involved an electric fan blowing air through dampened pads or screens. By adding moisture to dry air, these so-called swamp coolers increased evaporation and lowered temperatures between 20° and 40° F. Commercial production of evaporative coolers began around 1936 in Phoenix, and soon there were five large manufacturers that together grossed $15 million annually. By the early 1950s, more than 90 percent of Phoenix-area homes had evaporative cooling, and the technology became an integral part of the unique cultural and environmental legacy of Phoenix and the Southwest.[30]

At the end of the 1930s, Phoenix was still a small regional service center with a large and prosperous agricultural hinterland. The ingredients for large-scale urbanization were, however, in place—a stable water supply, abundant land, aggressive leadership, a growing national reputation as a tourist retreat, the means to quell the desert's sweltering summer heat, and a network of agricultural settlements around which later suburbanization would be organized.

DEFENSE AND THE POSTWAR BOOM

At the start of World War II, Phoenix was again able to capitalize on its formidable natural assets to attract military installations and defense industries. The average annual percentage of possible sunshine in Phoenix is 85 percent compared to 76 percent in Albuquerque, 73 percent in Los Angeles, 70 percent in Denver, 59 percent in New York City, 54 percent in Chicago, and 46 percent in Seattle.[31] Precipitation averages slightly less than eight inches per year, but falls below ten inches more than 80 percent of the time. The light winds, coupled with the flat topography, make the local environment well suited for flight training and military operations. In addition, its inland location provided security from foreign attack. In 1941, Luke and Williams Airfields were opened. By the end of the war, Luke was the world's largest flight-training school. Other facilities included Thunderbird Field north of Glendale (later the Thunderbird School of International Business), Thunderbird Field II north of Scottsdale (later Scottsdale Municipal Airport), and Litchfield Naval Air Facility. In addition, army bases, Camps Horn and Hyder, were established in the Phoenix area. At the peak of war deployment in 1943, more than 30,000 troops were stationed at Camp Hyder, and as many as 15 military trains passed through Phoenix daily.[32]

The desert city hummed with activity during the war years. In addition to military personnel, tens of thousands of men and women moved to Phoenix to work in war industries. Defense contractors were encouraged to decentralize and move inland as protection from possible air strikes. The Allison Steel Company, operating in Phoenix since the 1920s, began wartime production of portable bridges. In 1941, the Goodyear Aircraft Corporation began producing airplane parts and balloons in Litchfield Park, employing some 7,500 workers by 1943. Another 3,500 people worked at the Alcoa aluminum extrusion plant at Thirty-Fifth Avenue and Van Buren. Garrett Corporation built AiResearch, an airplane parts plant located south of Sky Harbor airport, and employed 2,700 workers at peak wartime production.[33] All these new people and increasing economic activity strained housing and city services. In 1942, the Phoenix War Housing Committee registered all residential quarters and appealed to the local citizenry to make extra rooms available to those working in the war effort. This effort fell short, however, as a severe housing shortage plagued the city throughout the war years.[34]

By the end of the war in 1945, the scale and nature of life in Phoenix was forever changed. Some of the war plants closed temporarily but were reopened quickly by private industry. Many servicemen and -women who trained in Phoenix returned with their families to start new lives and work in the new defense-related industries. City boosters began an aggressive campaign to lure electronics manufacturers and build an industrial base. In 1948, the local Chamber of Commerce established an industrial department to publicize the advantages of Phoenix. They touted the region's strategic location midway between aircraft manufacturers in Southern California and the atomic testing grounds in New Mexico. The federal government's desire to decentralize production sites in the face of Cold War threats and the city's wartime production record were also important selling points for Phoenix. Motorola, a major manufacturer of radios and electronic parts, opened its first plant on 14 acres on Fifty-Sixth Street between Thomas and Indian School in March 1950, followed by three more facilities by 1968.[35] In 1955, immediately after city boosters pushed through a right-to-work amendment to the Arizona constitution, Sperry Rand announced plans to move to Phoenix.[36] Between 1948 and 1960, three hundred new manufacturing plants began operations in Phoenix. Manufacturing supplanted agriculture as the region's leading sector, and the City of Phoenix mushroomed from 65,000 residents in 1940 to 439,000 in 1960.

Desert life in Phoenix was eased by the discovery and widespread acceptance of air conditioning. The technology for commercial refrigeration actually was developed early in the twentieth century for industrial purposes and later expanded for use in movie theaters. Although the knowhow for residential window units was perfected between 1928 and 1940, the Depression and wartime rationing of consumer goods severely restricted its use. In many parts of the country, there was an innate resistence to the idea of artificial air and sealed windows. People preferred more traditional ways of cooling off at night such as a dip in the pool, splash at the beach, walk in the park, or just plain sitting on their front stoop or porch. After the war, Phoenix was one of the nation's first places to embrace refrigeration technology, as the tradition of artificial cooling had already been established with swamp coolers in the 1930s and early 1940s.[37] Many Phoenicians abandoned their more energy-efficient evaporative coolers in favor of refrigeration, although some people continue even today to use swamp coolers during May and June, when humidity is low, and then switch to refrigeration during the more humid months of July and August, when the winds shift, bringing more moisture from the Gulf of Mexico to central Arizona, a season known locally as the Arizona Monsoon.

A homegrown industry soon emerged to meet the housing needs of the city's burgeoning postwar population. Phoenix's Levittown was engineered by a man named John F. Long. Long was the first child of German immigrant parents who came to the valley in 1910. Laboring on the family farm taught him how to work with his hands. After he graduated from Glendale High School, Long rode the rails looking for work at the end of the Depression and then joined the military and became an engine mechanic in World War II. He returned to the Phoenix area after the war and married his high school sweetheart, Mary Tolmachoff. In 1947, John and Mary used money from a GI loan and tools borrowed from Mary's father to build a home for themselves. Before moving in, they received an offer of $8,400 for the house, leaving them with a tidy profit of more than $4,000. By carefully reinvesting the profits, John and Mary built more homes, completing the work themselves. Mary was to wait three years for a home of her own, but John F. Long Homes became a thriving business.[38]

Long began his first subdivision in 1949, pioneering mass-production techniques that allowed him to deliver the most house for the lowest cost. These techniques were based on his own experiences laying pipe, installing electrical systems, and pouring cement. He was the first to use roof trusses, develop equipment to pour continuous sidewalks, and design plastic plumbing. His innovations also included component wall sections, modular bathrooms, and custom cabinetry. Every tool and laborer was assigned a duty that allowed for complete efficiency. Equipment was in continual use, making the most of every dollar. Building materials were pre-cut and then taken on site to speed the assembly-line process. In 1954, Long began construction of the region's first master-planned community on 2,000 acres of irrigated farmland on the westside. He named the community Maryvale, after his wife. The efficiency of the young developer's production methods allowed him to offer contemporary homes at affordable prices. At Long's first open house, dubbed the "Greatest Home Show on Earth" a three-bedroom, two-bath home sold for $7,950; homes with a swimming pool went for $9,800.

John F. Long pioneered not only the construction of a planned community, but its marketing as well. New home expos drew scores of potential home buyers. Billboards advertised home prices starting at $7,950, low down payments, and quality amenities. "Futuramas," as they were called, had a carnival-like atmosphere designed for young families seeking to buy their first homes. Radio and television spots as well as newspaper advertisements captured attention and drew newcomers to Long's home shows. Upon arriving, families could leave their children with a babysitter and tour model homes with knowledgeable and attractive young women called "house consultants." As parents enjoyed refreshments and toured model homes, children were entertained by clowns, balloons, and activities.

Beyond the showmanship, Long offered a good deal to young American families hungry for luxuries after the sacrifices and shortages of the war years. His homes had permanent, built-in appliances supplied by respected companies like General Electric. Other amenities were colorful bathroom fixtures and garages with overhead doors. The streets, parks, schools, shopping centers, and hospitals were laid out in detail. Maryvale was the epitome of the ideal, family neighborhood. Long would sell up to 125 homes per week.[39]

To ensure that developments like Maryvale stayed within the city's boundaries, Phoenix began an aggressive program of annexation after 1950. The city lacked a strong historic downtown because of the newness of its development. As a result, it was easy to look outward for future development. The city also was fearful of being choked off from future growth by suburban expansion, a trend easily observed in more established urban areas. To assure itself a northern growth corridor, the city increased its land area from a relatively compact 17 square miles in 1950 to 190 square miles just ten years later. While larger and older cities declined during this period, Phoenix quadrupled in population, and its land area grew by a factor of 11.[40] The ability to capture new growth, and the temptation to compete with suburbs on their own terms, ultimately led to an identity crisis for Phoenix. Even today, the city has trouble differentiating itself from surrounding suburbs and defining itself as the psychological heart and premier center of the urban region. Phoenix has been accused of being a supersuburb rather than an urban place of distinctive Southwestern character.[41]

By the 1950s, Phoenix had become the largest population and industrial center between Los Angeles and Dallas-Fort Worth. Sky Harbor was one of the busiest airports in the nation, served by five national carriers. Local historian Edward H. Peplow, Jr., proclaimed in the April 1947 issue of the magazine *Arizona Highways* that Phoenix combined the attractions of a cosmopolitan metropolis, thriving industrial center, productive agricultural region, and delightful resort while maintaining its Southwestern charm.[42] This latter quality became increasingly difficult to maintain with massive in-migration, postwar industrial development, planned communities, air conditioning, and all the other trappings of modern American life.

With growth and modernization, the city's relationship with its desert setting became increasingly tenuous. The Salt River Project, in an effort to conserve water, lined the canals with concrete and prevented access to canal banks to promote public safety. Without the seepage from the canals, the trees lining the banks could not be sustained, and more than 50,000 were removed. The unintended effect transformed the canals and their immediate environments from quasi-public settings, where people could commune with water in the desert, to sterile, utilitarian spaces off-limits to the public.[43] In its quest for modernity, efficiency, and growth, Phoenix was losing touch with the water that was so crucial for sustaining life in the desert.

RETIREMENT MIGRATION

The environmental transformation of the valley was accompanied by a significant social transformation, inspired by the development of retirement communities. The nation's first retirement community was the brainchild of Phoenix real estate salesman and entrepreneur Ben Schleifer, a Russian immigrant from New York. While visiting an elderly friend in Rochester, "Big Ben" had been disturbed by the lifeless days and spirit-crushing loss of independence that awaited Americans in their old age. When he moved to Arizona in 1947 to find a cure for severe asthma, he set out to build a place where retirees could pursue leisure activities such as bowling, dancing, swimming, and bingo away from the hustle-bustle of big-city life and be free from responsibilities for children and grandchildren. In 1954, he bought the Greer Ranch, a 320-acre cattle ranch northwest of Phoenix, and founded Youngtown, naming it "to make elderly people not feel old."[44] Youngtown residents were encouraged to establish clubs and organizations, and they did. The Youngtown Players (a theatrical group), the Ladies Tuesday Night Card Club, and the Saturday Night Sing and Dance Club were among Youngtown's earliest associations. Residents of this blue-collar retirement community fished in an artificial lake, played shuffleboard, enjoyed potluck dinners, and, in essence, pioneered the concept of active retirement. In response to the question: what is Youngtown, one resident answered: "It's the place where the people killed loneliness instead of dying from it."[45]

Schleifer's concept of active retirement did not include proximity to grandchildren—or children of any kind, for that matter. Youngtown's homes carried deed restrictions that required one member of each household to be over sixty years of age and prohibited children under eighteen. Residents were migrants from other states who were attracted to the Phoenix area by Schleifer's new concept of active retirement.[46] The idea of migration and escape are captured in one early resident's response to why she moved to the Phoenix area and Youngtown:

[What brought you here?] My grandchildren. [Oh, you wanted to be closer to them?] No. I wanted to be farther away from them. I reared eight children of my own, and I have no intention of rearing 22 grandchildren.[47]

Youngtown's success demonstrated that there was a viable market for active retirement and encouraged Del Webb to open Sun City on 20,000 acres of alfalfa and cotton fields adjacent to Youngtown. The idea of active retirement for the masses was, in no way obvious, as the Del Webb Corporation had assembled a team of experts from the Urban Land Institute who argued that "Old people want to be with their families, not together in an isolated community."[48] On its inaugural weekend in January 1960, more than 100,000 people packed Sun City's sales office and visited model homes; 237 units were sold. Sun City received front-page treatment from the media. Bob Considine, a nationally syndicated New York columnist, devoted an entire article to Sun City, and it appeared in hundreds of newspapers across the country. Stories followed in the *Chicago Tribune*, the *San Francisco Chronicle*, and the *Los Angeles Times*. Many of Sun City's first residents were retirees who had been spending winters in the Phoenix area, but soon retirees around the country were reading about Sun City in their doctors' offices and in hometown newspapers. Comedian Bob Hope came to Sun City to play golf, and *Rowan and Martin's Laugh-In* spoofed the new active lifestyle for seniors.[49]

In Sun City, Del Webb sold a lifestyle of active leisure, social interaction with age peers, and insularity from urban life. There was the spirit of starting a new life in Sun City. People were surprised to learn that their neighbors came from all walks of life, including several millionaires. The focus was on the future, not on where you came from, what you did for a living, or how much money you had. The first generation of Sun City pioneers included doctors, dentists, chiropractors, attorneys, merchants, manufacturers, retired military officers, government employees, executives, bankers, company presidents, ranchers, farmers, contractors, carpenters, and construction workers. What they had in common was the search for companionship and activity, and the quest for a new life in a new place.

The original Sun City contained bungalows intended for retirees of modest means, but new residents quickly set about adding screened-in patios, garages, and swimming pools. It was clear that there was sufficient demand for a much larger range of home styles, with more luxurious units at the top. By 1970, buyers could choose from a variety of single-family homes, duplexes, garden apartments, villas, quads, chalet apartments, patio homes, and ranch estates. The social class and income structure of Sun City today reflect this evolution. Those with more modest means live in the bungalows of the older neighborhoods, the more affluent in newer neighborhoods.[50]

When the original Sun City was completed in the late-1970s with around 40,000 residents, construction began on neighboring Sun City West with a target population of 28,000. And with completion of Sun City West in the late-1990s, the construction of Sun City Grand began. None of the Sun Cities were homegrown communities in the sense that they drew from a native-born, local market. Del Webb aggressively advertised Sun City in newspapers nationwide (especially in the Midwest) and instituted the notion of "vacation specials." Advertising in newspapers and magazines

and on television and radio stations across the country proclaimed: "Enjoy a wonderful vacation in a lovely apartment in
beautiful Sun City. Enjoy resort living, tour the models, enjoy a
completely furnished air conditioned apartment. Free guest activities, two free games of golf." These vacation specials were enor-
mously successful in spreading the image of Sun City nationwide,
and introducing visitors to the Sun City lifestyle.

CENTRAL ARIZONA PROJECT

The growth of Sun City, Youngtown, Maryvale, and the region's
other new communities would demand new supplies of water. The
Central Arizona Project (CAP) was constructed between 1973 and
1993 to bring Colorado River water to the desert cities of Phoenix
and Tucson. The idea of tapping into the Colorado River actually
began much earlier when, in 1922, the states bordering the Colorado River agreed with the federal government upon a plan for
water management called the Colorado River Compact. In 1928,
Congress allocated 2.8 million acre feet per year (one acre foot
equals 325,851 gallons, the amount estimated to be used annually by a family of four) to Arizona, far more than the state could
possibly use at the time, but seen as important to future growth.
To fully use its allotment, and to keep thirsty and greedy southern
Californians from using more than their share, Arizona looked for
a way to transport Colorado River water to the central part of the
state.

In 1968 at the behest of the Arizona congressional delegation,
Congress passed, and President Lyndon Johnson signed a bill approving the construction of an aqueduct from the Colorado River
to central Arizona. Construction of CAP began in 1973, with the
first Colorado River water pumped in 1985. With the capacity to
deliver some 1.5 acre feet of water annually, CAP became a critical
source of water for current and future population growth. The

problem, of course, is that the Colorado River's actual flow is less than the 16.4 million acre feet per year upon which the Colorado River Compact was based. In addition, Arizona has the lowest priority of the lower-basin states of Nevada, California, and Arizona, and its allocation will be the first cut in times of shortage. Arizona agreed to this provision in exchange for federal authorization of the CAP. In a series of legal cases and acts of Congress, the state's thirteen Indian tribes, who claim prior use of water, are now in the process of settling their claims and are about to receive almost half of the state's share of Colorado River water, making them key players in Greater Phoenix's future growth.

ENVIRONMENTAL CHALLENGES

With burgeoning postwar population growth, came a new set of environmental challenges. The desert is not by nature an obvious place to put a city of 3.6 million people. Problems of aridity are chronic. Floods can be absent for many years, and then reappear suddenly in an environment altered by large-scale urbanization. This scenario is precisely what occurred during a series of calamitous floods during the late 1970s. Postwar urbanization coincided with an unusually arid period: between 1942 and 1965, when the bed of the Salt River was for all intents and purposes dry. New migrants had no experience with the counterintuitive notion of too much water in the desert, and long-time residents had forgotten about the river's epic force. People built homes, not only in the flood plain, but in the river channel itself. Cities built roads across the river bottom to avoid the cost of expensive bridges. Sand and gravel pits were excavated in the empty river channel, and the flood plain was used for a new airport runway, parking lots, and farming operations. A wake-up call was sounded in 1965 in the form of a moderate-size flood, but people paid no heed. Despite traffic disruptions and damage to homes and property, individuals and communities simply rebuilt in place, underestimating the flood risk.

Two monster storms in 1978 laid this naive view to rest. Heavy rains in March drenched the watershed and unleashed a torrent of water through the heart of Phoenix. Three people died directly from the storm, and a woman was asphyxiated by automobile exhaust while waiting to cross the river on a local street. The city was crippled economically, with only three north-south bridges in a metropolis of almost 1.5 million people. Workers could not reach their jobs. Businesses were cut off from customers. Several corporations hired helicopters to shuttle workers to and from their jobs; many workers stayed temporarily with colleagues on the "right side" of the river. Railroad passenger service was temporarily activated to run across the river on a train called the Hattie B, named after Governor Bruce Babbitt's wife. Phoenicians were reminded that their desert city was divided by an intermittent dryland river that could suddenly disrupt daily lives and damage property.

Especially hard hit was Allenville, a close-knit westside community of 51 families founded in the 1940s by John Allen as a settlement for black farm laborers whose skin color prevented them from living in the nearby town of Buckeye.[51] Located in the channel of the river, Allenville bore the full brunt of flood waters. Residents were evacuated as the waters rose, and their homes were severely damaged. They vowed to return, rebuild their homes, and maintain the close-knit community. In a cruel twist of fate, just as residents were returning to their homes in December, 1978, the town again was inundated by storm waters. A dense snow pack in the mountains caused heavy runoff, and soil saturated from the previous storm caused severe flooding. The all-too-familiar drill of evacuation followed. This time, however, Allenville residents and local government officials acknowledged the folly of rebuilding on the same hazard-prone site. The local office of the Army Corps of Engineers relocated the entire town to a plot of state-owned land eight miles northwest of Buckeye, and the new community of Hopeville was established.

After these disasters, the risk of flood damage was reduced through engineering solutions. Urban residents, unwilling to tolerate disruption in their daily lives, built large bridges immune to all but the most extreme natural events, and channelized much of the lower Salt River. Levees protect 19 of the 53 miles of the Salt River from Granite Reef Dam to the confluence with the Gila.[52]

An innovative response to the desert's climatic variability—one that adjusts to uncertainty rather than engineers it away—is Scottsdale's Indian Bend Wash. From its beginnings, Scottsdale was bisected by a desert wash that delivered water from large mountain watersheds in the Phoenix and McDowell Mountains to the north into the Salt River south of the city. Indian Bend Wash was, in its natural state, a wide sandy strip with a shallow channel and tiny banks unable to contain runoff from high-intensity rains.[53] During a storm, water would overflow into nearby neighborhoods, preventing children from getting to school and disrupting emergency medical services. Even in dry years, the wash was an eyesore, highly eroded and overgrown with weeds and mesquite. Local residents hunted rabbits there and called it the "Slough."[54]

Floods were not a hazard when people did not live in the wash, but by 1970 Scottsdale had grown rapidly, and 60 percent of the flood plain had been developed. Scottsdale residents clamored for a solution and enlisted help from the state's congressional delegation. Congress directed the local office of the Army Corps of Engineers to provide a solution. In 1961, the Corps proposed lining seven miles of the wash from the Arizona Canal to the Salt River with concrete, creating a channel 125 feet wide and 25 feet deep. Scottsdale residents abhorred the idea, fearing a repeat of the Los Angeles River debacle of building an ugly, concrete channel through the heart of the city. In 1965, citizens defeated a bond issue intended to line the channel. A citizens group suggested turning the wash into a greenbelt, adding golf courses, ball fields, playgrounds, and hiking and equestrian trails. The proposed system would intercept flood waters originating in the McDowell Mountains and channel them into the wash and downstream 4.5 miles to the Salt River. The floodway would range from 800 to 1,200 feet wide and from 5 to 8 feet deep and be lined by earthen berms designed to confine flows up to a 100-year flood. The greenway was to consist of parks, golf courses, playgrounds, and hiking trails with features that would withstand rushing flood waters one day and be restored to recreational use the next (Figure 7). Maricopa County Flood Control District agreed to acquire the necessary land, and the Corps of Engineers agreed to build the flood-control structures and pay for half of the recreational features. Scottsdale pledged to pick up the tab for developing the other half of the recreational features and to build a series of east-west bridges capable of withstanding a 100-year flood.[55]

As plans for the project unfolded, and as Scottsdale sought public support for its share of the project, a 70-year flood hit the area in June 1972. Water backed up behind the Arizona Canal, causing damage to homes and a local resort; guest suitcases were seen floating in the parking lot. The area between Indian Bend Wash and Sixty-Fourth Street was inundated, 17 families in an adjacent settlement of low-income Yaqui Indians were left homeless, and one man drowned. Residents were unable to commute across the wash, many were cut off from emergency medical services, and children were unable to get to school. In April 1973, Scottsdale residents overwhelmingly approved a $10 million bond issue to support flood control by a margin of seven to one. By 1975, most of the recreational features were in place, as were several bridges. By the mid-1980s, the flood control features were completed.[56] Indian Bend Wash today serves as a model of intergovernmental cooperation, innovative urban design, and effective

Figure 7. Indian Bend Wash in Scottsdale is designed for both recreation (above) and flood control (below). Author's photographs.

flood control. What was once a physical and psychological barrier dividing Scottsdale became a community focal point and intensively used public space. The main criticism is the wash's lush greenery fails to convey a sense of the desert and requires heavy watering.

A second environmental threat involved mining of the region's underground aquifers. The Salt River Project's early twentieth-century plumbing system of dams and canals supported a prosperous agricultural society and postwar growth, but a crisis situation had arisen by mid-century. Until 1955, most of the region's urban growth had occurred in SRP's service area. Because it takes somewhat less water to support an acre of single-family homes than to grow an acre of cotton or alfalfa, the transition from rural to urban did not overly strain the region's water supply. After 1955, new development occurred outside the SRP service area on desert land as opposed to farmland. New supplies of water were required to support these new residential subdivisions. In addition, SRP was unable to meet the needs of its service area consistently and pumped a great deal of groundwater, especially during a long dry spell between 1941 and 1965, and agricultural users outside SRP's service area increased dramatically. The successful agricultural economy in SRP territory attracted other farmers and investors to try agriculture outside the service area, with new districts springing up from the 1920s to the 1950s. These districts were heavily dependent upon groundwater.

Tensions mounted from the escalating demand for water from SRP, municipalities, and farmers. By 1980, the state was consuming almost five million acre feet of water a year, twice the annual renewable supply.[57] Even with the Central Arizona Project coming online in the mid-1980s, there still would be a deficit, assuming prevailing levels of consumption. Land subsidence resulted in damaged roads and building foundations in many parts of the valley. Groundwater depletion also caused aquifer compaction, a reduction in overall storage space, and a decline in water quality. Cities understood that continued growth would require groundwater conservation, but knew that they consumed only 5 percent of the state's water supply. The major concessions to maintain growth and avoid an environmental disaster would need to come from the farmers who used 89 percent of the state's water supply.

Resolution of this problem signaled a shift in the balance of power from farmers who controlled a large majority of the state's water to cities that housed 80 percent of the state's population and voters. Early efforts to mediate the dispute revealed deepseated suspicion and distrust on all sides. The cities and mines accused the farmers of being water monopolists. Farmers felt that cities and mines were openly hostile to agriculture, and they preferred the status quo. Despite these differences, the momentum for groundwater reform was strong as urban growth eventually would be curtailed by water shortages.

In February 1977, President Jimmy Carter proposed to cancel the funding of 19 Western water projects, including CAP. In November 1977, a 25-member commission was set up to study the problem of groundwater depletion and draft a proposed law. At the crux of the debate was whether farmers' right to use groundwater was a property right or, as the cities and mines argued, a public resource governed by the same rules as surface water. Secretary of the Interior Cecil Andres warned that he would not allocate CAP water until Arizona passed a groundwater bill. Moreover, allocations had to be made in 1980 to keep the CAP on schedule. Secretary Andres visited Phoenix in October 1979 and declared in no uncertain terms: no groundwater code, no CAP.[58]

Then Governor Bruce Babbitt assembled stakeholders, including leaders of the legislature and representatives from cities, mines, and agriculture. This so-called "rump group" met in private for hundreds of hours. Babbitt was able to broker a delicate compromise among the three powerful antagonists (cities, farm-

CHAPTER 2

ers, and the mines), first because he was a skilled negotiator and knew a great deal about western water issues, and second, because there was simply no choice but to settle if the state was to continue to grow. The state legislature passed the Groundwater Management Act on June 11, 1980, and the governor signed the bill the next day. Because it was passed by an 80 percent majority, the Act went into effect immediately.[59] The code provided for strong state management and a program of conservation. It defined rights to use and transport water and a method of administering and enforcing the law. No group was completely satisfied, but all could live with the final result. The Ford Foundation named this Act one of the nation's ten most innovative programs in state and local government.

Drafters of Arizona's Groundwater Code identified four areas in the state, including Phoenix, Pinal County, Prescott, and Tucson, where groundwater problems were most severe and designated them as Active Management Areas (AMAs). A fifth AMA, Santa Cruz, was added in 1994 from a portion of the Tucson AMA.[60] The overriding goal was to achieve safe yield, considered an even balance between withdrawal and recharge by 2025 in three of the four original AMAs. In the Pinal AMA, the goal was to allow the development of nonirrigation water uses, extend the life of the agricultural economy for as long as possible, and retain water supplies for future urbanization.[61] In a series of management plans, farmlands were to be retired and higher levels of conservation achieved through the reduction in per capita water consumption in urban areas. The Act required developers to guarantee a 100-year water supply from renewable sources before a plan can be approved and offered three options for securing that supply. The simplest option is to develop new subdivisions within a municipal service area where the city is designated as the water provider. Once a developer obtains a water permit from the city, he or she satisfies the assured water-supply requirement. A second option is to retire farmland from production and convert irrigation rights into what are called Type 1 rights. The third method is to use the Central Arizona Groundwater Replenishment District (CAGRD) to augment supplies depleted by district members. The CAGRD has been very popular and has allowed development in areas that have no access to CAP water. Of concern are CAGRD's capacity to store water in places distant from where it will be used and its reliance on surplus water rather than permanent supplies to support future growth. With the creation of the Arizona Water Banking Authority in 1996, the state is taking its full Colorado River allocation, and it is banking a portion to ensure a 100-year water supply for new developments. This begs the question of what happens when allocations are fully allocated twenty to thirty years from now.

Also significant is whether healthful air quality can be maintained in the face of large-scale urbanization of the desert. During the past decade, unhealthful levels of atmospheric ozone across the Phoenix area attracted the attention of the U.S. Environmental Protection Agency (EPA) and the local population. Ozone is a colorless, slightly odorous gas. In the stratosphere, ozone blocks harmful ultraviolet radiation. In the urban atmosphere, it forms from the reaction of hydrocarbons from combustion and nitrogen oxide through heat and sunlight. Ozone pollution is mainly a summertime problem in Phoenix because the radiation is strong enough to trigger the photochemical process. Exposure to ozone can make people more susceptible to respiratory infection and lung inflammation and exacerbate conditions such as asthma. These conditions are dangerous to children because they spend so much time outdoors, and to the elderly because they are weakened by preexisting medical conditions. Joggers and exercising adults can experience throat dryness, chest tightness, cough, and shortness of breath. Ozone also is a significant cause of plant damage, being responsible for more than 90 percent of plant injury from air pollution on a global basis.[62]

The physical geography of Phoenix is uniquely well suited to produce and concentrate ozone. The region's high temperatures and clear, dry air promote the photochemical process in which nitrogen oxide combines with molecular oxygen to form ozone. The prevalence of light winds and an urban area surrounded by higher-elevation terrain prevent easy dispersion of ozone once it is produced. In 2002, the Phoenix area failed to meet EPA's standard for healthful ozone levels on 14 days, but this figure was down from 35 days in 1998.[63] Ozone has been reduced through automobile engine modifications, better engineered fuel tanks, a vehicle inspection program in the Phoenix metropolitan area, vapor recovery systems at retail gas stations, and reformulated gasoline. Despite these efforts, population growth and natural conditions make it difficult for Phoenix to meet the current eight-hour federal standard. In addition, because of the complex terrain and local circulation patterns, some parts of the urban area are more negatively affected than others. During hot, dry high-ozone days, local circulation is directed toward the higher elevations in the eastern part of the valley, and embedded in this flow is a plume of high-ozone concentration over the eastern suburb of Mesa.[64] The nature of Phoenix's circulation system means that unhealthful levels of ozone can appear far from the actual sources of pollutants. Massive population growth and increasing automobile emissions on the westside are causing high ozone concentrations on the eastside.

Air quality also is at risk from high particulate counts. Particulate matter involves solid particles and liquid droplets found in the air. Many artificial and natural sources emit particulates. Particles less than 10 micrometers in diameter pose the greatest health risk because they are inhaled and accumulate in the respiratory system. Very fine particles of less than 2.5 micrometers are responsible for the "brown cloud" that hovers over Phoenix on many calm days. It is primarily a fall and winter problem. The West Valley tends to have the highest particulate counts because of the presence of construction and industrial activity there. Although the region has been successful in lowering ozone and carbon monoxide emissions with the use of specially formulated gasolines, the percentage of days with high counts of the very fine particulates increased from one per year in 1999 to four in 2001 and five in 2002.[65] In 1995, the Arizona Comparative Environmental Risk Project estimated that small-particulate concentrations were responsible for more than 900 premature deaths annually and were observed in recent increases in hospital admissions for respiratory disease, asthma episodes, lower respiratory symptoms, and coughs.[66]

Arguably, the "hottest" challenge on the region's current environmental agenda is the growth of an urban heat island. Large-scale urbanization has caused the desert surfaces and the boundary layer atmosphere above to heat up, especially at night. This phenomenon happens because the city's buildings and paved surfaces absorb more sunlight and store the resulting heat energy more efficiently than natural vegetation. At night, city surfaces are slower to release this heat, preventing the temperature from falling as fast as in rural areas. The effect is strongest in the city center, where urban canyons, or clusters of high-rise buildings, are concentrated and heat absorption is greatest. Parts of Phoenix presently experience nighttime temperatures that are 12° F warmer than surrounding rural areas.[67] The heat island is more extreme in Phoenix than in temperate cities of similar size due to clear, calm weather, low-latitude, intense sunshine, and abundant heat-absorbing surfaces.

Longtime residents of Phoenix know that it takes less time to heat up in the mornings, and evening cooling is slower. The average number of hours per day between May and September with temperatures over 100° F—called "misery hours"—has nearly doubled since 1948, from 1.8 to 3.4. The number of hours with temperatures over 100° F during July and August increased from 3.6 to 6.4.[68] Heightened temperatures affect human comfort, as Phoenicians typically schedule daily exercise during the cooler morning and early evening hours. Also affected are energy demand and water use because more electrical power is required to maintain comfortable indoor temperatures, and high temperatures increase evaporation and the need for outdoor plants to be watered more often. The urban heat island threatens Phoenix's recent attempt to market itself as a year-round tourist destination, although temperatures at many resorts are considerably cooler than that of the city's official weather station at Sky Harbor Airport because they are at higher elevations and surrounded by dense, cooling vegetation.[69]

Although the heat island occurs at the regional level, there are quite startling and informative temperature variations across the urban area that may point to land-use strategies for mitigating the heat island effect. Phoenix's mosaic of wet and dry surfaces creates vastly different microclimates and thus human comfort levels. Areas with extensive watering provide longer periods of cooling and thus provide greater comfort. These examples suggest that heat-island-induced discomfort may be ameliorated, at a very small scale, with large amounts of greening, shading, and the altering of hot materials used for building and paving.[70]

The modern history of Phoenix is a story of how humans have confronted one environmental obstacle after another to build a metropolis of 3.6 million people in one of the most physically challenging places on Earth. Phoenicians constructed a sophisticated water infrastructure to tap into supplies from faraway watersheds, moderated desert heat with swamp coolers and air conditioning, protected themselves from episodic flooding by bigger bridges and through creative urban design, and developed innovative public policy to prevent the depletion of underground banks of water. To gain immunity from the vagaries of desert life, Phoenicians altered the local climate, topography, and vegetation, but in the process, they began to lose touch with the essence of desert life: its plants and animals, the unpredictability and extremes of its climate, the grandeur and beauty of the natural landscape, and the centrality of water to sustaining life in the desert.

Historical experience supports the view that desert dwellers can, through cooperative action and a unified purpose, moderate and accommodate their difficult environment to support large-scale urbanization. A significant issue for Phoenix's future is whether an increasingly diverse and socially balkanized population can make environmentally sound decisions in the face of increasing climatic uncertainty and a rapidly growing population.

An Ever-Changing Social Dynamic

Phoenix is not a sentimental city, focused on past traditions, heroic leaders, or memorable events. It is an ever-changing, ever-growing fusion of newcomers and old timers, all with an eye toward the future. When the great western author Wallace Stegner likened Westerners to "rolling stones that gather no moss," he captured the soul of many Phoenicians—always on the move. Rapid growth and constant turnover lead to a culture of migration, emphasizing change, innovation, adaptation, and the future. Such dynamism also leads to a weakened sense of place and conflicted loyalties, because many residents stay connected to the cities they came from, and expect to move again. Phoenix is like other Western cities in that many residents do not have close family members living nearby. Social discourse often begins with a rendition of residential histories. Friendships are formed among those who share connections with Wisconsin, Minnesota, Illinois, or even a particular neighborhood of Chicago or Cleveland.

Regional retailers, like Bashas supermarkets, are disadvantaged, having to spend more money to advertise their presence to an ever-changing mix of people more familiar with national brands like Safeway, Home Depot, and Wal-Mart. When the National Football League's Arizona Cardinals play the Dallas Cowboys or when the Arizona Diamondbacks baseball team plays the

Chicago Cubs, local broadcasters and team officials lament the loss of home field advantage because so many transplants from Texas and Chicago continue to cheer for their "hometown" teams. Even newcomers from abroad find it easy, because of advanced communications technology, to maintain ties to their homelands. They lead what anthropologists call transnational lifestyles, in other words, their lives transcend international borders. Everyday life includes reading hometown newspapers on the Internet, sending money home, and staying in close touch with the people and places they left behind.

Phoenix is in the process of becoming one of the nation's largest metropolitan areas. With this transition in status comes a huge influx of people and growing racial and ethnic diversity. Increasing diversity has the potential to transform Phoenix into one of the great cosmopolitan cities of the twenty-first century or, alternatively, into a socially fragmented place where affluent whites retreat into gated and guarded enclaves at the urban fringe to avoid confrontation with the inevitable ambiguities of modern urban life. Phoenix has a dismal early record of racial and ethnic intolerance. In the late nineteenth and early twentieth centuries, Phoenix was an ethnically diverse city populated by Native Americans, Mexicans, Chinese, African Americans, Mormon colonizers from Utah, and Anglo-European migrants from California and the Midwest. Eager to reshape the city's image from a primitive western outpost into a prosperous American town, the rapidly growing Anglo majority systematically purged minorities from public life and confined them to the least desirable, most flood-prone neighborhoods. Today's international migrants encounter a society that is open to newcomers, but not one that has, in the main, embraced multiculturalism, tolerance, or diversity.

Gated and master-planned communities proliferate on Phoenix's urban fringe. These communities promote a much-needed sense of belonging for newcomers, but impede regional cohesion. The new planned community of Verrado on the westside touts itself as a place "to press the fast-forward button, so that the community will have all the attributes of a clearly defined small town without waiting several generations for it to occur."[1] Civic leaders in outlying suburbs bemoan the fact that the residents of these places are more deeply involved in their immediate neighborhoods and communities than committed to the municipalities empowered to collect their taxes, provide public services, and plan for the future.

A LEGACY OF SEPARATION

Early Phoenix's prosperity drew Anglo-European settlers into a town that, unlike other cities of the Southwest, had not existed during the Spanish and Mexican periods. As a result, the new Anglo majority easily imposed their cultural system on the local population and denied the city's minorities a meaningful place in public life. Like other Western towns at the time, early Phoenix was in fact a melange of racial and ethnic groups who migrated to the city after working on the region's farms, in gold and silver mines, as construction workers on the transcontinental railroad, and as cowboys and soldiers at military posts. Rather than embrace this stunning array of humanity, early city leaders scrupulously reframed the city's image into one of a "progressive American town" and disparaged the behavior and cultural traditions of those who did not fit this image. A 1872 article about Phoenix in the *San Diego Union* set the tone for the new community's attitude toward people of color: "the Indian is now a nuisance and the Sonoran a decided annoyance, but both are sure to disappear before civilization as snow before the noonday sun."[2]

NATIVE PEOPLES

In 1876, the city's native peoples were described by Prescott's *Arizona Miner* as "idle, lounging Pima and Maricopa Indians continually about the streets or lying under some convenient shade, and apparently living on melons, pumpkins, and other cheap vegetables."[3] A 1889 ordinance made it illegal for Indians to appear on city streets scantily dressed, or to be out after dark unless employed by a Phoenix resident.[4] Discriminatory practices such as Indian seating areas in local theaters codified the reality of separation. Arizona denied Indians the right to vote until the state's constitution was reinterpreted in 1948.[5]

The Phoenix Indian School was established in 1892 to "Americanize" indigenous peoples, and, by 1900, the school enrolled some 700 students on its campus at Seventh Street and Indian School Road.[6] In an environment in which Indians were unwelcome on city streets after nightfall, many students became familiar with Phoenix neighborhoods through the school which operated an "outing system," initially to acquaint them with American customs and work life. Some students worked in adjacent orchards, while others worked in local homes where it was considered fashionable at the turn of the century to employ an Indian servant. Eventually, the program became a job-placement service for Indians and a source of cheap labor for Phoenician households.[7] Until its closure in 1990, the Phoenix Indian School served as point of entry for thousands of Native Americans moving to the city. Despite its harsh institutional setting and goal of eradicating Indian culture, the Indian School was a symbol of Indian solidarity and a gathering place for native Americans in the city.[8]

Many early twentieth-century Indians lived in poor inner-city neighborhoods, though a middle-class cluster of homes grew near the Phoenix Indian School. One former resident of the latter

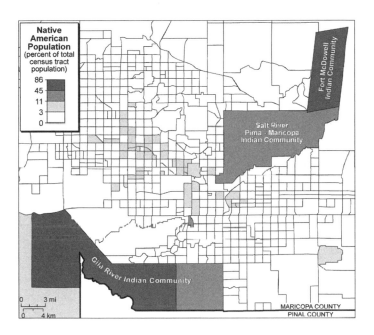

Figure 8. Phoenix's Native American population in 2000. U.S. Census 2000, Summary File 1.

neighborhood recalled "a real community. It was just like a little village, a little center. And then . . . there was a drug store, a beauty shop, and of course there was the tavern. It was just basically a little self-contained community."[9] Neighborhoods surrounding the old Phoenix Indian School site contain today's strongest residential concentrations of Native Americans, except for Guadalupe, a community of Yaqui Indians adjacent to Tempe, and the region's Native-American reservations (Figure 8). Nearby are the Phoenix Indian Hospital at Indian School Road and Sixteenth Street, social service agencies catering to Native Americans, and several classic Indian businesses such as a fry bread shop and art galleries. This cluster is fairly weak, however, with non-Indians greatly outnumbering Native Americans. Native Americans are dispersed throughout the city's low-income neighborhoods. In 2000, there were 45,703 Native Americans in Greater

Phoenix, up from 32,270 in 1990.[10] Nearly 50 percent lived inside the City of Phoenix, another 30 percent lived on reservations, and 12 percent were scattered across the older neighborhoods of suburban Mesa.

It is overly simplistic to see the treatment of Indians as a result of racism, discrimination, and Anglo domination, as the City of Guadalupe, sandwiched between Tempe and Phoenix, reflects both Anglo paternalism and Indian solidarity. Yaquis are Indians of Mexican descent. For hundreds of years, they cultivated fields along the Yaqui River in Sonora, Mexico. Beginning in the 1880s, they sought employment outside the "Eight Pueblos" of Sonora in the mines, on local haciendas, and in Arizona, where the climate was similar and the border was not patrolled. Under pressure for economic development and land reform, the government of Mexican dictator Porfirio Díaz brutally seized Yaqui land. Some Yaquis sought refuge in nearby mountains and formed a guerilla movement to fight the government. Others sought work in Arizona to help finance the resistence. Frustrated by the Yaqui guerillas, the Mexican government adopted a formal policy of deportation and extermination, and expelled hundreds of Yaquis to the Yucatán Peninsula in 1906. After the fall of Díaz, the Mexican Revolution continued to persecute the Yaquis, and many escaped to Arizona where family and friends had already established homes.[11]

Yaquis built four settlements near Tucson and Guadalupe south of Tempe. The founders of Guadalupe arrived in Arizona in the 1880s, and sought help from Franciscan friars. A friar brought them to the Phoenix area, where a Tempe homesteader relinquished five acres to the Catholic Church for one dollar. Under the friar's direction, Yaquis contacted friends and relatives and encouraged them to settle on church land. They built a church and central plaza and a cemetery nearby and named the village after the patron saint of their homeland, Our Lady of Guadalupe.

Fearing deportation to Mexico, the original Yaquis initially kept a low profile, but when they realized that the U.S. government had no intention of sending them home, they revived their cultural traditions. These traditions were centered on large extended families, Spanish language, and a unique form of Catholicism that combined Spanish and Indian traditions. After a dispute with a neighbor in 1914, Yaquis moved to a new 40-acre site, the current town site of Guadalupe.

Many Yaquis worked for the Salt River Valley Water Users Association (SRVWUA), the organization charged with maintaining the irrigation canals after Roosevelt Dam was constructed. SRVWUA had a hard time finding sturdy, willing workers to perform the dirty, arduous work of clearing and cleaning canals. First, they recruited Apache Indians but concluded they were sheep herders and cattle raisers and unsuited for settled agricultural work. Later, Puerto Ricans were recruited to work, but they too had little experience in agricultural tasks and expected better working conditions than local employers provided. SRVWUA hired Yaquis who proved to be loyal and industrious workers. Irrigation work was familiar, and they were accustomed to the climate, used tools with dexterity, and even seemed immune to scorpion bites. In addition, refugee status protected them, unlike other Mexicans, from deportation by U.S. authorities. Lee Webb, a SRVWUA construction supervisor familiar with the Yaqui's reputation as good workers and with their favorable immigration status, traveled to Mexico and Tucson between 1922 and 1924 to recruit Yaquis for canal work. The Water Users Association became the major employer of Yaquis in Phoenix. Despite their reputation as industrious workers, Yaquis were still Indians and Mexicans, and few were promoted.[12]

The Association decided in 1927 to establish permanent camps for canal-maintenance crews at two sites: "Northside" north of the Salt River at the confluence of the Crosscut and Arizona Ca-

nals in south Scottsdale and "Southside" south of the river between Tempe and Chandler. These camps were in no way unusual,
as some 80 labor camps dotted the cotton belt of Maricopa
County, extending some 50 miles west of the city. Guadalupe remained the focal point for Yaqui culture, but its year-round resident population was quite small, as many Yaquis circulated
among the camps and farm fields of Greater Phoenix. Hourly work
was extended into year-round employment by cleaning canals in
the summer and winter and picking cotton in the spring and fall.
Guadalupe was the center for Yaqui social life, and community
members returned often for festivals, church, burials, visits with
family, and religious holidays, particularly during Lenten and the
Easter season. The SRVWUA camps provided political sanctuary
and stability for a displaced people who sought to preserve their
cultural traditions, but living conditions were very primitive. Yaqui
workers lived in tents, shacks, and houses made of sticks, wood,
and cardboard.[13] Only after World War II started and Yaquis began
to leave the camps for better paying jobs did the housing conditions improve. SRVWUA fostered segregation, albeit it in benign
way, through camp activities, by allowing workers time off for
fiestas, and by publishing a Spanish-language newspaper.[14]

By the 1950s, the camps were more of a burden than a help
for the SRVWUA. New chemicals and machinery lessened the
need for human labor to keep the canals clean. Postwar urban
expansion spawned conflicts between primitive camps and neighboring subdivisions and businesses. Many Yaqui bought homes
and moved out of the camps, and camp housing conditions deteriorated. Camp children had problems in public schools because
they could scarcely speak English. In 1956, SRVWUA's board
voted to abandon the camps and sent a 30-day notice to the 37
remaining Yaqui households. Many moved back to Guadalupe,
while others found housing in south Scottsdale near the old
Northside camp. Some took jobs in construction, maintenance,

and the service industry, while others continued to work for the Salt River Project.

When adjacent Tempe attempted to annex Guadalupe in 1974, residents objected, fearing their deteriorated housing units would not meet Tempe's housing code and not wanting to pay higher taxes for Tempe services. Guadalupe incorporated as a freestanding community later that year. Self-determination has proven rocky, as Guadalupe's municipal history has been riddled with political squabbles, infighting, and corruption. Modern subdivisions, an outlet mall, fast food restaurants, and other trappings of mass American culture now surround the town. Within its borders, however, remains a unique community with deep roots in the region's agricultural past and first-hand experience with its legacy of discrimination and social segregation.

MEXICAN AMERICANS

Mexicans were equally important to the nineteenth- and early twentieth-century history of the valley, and were similarly set apart by the growing Anglo majority. The city's first Mexicans were called Sonorans because they moved north from the Mexican state of Sonora. They settled first at Fort McDowell working as post guides, translators, laborers, and volunteers for the military forces in the 1870s and labored in the hay camps of the Salt River Valley. Jack Swilling's wife, Trinidad Escalante Swilling, was Mexican, giving him influence among local Mexicans. In 1870, Mexicans comprised half of Phoenix's population, and they played an active role in the city's commercial and civic life, as illustrated by the election in 1881 of Henry Gárfias as city marshal.[15] Gárfias also served in other city offices, including constable, tax collector, and street superintendent. He published a local newspaper, *El Progresso*, which helped him reach out to Mexican voters.

Early Mexican migrants to Phoenix considered themselves to

be sojourners and intended to return to Mexico eventually. Ethnic identity was maintained by congregating in ethnic neighborhoods or barrios. In 1881, Mexican workers built the original St. Mary's Catholic Church, an adobe structure, on East Monroe on land donated by Jesús Ortero, a local businessman. A district of Mexican homes and businesses along East Monroe, known locally as the "Sonora corner of Phoenix," celebrated Mexican Independence Day on September 16 with fireworks, bonfires, dancing, singing, and drinking.[16]

As Anglo-Americans streamed to the area in the late nineteenth century to homestead and farm, Mexicans declined as a proportion of the population and became increasingly segregated, both socially and spatially. After the great flood of 1891, when the Salt River reached Washington Street, Anglos moved to high ground, away from the potential for flood damage. Enterprising real-estate developers and land speculators encouraged this trend and constructed new trolley lines to the north. Poorer Mexicans continued to build homes in the lower flood-prone districts south of the downtown amidst the city's railroads, warehouses, and stockyards. The new economic order dictated that Mexicans would provide cheap labor for the rapidly growing city and its surrounding farmlands.

The concentration of Mexican barrios south of downtown served the Anglo need to present Phoenix as an American town. From the Mexican perspective, concentration provided the market base to support ethnic businesses and to establish Spanish-language newspapers, benevolent societies, employment bureaus, and other cultural institutions. In addition, geographic concentration afforded a measure of political power in an increasingly Anglo community, as minority residents dominated two of the city's four wards. Mexicans lost this toehold on political power in 1913 when Progressive Anglo reformers succeeded in revising the city charter from ward-based to at-large elections. After the reform, representatives from the more populous and affluent northern neighborhoods dominated city leadership. In 1982, the city returned to district elections, and Hispanic influence on city government increased, though modestly.

By 1940, Mexican settlement in Phoenix was concentrated in two neighborhoods: between Sixteenth and Twenty-Fourth Streets, from Washington Street south to the Salt River and between Second and Fourth Avenues south of Washington. Barrios contained residences, shops, churches, schools, societies, and institutions vital for survival in an increasingly Americanized community. Physical separation of Mexicans was enforced by signs that warned: "No Mexicans Allowed" or that restricted Mexican use of public facilities to particular hours of the day or days of the week. Longstanding Latino residents recall being limited in their use of city pools to just before the water was changed, when it was too dirty for Anglo children.[17] In a particularly egregious act, Irish priests at St. Mary's Church relegated Mexican parishioners to the basement of the church that their parents and grandparents had founded and built.[18] Eventually, they left St. Mary's for their own churches, which became the new centers for Mexican Catholic life in Phoenix. The new St. Mary's Basilica, dedicated in 1915, became the focus of Anglo Catholicism (Figure 9).

The story of the Golden Gate Barrio's unsuccessful struggle for survival in the face of Phoenix's quest to expand Sky Harbor Airport is a sobering tale of the domination of Anglo economic interests over Mexican cultural traditions in the city's development. Located between Sixteenth and Twenty-Fourth Streets north of Buckeye Road, the Golden Gate Barrio was firmly established by 1933. Mexican families owned homes on small lots that were constructed of cheap materials by the residents themselves or by a local Mexican contractor. Roofs were made of corrugated metal, plumbing was lacking, and dirt floors were common. Urban amenities were sparse; Golden Gate had no sidewalks, water, or

Figure 9. Saint Mary's Basilica, dedicated in February 1915, is the oldest Catholic church in the city of Phoenix. Courtesy of Phoenix Museum of History, St. Mary's Basilica Collection.

sewer facilities. Water came from backyard wells, and wood was the main source of heat and fuel. On hot summer nights, beds would be moved outside for cooler sleeping.[19]

Despite these primitive conditions, a sense of community thrived in Golden Gate. Phoenix's Mexican American community was active in the war effort, providing servicemen and participating in warbond drives. Golden Gate emerged as a distinct place in its drive to build a neighborhood church. The barrio held fund drives in the late 1930s, and one resident donated land for the much-sought-after building. By the 1940s, an old store had been converted for church use. Community activism grew when Father Albert Braun, a Franciscan priest, moved to Phoenix after World War II and took a special interest in Golden Gate's campaign for its own church. After a good deal of sacrifice and persistence, Sacred Heart Church, a rectory, and school were constructed in

CHAPTER 3

the mid-1950s. Original plans called for the adobe brick construction, but when the bricks dissolved during an untimely rainfall, Father Albert started a program whereby everyone, even children, would buy at least one red brick for church construction. Building the church thus became a community effort. In addition to religious services, the church sponsored fiestas and became a focus for Mexican life and social activism. In 1972, when Governor Jack Williams signed legislation that would prevent farm workers from striking during harvests, United Farmworkers Union leader César Chávez began a "fast of life" at Saint Rita's Center in Sacred Heart Church. He was visited by U.S. presidential candidate George Mc-Govern, Coretta King, widow of Martin Luther KIng, Jr., and a host of national dignitaries and activists. Although efforts to overturn the law were unsuccessful, the event demonstrated the significance of Sacred Heart Church and Golden Gate to Mexican American life and activism in Phoenix.[20]

Golden Gate's period of community building coincided with the City of Phoenix's desire to expand Sky Harbor Airport—with devastating consequences for Golden Gate. The city had long coveted Sky Harbor as an engine of economic development. Expansion of the airport was seen as inevitable. The airport served as a base of U.S. Army operations during World War II. Two of Phoenix's leading economic sectors, defense manufacturing and tourism, were heavily dependent upon air travel. Local boosters pressed the city to enlarge and beautify the airport, even before the Army left Sky Harbor in 1944. The city vigorously and successfully sought federal matching funds to support airport expansion.[21]

When, in 1968, Phoenix City Council passed a new master plan for airport expansion, the federal government required, for the first time, an environmental impact assessment. As part of this process, residents east of the airport in suburban Tempe and Scottsdale raised concerns about noise and pollution and succeeded in delaying construction for three years. After the environmental impact assessment finally was approved in 1974, residents west of the airport in Golden Gate complained about airport expansion. The city acted quickly to relocate barrio residents to new neighborhoods without seriously considering the consequences of relocation for this close-knit Mexican American community or the alternative of developing a less centrally located regional airport to reduce pressure on city neighborhoods. From the city's perspective, Sky Harbor's expansion was crucial for continued economic growth. The city's eye was on the future. The perceived common good outweighed the interests of any particular group or neighborhood, particularly a poor Mexican barrio with dilapidated housing. From the residents' perspective, the city forced them to sell land and homes at below-market prices under threat of condemnation, lowered property values by organizing the relocation in phases, and callously denied the community's request for group relocation. Golden Gaters were scattered across the city's low-income neighborhoods, and a place with meaning in the everyday lives of barrio residents was razed.[22] Only Sacred Heart Church remains today—boarded up behind a chain link fence and surrounded by vacant lots and telephone call centers. It is an eerie reminder of a once vibrant Mexican community and of the dominance of Anglo economic values over Mexican American traditions and community identity.

The Hispanic population of metropolitan Phoenix hovered between 10 and 15 percent of the total population for much of the early and mid-twentieth century. As Mexican and Central American immigration mushroomed, the region's Hispanic population grew from 112,225 in 1970 to 199,803 in 1980, 345,498 in 1990, and 763,341 in 2000.[23] To accommodate this growth, particularly between 1990 and 2000, the original barrios south of Washington Street spread out to encompass much of central and west Phoenix, and a secondary core of Hispanic settlement expanded in

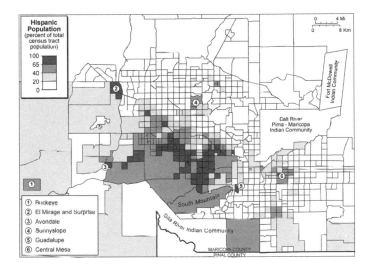

Figure 10. Phoenix's Hispanic population in 2000. U.S. Census 2000, Summary File 1.

central Mesa (Figure 10). Hispanic concentrations also are found in several of the old farming settlements at the urban fringe, including El Mirage and Avondale.

CHINESE AMERICANS

Although the Chinese of early Phoenix were isolated and excluded from public life, they eventually improved their economic and social status and moved first into black and Mexican neighborhoods where they owned businesses and later into affordable neighborhoods throughout the city.[24] Between 1848 and 1882, more than 300,000 Chinese entered the United States looking for work, first on gold placers and later on railroad construction gangs, in laundries, and as cooks, domestics, and truck farmers.[25] Chinese immigrants were a familiar feature in developing the American West. Nearly all were men, as it was common in China for men to travel to other cities and abroad to work, leaving their wives at home, sometimes staying for decades. Like Mexicans, Chinese saw themselves as sojourners and hoped to save enough in America to return to China to live in comfort with their families. With distinctive dress and appearance (shaved heads and a single long braid of hair), bachelor lifestyles, and the desire to maintain their culture, the sojourners lived apart from their Western neighbors. During the economic hard times of the 1870s, white workers feared competition from the Chinese for jobs, and cries of "yellow peril" echoed throughout California and the West. Western newspapers exaggerated problems of prostitution, opium use, and public health problems in the Chinese communities.

Chinese were a part of Phoenix's history from the early days of Jack Swilling's canal building. The *Arizona Weekly Miner* reported in 1872 that two Chinese had opened a laundry in Phoenix.[26] Construction of the Southern Pacific Railroad brought more Chinese to the state where some abandoned railroad work and drifted to the city. By 1880, there were 109 Chinese living in Phoenix, representing four percent of the city's population. Local Chinese operated laundries, groceries, bakeries and worked as household servants, cooks, gardeners, small farmers and vegetable peddlers.[27]

During the 1870s and 1880s, Chinese settled in an area bounded by Jefferson, Monroe, First and Third Streets. The first Chinatown was located around First and Adams, serving the needs of the community's bachelor society with restaurants, tenements, gambling parlors, and opium dens. The local Anglo population held a negative perception of Chinatown. Newspaper editors complained about Chinese monopolies of the restaurant and laundry business and implored white residents to open their own businesses. Chinese buildings were described as "unsightly," "unhealthy," and a "public nuisance."[28] In 1890, the *Arizona Republican* declared that the "wily Mongolians should be kept in as small an area as possible."[29] When the new street railway was built with its terminus at First Street and Adams, civic leaders forced the Chinese to relocate to a less conspicuous site, and their buildings were demolished.

The new Chinatown developed between First and Third Streets and Madison and Jackson with a temple, restaurants, laundries, and boarding and tenement houses. The area also housed the Chinese Chamber of Commerce to manage the affairs of local Chinese merchants. Land transactions often were conducted under the names of American-born children of Chinese residents because national legislation barred the Chinese from owning property. Chinese also specialized in the grocery business. Eventually, many families left Chinatown to open businesses in other parts of the city, particularly in Hispanic and black neighborhoods. In 1929, there were 53 Chinese business establishments outside Chinatown, up from 34 in 1921 and 18 in 1900.[30] As time passed, the laborers, gardeners, laundry workers, and grocers of the first generation of Chinese gave way to middle class, professional children and grandchildren who preferred to live more autonomously. Chinatown began to fragment in the 1930s and early 1940s. In 1943, repeal of anti-Chinese legislation and China's status as a wartime ally of the U.S. lessened prejudice and furthered the upward mobility and geographic dispersal of Phoenix's Chinese population.

Today, Chinese are the most numerous Asian nationality in Phoenix with a population of 15,020, but they are, by no means, a majority of the city's Asians. Recent immigration from abroad has created a pan-Asian population with 11,516 Filipinos, 11,370 Asian Indians, 10,102 Vietnamese, 5,878 Koreans, and 4,875 Japanese.[31] There is great diversity in language, religion, and income and educational status, even within the national groups themselves. Highly educated Chinese graduate students, the "uptown Chinese," have an entirely different background than "downtown Chinese" who work in restaurants and factories. In 2000, Asians

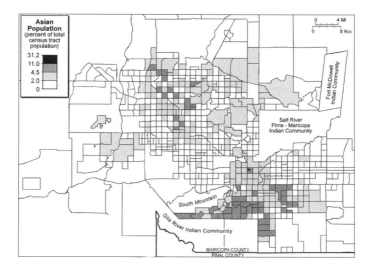

0   4 Mi
0   8 Km

Fort McDowell
Indian Community

Salt River
Pima - Maricopa
Indian Community

South Mountain

Gila River Indian Community

MARICOPA COUNTY
PINAL COUNTY

Figure 11. Phoenix's Asian population in 2000. U.S. Census 2000, Summary File 1.

in Phoenix were concentrated near high-tech employment clusters and adjacent to Arizona State University where many Asian students attended school (Figure 11).

AFRICAN AMERICANS

African Americans first moved west to join the Gold Rush in the mid-nineteenth century. Many early black settlers to Arizona landed first in rural areas where they were homesteaders, soldiers, cowboys, and miners. Escaping oppression and racism in the South, they were attracted to Arizona by the same forces that beckoned Anglo settlers: wealth, the chance to start over, and the possibility of social advancement. Gradually, they made their way to Phoenix and formed a cohesive black community. Phoenix's first African American was Mary Green, a domestic who accompanied the Columbus Gray family from Arkansas to Phoenix in 1868. Although most African Americans worked in semiskilled and unskilled occupations, a cadre of black entrepreneurs and community leaders emerged by the end of the century. Robert Stevens, who migrated to Phoenix in the early 1880s established a department store. Frank Shirley, who arrived in 1887, opened a barber shop near Adams and First Street. Other black-owned businesses included a farm, hotel, and fruit and produce enterprise.[32]

African American leaders established the social structure of community organizations. A colored baseball league was organized in 1897. The local black community had many clubs, including the Horseshoe Literature Club, the Colored Lecture Forum, the Colored Glee Club, Black YMCA, Black Boy Scouts, and Black Campfire Girls. The *Phoenix Tribune*, founded by Texas-born English teacher Arthur Randolph Smith in 1918, was the first black newspaper in Arizona. It was followed by the *Arizona Gleam* in 1919 and the *Phoenix Index* in 1936.[33] Churches were the center of African American life in Phoenix. In addition to spiritual guidance, they offered rooms for community events and political gatherings. The African Methodist Episcopal Church was constructed in 1899 at the corner of Jefferson and Second Streets. By 1911, black settlement had spread eastward to Twelfth Street, and a second community had formed between Twelfth and Eighteenth Avenues along Buckeye Road.

As the number of blacks grew from just 54 in 1890 to 1,075 in 1920, Phoenix's elite imposed harsh social rules to define race relations. The city's leaders systematically separated blacks from the dominant white society through segregated theaters, churches, saloons, restaurants, and hotels. Responding to the growing number of Chinese and black men in the territory, Arizona law in 1901 prohibited "the marriage of Caucasian blood with a Negro or Mongolian."[34] In 1909, the territorial legislature passed a law allowing local school districts to segregate students of African ancestry from other races. Although few districts in Arizona endorsed this provision, the Phoenix School Board adopted a segregation policy.[35] In 1910, over the objection of the local black community, Phoenix opened the Frederick Douglass Elementary School for "colored children." Phoenicians voted to establish a segregated high school as well, starting with a "colored room" at Phoenix Union High School that led to a separate campus in 1926. Writing to the *Arizona Republican* in 1915, local resident Frank Smith noted in 1915 "that there is more race hatred right here in Phoenix to the square inch than in any city I have lived in."[36]

Due to discriminatory practices by lenders and real-estate agents, most African Americans in Phoenix lived in segregated neighborhoods until quite recently. Early advertising listed properties for sale as "highly restricted" or with "race restrictions." Ads stated boldly that "the couples must be white Americans." The Phoenix Real Estate Board in 1924 adopted the code of ethics of the National Association of Real Estate Boards which stated that they "never be instrumental in introducing into a neighborhood members of any race or nationality, or any individual detrimental to property values in that neighborhood."[37] In 1960, half of Phoenix's 21,000 blacks lived in just three of the city's 92 census tracts.[38]

Phoenix's black population kept pace with the city's growth and maintained a steady proportion of the local population—between 3 and 4 percent. After 1980, blacks dispersed from traditional neighborhoods in South Phoenix with few dense concentrations remaining in 2000 (Figure 12). Phoenix's experience in this regard was quite typical of other U.S. cities as affirmative action programs, the rise of the black middle class, and declining housing discrimination led to widespread black suburbanization during the last two decades of the twentieth century. Also, push factors in cities like Los Angeles and Phoenix led to racial and ethnic succession, as new immigrants from Mexico and Central

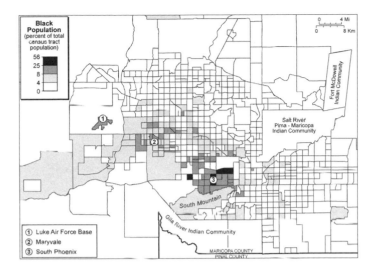

Figure 12. Phoenix's African American population in 2000. U.S. Census 2000, Summary File 1.

America moved into neighborhoods traditionally occupied by blacks who, in turn, moved to neighborhoods vacated by whites who moved to new residential subdivisions on the urban fringe.

Large-scale immigration and demographic change in Phoenix generate a pattern of racial succession in which white Anglos move continuously outward (Figure 13). This pattern is reminiscent of early-twentieth century social structures in which minorities dominated the inner city, while affluent whites sought new homes on higher ground and in more aesthetically pleasing areas at the urban fringe. The urban architect and critic, Dolores Hayden, calls this a "clustered world" to describe a segregated metropolitan region with affluent, white people in distant suburbs and people of color concentrated in poor, inner-city neighborhoods.[39] By 2000, minorities dominated the inner cores of Phoenix and Mesa, while Anglos occupied suburban neighborhoods, especially to the north and east where temperatures are cooler

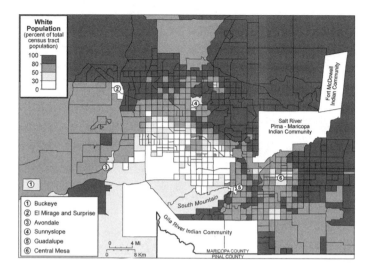

White
Population
(percent of total
census tract
population)
100
80
50
30
0

① Buckeye
② El Mirage and Surprise
③ Avondale
④ Sunnyslope
⑤ Guadalupe
⑥ Central Mesa

Fort McDowell
Indian Community

Salt River
Pima - Maricopa
Indian Community

South Mountain

Gila River Indian Community

MARICOPA COUNTY
PINAL COUNTY

0   4 Mi
0   8 Km

Figure 13. Phoenix's white Anglo population in 2000. U.S. Census 2000, Summary File 1.

and views are better. Minorities are virtually absent from areas of new development, especially in places like the Sun Cities, Ahwatukee, Fountain Hills, North Scottsdale, and Rio Verde.

CHURCH OF JESUS CHRIST OF LATTER-DAY SAINTS (MORMONS)

Yet another component of the early cultural history of the Salt River Valley was the settlement of members of the Church of Jesus Christ of Latter-day Saints (LDS), also called Mormons. Today's 160,023 LDS adherents are Greater Phoenix's second largest religious denomination, after 562,213 Catholics.[40] Local Mormons are active in political life, sending church members to the U.S. Congress and the state legislature in numbers far exceeding their proportion of the population. The magnificent LDS temple in Mesa and religious buildings throughout the valley are an important feature of the local cultural landscape and reminders that Mormon roots run deep in the Phoenix area.

The broad outline of Mormon history involves Joseph Smith's revelation in upstate New York leading to the group's trek through Ohio to Missouri and Illinois through persecutions that culminated in the murder of Joseph Smith. Brigham Young then led the sect to the Salt Lake Basin, where they diverted water from the mountains to the dry but fertile valley and made "the desert bloom." Missionary fervor and the dearth of arable land in the Salt Lake area led the church to send colonizing groups north and south along the Rocky Mountains. Mormons colonized 350 settlements in Utah, Nevada, Arizona, Wyoming, and Idaho and established industries to support their system of self-sufficient agricultural economies. The Mormon Battalion, LDS members who joined the U.S. Army to fight in the Mexican War, had crossed the Arizona Territory in 1846–47 and were impressed with what they saw. Early missionaries first settled the upper reaches of the Little Colorado River in eastern Arizona.

In 1876, Mormon church officials asked Daniel Webster Jones to lead a colonizing group south into Mexico. He had explored parts of Arizona and Mexico in the past, and requested that his colony consist of poor families with many children so they would not be able to resettle easily. After a rugged and hardship-prone three-month journey through southern Utah and northern Arizona, his Lehi company reached the Salt River Valley in March 1877 and found canal diggers, farmers, Indians, and early entrepreneurs like Charles Trumbell Hayden of Tempe. Phoenix had a reputation as a rowdy town at the time, so to avoid trouble, Jones led his party to a site north of the buttes, in what is now known as Papago Park, to camp for the night. The group, having reached the end of their endurance, decided not to proceed on to Mexico, but to settle permanently in the Salt River Valley, east of Hayden's growing settlement in Tempe. On March 6, 1877, the town site of Utahville was established north of the Salt River, and the settlers celebrated by taking a swim in the free-flowing Salt River.

That night the group designed a rough layout for the Utah Ditch, and began to clear away the brush. Jones developed a friendly and productive working relationship with local Pima Indians and hired them to help in canal digging. Neighbors complained to the local Indian agent that Jones was housing Indians who were stealing their crops and livestock. Some in Jones's party also objected when the Indians made their home in the fort at Utahville. These disgruntled souls left the group and headed southeast for the San Pedro Valley where they experienced hardship and extreme deprivation. With their numbers depleted, the Lehi group also had a difficult time surviving.

In September 1977, another group of 85 Mormon pioneers arrived in the Salt River Valley and settled upstream and south of the river where another workable site was identified. Jones invited them to stay in Utahville, but the group decided to move up to the nearby mesa or plateau above the valley floor. Captain John Hancock, the same surveyor who platted the original town site of Phoenix, was called in to plat the new town site of Mesa. He believed that, even if new settlers could get water into the canal from this site, the work was beyond the company's capacity. Nonetheless, the group persisted, and one of its members, Theodore Sirrine, went to the Territorial Land Office in Florence to file a claim on Section 22, the square mile from Mesa Drive to Country Club Road and from University to Broadway Roads.

Brigham Young believed that the ideal town site employed the "City of Zion" town plan and should be one square mile with streets 132 feet wide separating blocks of 10 acres. The traditional belief was that the streets were to be wide enough for ox-drawn wagons to turn around without having to go to the edge of town to come about. Some believed that streets did not have to be so wide, but others contended that the city would be grateful later on for such wide streets. Work on the Mesa Canal began in February 1878 and was completed nine months later. When the great flood of 1891 destroyed much of Utahville and carried away acres of its low-lying farmland, Mesa became the dominant center of Mormon life in the valley.

The first school building was constructed at Second and Center Streets in 1882, and the town was incorporated in 1883. As the community grew, it was inconvenient to have the nearest post office six miles away in Tempe, so residents petitioned for the establishment of a formal Mesa Post Office in 1889. Polygamy was sanctioned by the Mormon Church until 1890 when Utah entered the Union, and there were a few polygamous families in Mesa. Pluralistic marriages ended with some turmoil, as five Mesa men were sentenced to brief terms at Yuma's Territorial Prison.[41] In 1970, the Lehi area (as Utahville later was known) became part of the city of Mesa, but has retained much of its rural character.[42]

Given the importance of Mesa to Mormon settlement in the region, the decision was made to construct a temple in Mesa in the 1920s. The building, designed in part as a replica of King Solomon's Temple, was completed in 1927 and remains today as the cultural center of Mormon life in central Arizona and as a local tourist attraction. At Christmastime, the temple is festooned with hundreds of thousands of lights, and thousands of Mormons and non-Mormons alike visit nightly to view the temple's landscaping and gardens. Mormon settlement in Mesa was solidified over the years and spread to other parts of the valley. In 2000, there were 390 LDS congregations in the Phoenix area, up from 273 in 1990. In 2000, Maricopa County contained the nation's fourth largest concentration of LDS adherents (153,980), after Salt Lake County (503,476), Utah County (236,893), and Davis County in Utah (173,172).[43] Although Mesa is generally thought to be the center for Mormon life in the valley, LDS members constitute just 10 percent of the city's present population and are far outnumbered by Catholics who are estimated at about 60 percent.

PHOENIX IN FLUX

In the words of the rock musician Jerry Lee Lewis, there is a "a whole lot of shak'in go'in on" in Phoenix. Turnover and churning in the population stem, primarily, from growth of extraordinary proportions. Between 1990 and 2000, metropolitan Phoenix added more than one million new residents, growing from 2.24 to 3.25 million people, and became the fastest-growing *large* metropolitan area in the nation. Among the top 50, Las Vegas and Austin grew faster but onto a much smaller base.[44] Between April 1, 2000 and July 1, 2003, another 340,000 were counted, adding 8,757 new residents per month and 288 each day.[45] Brash young Phoenix is about to surpass venerable, old Philadelphia as the fifth-largest city in America. This eventuality has occasioned a fair bit of sniping: "some cactus city sticking its prickly spines into our civic body as it climbs atop us in the population charts," and "who wants to be in the middle of nowhere. I can be nasty and ask what kind of culture they have in Phoenix, but I won't," but also some serious reflection about what growth and newness mean to an urban economy and civic identity.[46] Gilbert, a suburb of Phoenix, is the fastest-growing city in the nation with more than 100,000 residents. Three of the country's ten fastest growing "boomburbs," Gilbert, Peoria, and Chandler, are suburbs of Phoenix. Mesa is now the nation's fortieth largest city in its own right, ahead of Atlanta, Tulsa, Omaha, Honolulu, Minneapolis, and Miami.[47] Because momentum is built into the growth process, Greater Phoenix is projected to reach 3.9 million in 2010, 4.7 million in 2020, 5.6 million in 2030, 6.6 million in 2040, and 7.6 million in 2050.[48]

There are several demographic dimensions to this growth: domestic migration from other parts of the U.S., migration from abroad, and natural increase. All conspire to keep Phoenix in a constant state of flux. Domestic migration accounts for slightly more than half of all growth. High levels of in-migration and out-migration lead to rapid throughput and a continual population churning. Growth in Phoenix is less like adding bricks to a pile than it is about catching particles of sediment as they rush through a sieve. Between 1995 and 2000, Greater Phoenix attracted 518,000 out-of-state migrants, and lost 275,000 to other states, for a net gain of 243,000.[49] Annual numbers are highly volatile, rising and falling with the ebb and flow of the economic cycle and the state of Phoenix's economy relative to the rest of the nation.

Phoenix has always had strong ties with California and the Midwest, the Chicago area in particular. Former Chicagoans have been linked to highly visible civic projects and business ventures. John C. Adams, a Chicago lawyer, arrived in 1897 and set about building the "largest and most magnificent" hotel in the Southwest, the Hotel Adams in downtown Phoenix, with backing from Marshall Field. Early land developer Dwight Heard married Chicago socialite Maie Bartlett, and with her father, Adolphus Bartlett, head of the world's largest hardware company, channeled millions of dollars into the Phoenix mortgage market to finance farms, ranches, and urban development. Today, the Heard name often is associated with the world-famous Heard Museum of Native Cultures and Art in Phoenix. Former Chicagoans Charles and Warren McArthur established a car dealership, the Dodge Brothers, and sent for a third brother, Albert, who trained as an architect under Frank Lloyd Wright. The McArthurs built the Arizona Biltmore resort along the banks of the Arizona Canal in the shadow of a prominent hill where Chicago chewing gum magnate, William K. Wrigley, built a mansion.[50] Wrigley later bought the Biltmore when it went bankrupt during the Depression. In 1928, Chicago and Phoenix investors bought the airfield two miles east of the downtown that would become Sky Harbor International Airport. Motorola Corporation, based in the Chicago area, jump started postwar industrial expansion in Phoenix. Until recently, Motorola was the region's largest private-sector employer. The former farming community of Peoria, now one of Phoenix's fastest growing suburbs, was named after Peoria, Illinois. The list of Chicago and Illinois connections goes on and on—much like the list of people and business transactions that bind New York City and Miami.

Environmental historian and geographer William Cronon argues that no city played a greater role in shaping the landscape and economy of the West than Chicago.[51] The central story of the West was of an expanding metropolitan economy creating elaborate and intricate linkages between the city and countryside. In the empire-building mentality of the late nineteenth century, Chicago, with its favored location at the southwestern corner of Lake Michigan, was the Rome of the West, center of the newly emerging empire, and the place where the resources and energies of the West would be concentrated. Cities of the West were called by "high destiny" to combine their natural advantages with the progress of human populations to support the growth and development and the wealth of Chicago. Boosters believed that the Western territory ultimately would be absorbed into a commercial system that revolved around a small number of urban centers. They set about ensuring that their towns would be favored among these centers. They erected cities out of thin air and prophesied the emergence of a great urban civilization in the most unlikely of places: in Phoenix, for example. It is no coincidence that many of Phoenix's late nineteenth-century and early twentieth-century boosters and entrepreneurs were Chicagoans, imbued with the belief that the Windy City would spread the progress of the great American civilization across the West.

This legacy of migration, destiny, and economic development is expressed in the life of Phoenix local sports mogul, Jerry Colangelo. Colangelo grew up in the Hungry Hill neighborhood of Chicago Heights, played prep basketball in Chicago Heights before heading to the University of Kansas to play for the Jayhawks. He later transferred to the University of Illinois, where he played basketball for the Fighting Illini for two years and then found work in the front offices of the National Basketball Association's Chicago Bulls. Colangelo moved to Phoenix in 1968 to take over as general manager of Phoenix's expansion franchise, the Suns. From that position, he eventually acquired ownership of the Suns and orchestrated Major League Baseball's expansion in the Valley with the Arizona Diamondbacks. Colangelo's success was closely linked to the growth and progress of Phoenix. He assumed community leadership positions that were a logical outgrowth of his business interests, for example, as president of the Phoenix Downtown Partnership. His community interests also were related to a broader and deeper concern with community welfare. Like classic boosters of the past, Colangelo pushed for public initiatives that would both generate private profit and promote city progress, as in the building of downtown facilities for both the Suns and Diamondbacks.

Illinois today ranks second after California as a source of Phoenix's migrants (Table 1). Historically, Californians were less efficient migrants than Illinoisans in the sense that they returned home or moved on after a brief stay, while Illinoisans tended to stay put. After California's devastating recession in the early 1990s, however, the Phoenix sieve trapped far more Californians than it had previously. Texas and Colorado functioned more along California's inefficient lines, with high throughput. Like Illinois, Washington, New York, Michigan, and Ohio sent many more migrants to Phoenix than they received in return. Adjusted for size and distance, Chicago is metro Phoenix's major migration partner, followed by the Twin Cities of Minneapolis and St. Paul, Detroit, St. Louis, and Milwaukee in the Midwest and Portland and Seattle in the Pacific Northwest.[52] The predominance and persis-

TABLE 1. Migration to and from Metropolitan Phoenix between 1995 and 2000

Top ten states	In-migrants	Out-migrants	Net migrants
1. California	109,218	49,255	59,963
2. Illinois	35,862	10,112	25,750
3. Texas	26,977	22,466	4,511
4. Washington	21,851	12,266	9,585
5. New York	21,620	5,560	16,060
6. Colorado	20,746	18,391	2,355
7. Michigan	16,457	6,821	9,636
8. New Mexico	16,328	8,365	7,963
9. Ohio	13,891	5,967	7,924
10. Florida	13,793	10,079	3,714

SOURCE: U.S. Census 2000, "County-to-County Migration Flows."

tence of these longstanding migration streams account for the strong Midwestern, what-you-see-is-what-you-get character of Phoenix. This trait is reinforced by the fact that many California transplants are themselves Midwestern by birth.

Migrants tend to be young people in their 20s. It is during these years that people typically leave their parents' home to attend school, join the military, or take a job; leave college to find employment; change jobs; and marry and begin families. This is one reason why Phoenix's population is relatively young, contrary to the popular perception that Phoenicians are old. Only 11.7 percent are older than 65, in contrast to 12.7 for the nation. The median age is 33.0 years compared to 35.9 for the nation.[53] Phoenix's youthfulness is reinforced by the presence of a rapidly growing Hispanic population. There is a huge age gap between Latinos and Anglos in Phoenix. The median age for local Hispanics is 23.3, compared to 38.5 for Anglos.[54] This means that generational issues have an ethnic dimension and explains why some westside school districts have predominantly Hispanic student bodies and Anglo voting majorities.

After domestic migration, another 15 to 20 percent of Phoenix's population growth comes from international migration—both legal and illegal. This represents a sizable increase from the recent past and is the result of the changing geography of the nation's immigrant population. Until recently, most new immigrants to America settled in a few gateway cities, such as New York, Los Angeles, Chicago, San Francisco, Washington, D.C., and Miami. These cities are now struggling to sustain new immigrants as their cost of living soars and new job opportunities are limited. Immigrants are now leaving these gateway cities for places in the Southeast and West, like Atlanta, Phoenix, and Las Vegas with affordable housing and faster job growth.[55] Between 1990 and 2000, the Phoenix area's foreign-born population tripled from 152,000 to 457,000 and increased as a proportion of the population from 7.3 to 15.1 percent. Mexicans accounted for two-thirds of local immigrants.[56]

The arrival of large numbers of Mexican migrants and spectacular growth of inner-city immigrant neighborhoods transformed many declining 1950s strip malls into lively neighborhood shopping centers, often with a beauty parlor, joyeria (jewelry store), carniceria (meat market), herberia (natural herbs and remedies), and store selling Latino music. The whole scene of street vendors and open-air dining has been rediscovered in central Phoenix, although neighbors, complaining about noise, odors, parking, and litter, have lobbied the city for stricter regulation. The Arizona legislature recently extended the last call for ordering alcoholic beverages from 1 A.M. to 2 A.M. Mexican food vendors, regulated by the city, asked to extend their hours, arguing that many of their customers want to eat on their way home from a night of dancing and drinking. Neighbors, already fed up with this form of commercialism, have resisted. The city is forced to adjudicate a clash of cultures, pitting the interests of those who want to retain the more traditional separation of urban land uses and those who seek a more cosmopolitan, immigrant-oriented, 24/7 way of life for inner-city Phoenix.

Although most new immigrants cluster in central Phoenix, there are smaller, less visible pockets of Hispanic residence elsewhere. In Phoenix's highly segregated labor market, Mexican immigrants dominate entire employment categories. These immigrants work as landscapers and housekeepers at resorts, janitors and cleaners in upscale office and industrial parks, cooks in restaurants, maids and babysitters in "toney" homes, and laborers on construction sites. Sometimes these workers live in small immigrant residential districts, often in older apartment complexes. In Scottsdale, for example, there are several small immigrant neighborhoods interspersed in older parts of town.[57] They are invisible to most, first because they are small in size, and second, because they do not fit Scottsdale's image of a haven for the rich, an exclusive golf resort, "the West's most Western town," and center for the arts and culture. Mexican immigrant families in Scottsdale can be seen on Sundays at Indian Bend Wash picnicking, fishing, and playing soccer amidst Anglo roller bladers, skateboarders, bicyclists, power walkers, and Frisbee-golf enthusiasts.

Many Mexican immigrants live truly transnational lifestyles and maintain family and community responsibilities in Mexico. They are typical of the divided-loyalty dilemma that, on the one hand, breeds a cosmopolitan way of life and connects Phoenix to a broad array of places nationally and internationally but, on the other hand, diminishes interest in and responsibility for local concerns. The latter is visible in very low naturalization rates among Mexican immigrants. Only 31 percent of the Phoenix-area migrants who arrived in the United States prior to 1990 became citizens by 2000. This compares with figures of 71 percent for Asians, 69 percent for South Americans, 66 percent for Africans, 56 percent for Canadians, and 41 percent for Central Americans.[58] The reasons are many: some Mexicans work illegally, and a number do not speak English well. Others intend to return home eventually, and have significant personal responsibilities in Mexico. Whatever the reasons, the result is a low level of participation in public life and less influence over political decisions than the numbers alone would suggest.

While Mexico is the largest source of Phoenix's new immigrant population, a substantial and quite diverse refugee community has arisen in recent years. Local voluntary organizations, most notably the International Rescue Committee and Catholic Social Services, resettle several thousand refugees annually. Some refugees later sponsor family members, and numbers swell. Nationalities vary depending on the status of ethnic tensions and global political warfare. A substantial number of Vietnamese resettled in the 1980s and early 1990s, Iraqis after Desert Storm in 1990, Ethiopians in the wake of the Ethiopian Civil War, Sudanese "Lost Boys" in 1999, and Bosnians between 1993 and 2001.[59] Today, more than 6,000 Bosnians live in Phoenix, comprising the largest U.S.-based Bosnian community after Chicago.[60]

The story of Bosnians in Phoenix is one of rapid spatial assimilation, community building, and an evolving sense of becoming Phoenician. There was no existing Bosnian Muslim community in Phoenix, so early refugees arrived with no connections. They were settled into inner-city apartment complexes near refugee resettlement offices to be near employment sites, social services, and public transportation. Bosnians disliked these apartments, viewing the neighborhoods as unsafe, especially for children. Ironically, in light of the ethnic cleansing and civil war that drove them from the former Yugoslavia, Bosnians were appalled both by their personal experiences on Phoenix's streets and by the casual depiction of violence in local and national media. In the words of a young mother of three: "We see these school shootings on TV and we ask why, why, why. It makes us so afraid to send our children to school when we see these things. Why do kids shoot each other, can you tell me why?"[61] Another recalled an incident in which a Bosnian family moved from the resettlement district to another central city neighborhood, and someone shot the tires on the family car. The woman later refused to leave her children alone to go to the grocery store and despairs of escaping the cycle of violence that brought her to the United States.[62] Upon finding jobs and buying a car—both necessities for life in Phoenix—Bosnians dispersed quickly to suburban neighborhoods. When asked how they chose where to live, the need to feel secure trumped all else. In the words of a Bosnian father living in a suburban neighborhood: "We want a place where we can come home and where our children will be safe . . . where we are, this is nice."[63] They showed no desire to live in ethnic enclaves near other Bosnians, often commenting that they were from Sarajevo, a multiethnic, cosmopolitan city, and quite accustomed, therefore, to living in ethnically mixed settings. Bosnians quickly found housing in affordable single-family neighborhoods in the suburbs and in suburban-like parts of Phoenix.

Ten years after initial resettlement, a "spatially liberated" community has evolved. It is organized around extended family networks, Bosnian-dominated job sites, three Bosnian businesses (including two restaurants and Bosnian Delicious, a grocery store), and a part-time radio station, Radio Bosnie i Herzegovie. Bosnian-Phoenicians retain connections to the Bosnian homeland, but realistically accept that their lives are now in Phoenix. Unlike the typical migrant from Texas or Colorado, few anticipate returning home or moving elsewhere in the U.S. Many see the openness, focus on the future, and migration culture of Phoenix as compatible with their need for renewal after personal crisis. Several observe pointedly that Phoenix is perhaps the "new Yugoslavia" where people of different nationalities can learn to live together in peace.[64]

CHAPTER 3

While Phoenix is a place that has attracted large numbers of migrants, there is a substantial homegrown component to growth as well. Natural increase, the surplus of births over deaths, generates around one-third of the region's population growth each year. At its root, however, natural increase is linked to migration, because migration brings young people who are far more likely to have children than to die, and because the Mexican immigrant birth rate is high. The region's overall fertility rate, or the number of children a woman has as she passes through her reproductive years, of 2.4 belies important racial and ethnic differences. Anglo fertility is 2.0, African American and Asian is 2.4, and Hispanic is 3.2.[65] This is a stunningly high number in light of plummeting birth rates in Mexico where the fertility rate stands at 2.8.[66] Hispanic women account for 27 percent of the region's population but 41 percent of its births. The city's maternity wards, preschools, and classrooms are disproportionately Hispanic and are likely to become more so in the future. School districts in Phoenix and central Mesa face the demographic challenge of an increasingly Hispanic student body and a heavily Anglo electorate.

SOCIAL FRAGMENTATION

In the face of high mobility and growing diversity, many Phoenicians have retreated into communities with those who share their values, lifestyles, cultural traditions, and worldviews. This trend is not, to be sure, simply a reaction to diversity, nor is it limited to Phoenix. The growing fragmentation of urban social space that has gripped urban America finds special expression in Phoenix for many reasons: the sheer magnitude of recent growth; the proliferation of master-planned and retirement communities on the urban fringe; weak regional traditions and established neighborhoods; and the prevailing culture of migration that intensifies the need to settle quickly, make new friends, and move on with life—

the Verrado phenomenon mentioned earlier in which community development is fast forwarded, skipping generations of authentic human experience. Three case studies of Phoenix social life demonstrate narrow definitions of community, weak ties to the metropolitan whole, and the problems that can arise when regional problems are not met with regional solutions. The first of these cases involves the retirement community of Sun City West's takeover of its neighboring school district. The second involves the new master-planned community of Anthem—how it markets itself and how residents come to adopt an Anthem-oriented view of the world. The third addresses the homeless and how a regionwide problem has come to be seen as a small-scale, local problem for inner-city Phoenix.

There was a long history of exclusivity in the Sun Cities, leading up to Sun City West's takeover of the Dysart School District. The corporate image of retirement communities emphasized an idyllic, leisure-centered way of life for healthy, newly retired, middle-class Anglo couples, set apart from families with children. As seen earlier in the comments of the Youngtown grandmother seeking freedom from family responsibility, there was and is the sense that children erode the quietude, leisure orientation, sense of belonging, and housing values of retirement communities. In the original Sun City neighborhoods, age restrictions were encoded in deed restrictions or legal covenants that prevented selling to people who fail to meet the age requirements. Usually one person in the household had to be at least fifty-five years old, and children under eighteen were not allowed. Deed restrictions were imposed on a neighborhood-by-neighborhood basis, so enforcement was in the hands of individual homeowners and community associations, often acting in response to complaints.

In 1979, residents of the Sun Cities, recognizing the burden of enforcing age restrictions, persuaded the Maricopa County Board of Supervisors to pass a zoning ordinance designed to protect retirement communities from young people.[67] Under this ordinance, dwelling units in those districts had to be occupied by at least one person over the age of fifty. Children under eighteen were not allowed to reside there for more than ninety days, although a temporary use permit could be issued in exceptional circumstances. To be designated as a Senior Citizen Overlay District (SCOD), at least 80 percent of the dwelling units had to be occupied by people meeting the age criteria.[68] Today, five retirement communities, home to almost half of Maricopa County's unincorporated population, are designated as SCODs. Several municipalities offer age zoning in addition to the County, and age-restricted communities proliferate on the urban fringe.

Retirement communities have been aggressive in pushing the county to enforce age restrictions. Challenges have centered on the code provision that allows exceptions under "exceptional circumstances." Recent examples have included a widowed grandfather who sought an extension to allow his eight-year-old grandson to live with him while the boy's mother worked on a nursing degree, an elderly couple who took in their daughter and infant granddaughter for financial reasons, and a married couple with two teenaged children who moved to a seniors-only mobile home park to care for the mother's blind and disabled mother. Residents have been militant in demanding enforcement of age restrictions, and the County has been strict in executing their will. The County ordered the eviction of the family seeking to care for the blind mother, although the decision was overturned in County Superior Court by a judge who ruled that is unreasonable to expect an adult daughter to live separately from her husband and children in order to care for her ailing mother.

Age restrictions and their enforcement are part of an insider-outsider mentality that pervades Sun City's social life. Politically, this is expressed in the widespread belief that retirement-community residents should not be responsible for public education.

Figure 14. October 1985 cartoon spoofing Sun Citians for their failure to pay school taxes. Courtesy of the *Arizona Republic*.

They are, after all, migrants from Chicago, Minneapolis, St. Louis, and Fresno where they paid taxes and raised their children. As early as 1962, Sun Citians questioned their obligation to pay school taxes to the Peoria School District, arguing that few school-age children lived in their community and that they had already borne the burden of educating children in their former hometowns. Using the formidable strength of their voting bloc (45,000 highly motivated, geographically concentrated seniors), Sun City residents defeated 17 school bond issues between 1962 and 1974. Frustrated with their inability to raise funds for new schools, the district petitioned the County Superintendent of Schools to remove Sun City seniors, and their wish was granted. Sun City West followed suit with a similar strategy toward the Dysart School District and was allowed to de-annex in 1981.[69] There was, at the time, a community backlash, as seen in this cartoon from the *Arizona Republic* mocking Sun Citians for their unwillingness to pay local school taxes (Figure 14).

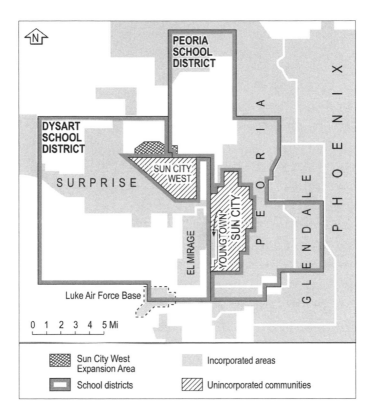

Figure 15. Sun City, Sun City West, and neighboring school districts.

The latest chapter in the Sun Cities' dispute with local school districts, culminated in a small section of Sun City West literally taking control of the Dysart School District in 1997. Sun City West was expanded in 1992 to include 1,733 units not included in the original agreement to de-annex from Dysart. Part of the area falls inside the Peoria District, and a second much larger part is inside Dysart (Figure 15). Caught up in the anti-tax fervor so prevalent in the Sun Cities, and resenting that they were paying school taxes when their neighbors did not, residents of the Sun City West Expansion Area formed the Citizens for Tax Equity in 1995. Using its small but effective senior voting bloc, Citizens for Tax Equity orchestrated the defeat of three budget override issues and two bond proposals. This action cut $2.5 million from the $16 million Dysart budget and forced cutbacks in school programs. The seniors wanted out of the district, but were thwarted by a growing sentiment among Dysart residents that affluent seniors should pay their share of local school taxes. Neighbors also worried about losing a huge chunk of their tax base and setting further precedent in an area ripe for further retirement-community development.[70]

Barred from leaving, Citizens for Tax Equity took over the district. On November 7, 1997, three Anglo middle-class retirees were elected to the five-member school board of a district in which three-quarters of the student population was minority (70 percent Hispanic and 5 percent black). One of their first official acts was to replace the Dysart legal counsel with the lawyer who worked for the Citizens for Tax Equity. Later they forced the resignation of the Hispanic superintendent and replaced him with his former assistant superintendent, an Anglo woman more in tune with their views of public education. Quickly, they instituted new management and accounting practices.

The social isolation between the seniors on the board and minority neighbors led the two groups to interpret the takeover of the school district differently. Retirees defined their community within the walls of Sun City West, and their sense of fairness was violated by having to pay higher school taxes than community peers. Moreover, they were hurt and dismayed when district parents and teachers did not appreciate their sincere but heavy-handed efforts at sound financial and educational practices. Parents and neighbors took an entirely different view. They felt violated by the seniors' takeover of the district and disenfranchised from their own community institution. They were mystified that the newcomers, particularly *because* they were seniors, would seek to withdraw from responsibility for the area's children.[71]

The situation was still smoldering in July 2001, when, in a huff, all the seniors on the school board resigned. Their decision protested a State Facilities Board decision not to relocate the District's thirty-nine-year-old high school away from the noise and accident zone near Luke Air Force Base. While school board members favored the idea of a new state-funded high school, district residents opposed the move, claiming that the high school's current location was vital to maintaining the community's sense of purpose. Moreover, having lived in the area for generations, they questioned whether the noise and safety issues were really that bad. One local woman whose family had lived in the area for more than forty years declared that "My son is in more danger of getting hurt on the bus to school then he is from a bomb or jet crashing at the school."[72]

The question of whether retirement community residents should pay school taxes is not an isolated issue born of the unique historical and geographic circumstances of the Sun Cities. It reflects social change in an increasingly diverse and socially disconnected metropolitan area where community responsibility is felt on a very small scale. Sun City West residents defined community and their public responsibilities to include the people and area within the boundaries of Sun City West itself. Residents of the Dysart District regarded their public responsibilities in broader terms to include the children of the school district. With conflicting definitions, the two groups were unable to reach a consensus regarding school district financing.

While the Sun City case study is perhaps the most dramatic example of social fragmentation in Phoenix, its story lines are being replayed in literally hundreds of places, most notably in master-planned and gated communities on the urban fringe. These communities promote and deliver an intense sense of belonging, albeit on a small geographic scale. Results of a recent study of migration and community ties in Phoenix would come as a rude shock to adherents of Jane Jacobs' and Lewis Mumford's traditional ideals of urbanism. The study showed that people on Phoenix's urban fringe were more familiar with neighbors, more likely to walk outdoors at night, and more likely to call upon their neighbors for help than those in longstanding, inner-city neighborhoods.[73] Master-planned communities are marketed as creating new lifestyles; and indeed, they do.

The second case study deals with life in Del Webb's master-planned community of Anthem. Built on fairly untouched Sonoran Desert land some 40 miles north of downtown Phoenix, Anthem leaped the built-up area by 12 miles. It occupies 6,000 acres and is intended for between 35,000 and 40,000 residents. Anthem markets itself as a multigenerational community, one in which retirees can live near their children and grandchildren and be part of their everyday lives. Drawing on nostalgic feelings about a quieter, simpler time, Anthem strives to be the kind of community where extended families have lived for generations. Marketing juxtaposes the over-fifty golfer, the young couple spreading a picnic blanket, and a small girl on a pier fishing, and declares that Anthem is "a remarkable new community for everyone."[74] Testament to its multigenerational aspirations is a list of activities in the *Anthem Monthly* including a Senior Potluck, Skate Night at the Hockey Rink, Anthem Teens in Action, Self Defense Classes, Stress Management Workshops, Marriage and Communication Skills, Glaucoma Awareness Month, and Martin Luther King Day Camp. Acknowledging the importance of lifestyle and family, Del Webb General Manager Ben Redman notes that: "Here at Webb, we have customers to serve and lifestyles to create. In many ways our promise is to deliver the Great American Dream."[75]

Anthem emphasizes the notion of community in its advertisements. It beckons outsiders to settle into an easy rhythm in a place where they can feel at home. At Anthem Country Club, the new resident can "feel part of something bigger and at the same time be part of something personal and intimate."[76] The idea is that you can join a special class of people who share your interest in golf and can afford a home in Anthem Country Club. You can feel a sense of belonging without having to invest in the civic responsibilities that usually accompany community membership. Anthem falls into the preexisting Deer Valley Unified School District, a semi-rural district, not known for its high test scores. Anthem sidestepped this problem by creating its own, well-equipped schools and drawing the boundaries to exclude non-Anthem students. Although a branch of the Maricopa County Public Library will be open to the public, it will be on site with the new high school, which in fact limits its access.

Not only does Anthem seek to evoke family histories that never really existed, it also creates an artificial natural environment of desert landscaping. The landscape has an engineered feel and look. "Designer desert," a landscaping treatment in which the ground is leveled and natural plants removed to be replaced by replanted saguaros, pruned palo verde trees, and arranged cacti and ocotillo—all watered to a lush state, is popular in Anthem. The developer is scrupulous about the importance of profitability and maintenance of property value and defines its target market as multigenerational families, and then creates a social and natural environment designed to meet the needs of this market.

The third case study is at the opposite end of the income and status spectrum and deals with Phoenix's homeless. Although services for the homeless are highly concentrated in central Phoenix, homelessness comes from all segments of society and indeed from all parts of the metropolitan area. Advocates for the homeless generally cite two major causes for increasing homelessness: the rise in extreme poverty that renders individuals and families vulnerable to medical, personal, and economic emergencies as well as the shortage of affordable rental housing.⁷⁷ The problem of homelessness is not, at its root geographical, but the community's response has been to concentrate it, make it as invisible as possible, and transform it into a geographical problem. Local experts on homelessness point to a critical period in the city's development when the Deuce, a notorious skid row area in downtown Phoenix, was razed to make way for the Phoenix Civic Plaza after 1970. More than 33 hotels were removed from the downtown area, representing a loss of between 3,000 and 4,000 inexpensive rooms for low-income residents. Social service providers tried unsuccessfully to disperse their activities across the metropolitan area but met with strong NIMBY (Not in My Backyard) reactions when more affluent and politically powerful areas opposed locating homeless shelters in their neighborhoods. Services moved west of the downtown to the Capitol Mall District, an area of turn-of-the-century homes near the State Capitol built to serve laborers working on the railroads and in the nearby industrial district. The area declined after World War II, when the middle class left the inner city for new developments sprouting up to the north, and when expansion of the state office complex nearby eroded its residential character. The district became known for prostitution, drugs, and gangs. Politically weak, and beset by an array of urban ills, the Capitol Mall area was unable to fend off the influx of homeless from the Deuce, and it now houses the largest concentration of homeless services in the region (Figure 16).⁷⁸

Local municipalities have zoning policies and occupancy restrictions that preclude the siting of homeless shelters and creatively enforce other policies to disallow homeless in certain areas. The establishment of a shelter requires a special-use permit that often requires public meetings that serve to galvanize neighborhood opposition. As a result, shelters locate in the poorest neighborhoods where opposition is weak. In 1987, the City

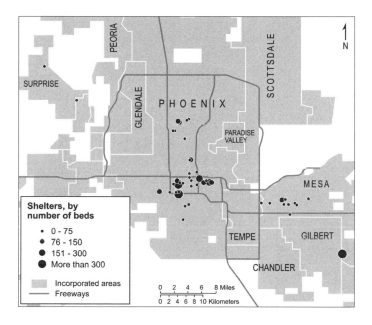

Figure 16. Homeless shelters in metropolitan Phoenix in 2000. Sarah JoAnne Brinegar, "Emergency Shelter Location and Homeless Family Displacement in the Phoenix Area," Ph.D. dissertation, Arizona State University, 2000.

of Phoenix used public safety concerns to bulldoze a homeless encampment in the bed of the Salt River. Its Parks and Recreation Board banned shopping carts in six city parks in 1994 and in 1997 banned outdoor charitable meals in a city park unless diners could be hidden from view—a poorly veiled move to eliminate the annual Thanksgiving Day holiday dinner for the homeless.[79]

When, after the demise of the Deuce, the city and homeless advocates struggled to find dispersed locations for homeless shelters, they encountered stiff opposition from suburban municipalities.[80] Mesa was the only suburb to operate shelters of significant size and, even there, negative public response forced the shelters to be as invisible as possible. During the 1980s, city officials opened the downtown armory for shelter use during the winter months; clients were bused in from a downtown community service center in the evenings and then back out again early in the mornings. In 1990, the Mesa City Council granted a special-use permit and funded the renovation of a dilapidated motel into a small family shelter along a depressed thoroughfare adjacent to Tempe, but even there, encountered opposition from neighborhood residents and local businesses.[81]

The favored suburban tactic for dealing with the homeless is to export them to central Phoenix. Glendale, Scottsdale, and Tempe all blocked early efforts to develop permanent shelters, preferring instead to refer homeless to neighboring communities and support out-of-town shelters.[82] Scottsdale opened a temporary overflow homeless shelter on the Tempe border in the winter of 1990 to help when the Mesa armory was full. In response to neighborhood protests, the city sought to make shelter residents as inconspicuous as possible. The site was enclosed by a chain link fence and locked at night. Guests were bused in during the evenings and out again in the mornings. The following year, Scottsdale declined to open its shelter and provided funds to the centrally located CASS (Central Arizona Shelter Service) facility in Phoenix.

The economic revitalization of downtown Tempe motivated the city to address its "homeless problem." Tempe's emphasis on pedestrian-friendly development makes it especially vulnerable to panhandling, loitering, public sleeping, and other behaviors endemic to homelessness. So-called "Mill Rats," who subsist on food from doggie bags, spare change, and bummed cigarettes, clash with Tempe's smart, upscale, revitalized image. Reacting to complaints from local businesses, Tempe City Council in 1998 banned urban camping and aggressive panhandling around bus stops and automated teller machines. It became a misdemeanor to sit, lie, or sleep on sidewalks within the downtown commercial district. "Anti-slacker" ordinances reflect a nationwide trend for cities to use legal remedies to remove homeless people from public spaces. Ordinances that ban sleeping and sitting in public, loitering in parks and on streets, and urinating in public places criminalize behaviors that homeless people use for their very survival.[83]

Phoenix's population is growing at breakneck speed, migrants come from across the nation and world, and their loyalties are divided. Cultural diversity is on the rise, and residential segregation is increasing for Hispanics and Asians. Anglo Phoenicians are retreating from the city center and are isolating themselves in gated and guarded master-planned communities, rather than confronting the challenges of diversity. There are few positive guides in the city's social history for how to absorb people of color and from different cultural backgrounds. Attitudes of segregation and discrimination toward Mexicans, Chinese, African Americans, and Native Americans provide an inadequate social context for a metropolitan community where Hispanics now comprise 25 percent of the population and a large and growing proportion of the labor force. Native Americans will play an increasingly significant role in the region's future growth, owing to their control of substantial land and water resources, and Asians are a vital and growing segment of the "silicon desert" and emerging knowledge economy. The great social challenge for Greater Phoenix is how to develop a culture of civic life and regional identity consistent with its large size, growing diversity, international linkages, and increasingly cosmopolitan lifestyles.

You Can Never Get Hurt in Dirt

The disorderliness of new land development in Phoenix has led to periodic efforts to manage growth, but Phoenix is not Portland when it comes to urban growth management. The people of Phoenix fashioned creative and effective public policy to manage their precious water supply during the twentieth century, but they have been less careful about land for several reasons. First, it is so plentiful, and there are few natural barriers to development such as coastlines, waterways, and impenetrable mountains. Second, space and land are vital to the region's low-density suburban lifestyle. Backyard pools, outdoor barbeques, basketball courts, and four- and five-car garages are part of the region's outdoor way of life, its individualist bent, and its automobile-oriented culture. And third, growth and real estate profits are central to the region's economy and prosperity. Market forces and the real estate industry dictate the timing, direction, and pace of growth. Municipalities vie with one another to attract new auto malls, shopping centers, and office complexes, offering developers substantial subsidies in the process. The development industry assiduously fights public initiatives to protect open space, prevent leapfrog development, and manage growth. The general public resists policies that would limit growth and thus access to affordable housing, although a minority of environmentally active citizens are behind these initiatives. Regional cooperation is complicated by the demographic issues raised previously: a peripatetic and increasingly diverse, migrant population whose loyalties are divided, a balkanized social structure, and an Anglo majority increasingly drawn to master-planned communities at the urban fringe.

Once the early entrepreneurs and boosters of Phoenix secured the water needed for their survival, they set about building a city that would capitalize on its second asset: abundant land. The civic and economic ethic centered on growth. The mythical phoenix bird rose from the ashes of the ancient Hohokam settlements as a place intricately, perhaps diabolically, programmed to grow at all costs. Like San Diego, Houston, and Seattle, Phoenix is a one-industry town, but the industry is not the military, oil, or software. It is growth. In one widely circulated 1988 article, an out-of-town analyst estimated that 20 percent of local jobs were involved in some form of land development, including home builders, construction workers, architects, real estate agents, mortgage loan officers, title companies, appraisers, and insurance agents.[1] In a recent study, the *Arizona Republic* estimated that one out of every three dollars in the region's $140 billion economy comes from some aspect of the housing industry.[2] Growth is taken for granted in Phoenix. When a reporter recently asked Mayor Phil Gordon to share his observations about Phoenix moving past Philadelphia to become the nation's fifth-largest city, the mayor noted it was business as usual at city hall and observed: "we can reinvent ourselves as the future demands; that's why we continue to grow. That's why people move here each and every day."[3]

Population growth has unleashed stunning changes in land use and the built environment. Between 1980 and 2000, a total of 720,858 new housing units were constructed in Greater Phoenix, most of them at the urban fringe.[4] The amount of urban land

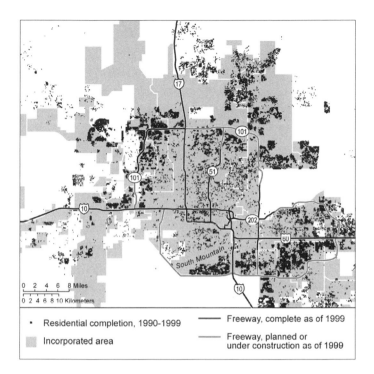

Figure 17. New residential construction between 1990 and 2000. Maricopa Association of Governments, Residential Completion Data.

Legend:
- Residential completion, 1990-1999
- Incorporated area
- Freeway, complete as of 1999
- Freeway, planned or under construction as of 1999

grew from 273 to 732 square miles between 1975 and 1995.[5] With few natural barriers to limit urban development, growth during the 1990s exploded northward far beyond the existing built-up area. Former farmland to the east was incorporated into the urban sphere. The 101 Freeway served as the focal point for new development in the northwest; and the glimmerings of a new growth corridor emerged along Interstate 10 in the west (Figure 17). The local development community's Holy Grail is its continuing ability to deliver an affordable detached single-family home on an attractive lot at the urban fringe. Housing in Phoenix is, in fact, very affordable relative to other large Western cities, although prices have risen significantly in the past year. Still, the average price of an existing single-family home during the first quarter of 2004 was $155,800 which compares very favorably to $224,900 in Las Vegas, $242,500 in Seattle, $277,000 in Sacramento, $387,700 in Los Angeles, $572,500 in Orange County, and $597,300 in the San Francisco Bay Area.[6]

The Phoenix area is judged harshly by urban critics and design professionals for the banality of its built environment. Acres of urban sprawl march across the desert and fail to evoke a sense of place, an urban life, or a recognizable identity for the nation's premier desert city. A sea of Spanish-style houses with red tile roofs, laid out in an endless grid, interspersed with commercial zones containing nondescript sheds and big boxes, linked by little more than parking lots and wide avenues, do not add up to a great city or a distinctive place. The quintessential Phoenix home is large, sits on a small, narrow lot with a shallow setback, and has a two- or three-car garage facing the street. Some call these "snout houses" because protruding garages take up most of the street frontage. Putting together ten of these creates a streetscape dominated by garage doors and a built environment that discourages neighborliness. New housing developments fail the "trick-or-treat test" in which children have to be able to find front doors on Halloween evening. Moreover, Phoenix lacks a viable urban core, a critical mass of exciting and meaningful public spaces, visual symbols of Southwestern urban life, meaningful historical landmarks, and a plan of what a desert city should look like. Its future is unclear: will it be an interesting and distinctive city or a big, sprawling mass of suburban development?[7]

NEW LAND DEVELOPMENT

The essential truth about land development in Greater Phoenix is expressed in the industry's mantra: you can never get hurt in dirt. Land for new development is seemingly limitless. Despite the booms and busts that naturally occur in any one-industry town, urban Phoenix has marched relentlessly into the desert, creating profits for developers of land and housing. The metropolitan area is projected to gain another 3.3 million people between 2000 and 2040, effectively doubling the current population.[8] This abstract number may seem innocuous until translated into the new land needed to support this growth under current conditions. Assuming that 2.67 people will occupy the average home, another 1.2 million housing units will be needed to accommodate future growth. If 60 percent of these housing units are single-family detached units built four to an acre, and the rest are a combination of single-family attached units, large and small apartments, and mobile homes built ten to an acre, it will take 235,000 acres of new urban land, or almost 367 square miles, to accommodate future housing demand. And this does not include land needed for streets, schools, supermarkets, employment sites, libraries, or parks!

Maricopa Association of Governments (MAG), an intergovernmental agency charged with regional planning and predicting the course of future growth, has simulated a future pattern of development based on the supply of available land, transportation access, and presence of nearby development. It is assumed that developers will continue to build at the urban fringe, that people will want to move there, and that fringe communities will continue to encourage development. MAG's vision of 2040 shows urban growth extending well beyond the physical borders of the Salt River Valley, particularly to the north and west (Figure 18). By 2040, metropolitan Phoenix will stretch to Apache Junction on the east, Carefree, Cave Creek, and New River to the north, and well beyond Buckeye to the west. Semirural places like Queen Creek, Laveen, Tolleson, Avondale, and Buckeye will be absorbed into the urbanized fabric, and pockets of new development will extend 55 miles northwest to Wickenburg and west to Tonopah. This far-

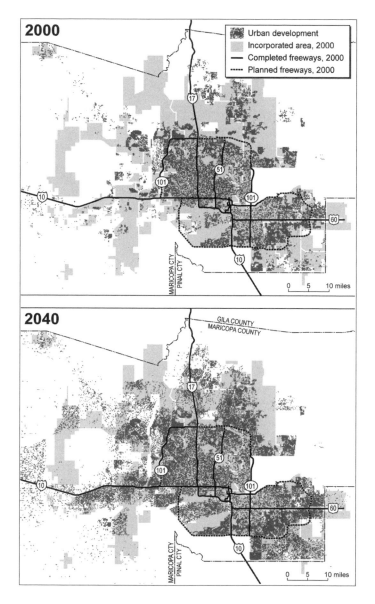

2000

Urban development
Incorporated area, 2000
Completed freeways, 2000
Planned freeways, 2000

0   5   10 miles

2040

GILA COUNTY
MARICOPA COUNTY

0   5   10 miles

Figure 18. Maricopa Association of Governments, built-up area in 2000 and projected built-up area in 2040.

flung pattern of development will translate into huge increases in travel times and levels of congestion. A trip from Chandler in the southeast to north Scottsdale during peak travel times will lengthen from 60 minutes today to 120 minutes in 2040 and it will take 93 minutes instead of the current 43 to travel from downtown Phoenix north to the 101 Freeway. The average speed during rush hour on freeways will fall from 35 to 16 miles per hour and on arterial streets from 24 to 12 miles per hour.[9]

Phoenix gets a bum rap, however, as the national poster child for low-density urban development. While the urbanized area is extensive, population density per square mile of *urbanized land* is on a par with cities of comparable size. When density is measured simply as persons per square mile in the metropolitan area, Phoenix's density is very low, but its land base includes all of Maricopa and Pinal Counties, including Indian reservations, agricultural land, pristine desert outside the built-up area, and uninhabited mountain and desert areas interwoven into the urban landscape. When only the urbanized portions of the metropolitan area are considered, Phoenix stacks up quite nicely against other large metropolitan areas (Table 2). Greater Phoenix's urbanized density of 3,638 persons per square mile is actually higher than in Washington, D.C. (3,401), Philadelphia (2,861), Boston (2,323), Detroit (3,094), and Atlanta (1,783). This is because most new perimeter developments in Phoenix are fairly dense—in the range of four homes per acre—and include condominiums and other related forms of higher-density housing. There is little of the one-home-per-acre type of development that occurs at the edges of many urban areas across the nation. A desert city must grow in a more concentrated fashion because of the need to connect to an established water source.[10] People cannot just dig wells helter-skelter, put in septic tanks, and develop anywhere they want, as they do elsewhere. Ironically, Los Angeles, the city that Phoenix has tried so hard not to emulate in terms of low-density urban sprawl, is

TABLE 2. Residential densities in built-up urbanized areas in 2000

	Urbanized Area	2000 Population	Density (per sq. mile)
1	New York	17,199,861	5309
2	Los Angeles	11,289,487	7068
3	Chicago	8,307,904	3914
4	Philadelphia	5,149,079	2861
5	Miami	4,919,036	4497
6	Dallas	4,145,659	2946
7	Boston	4,032,484	2323
8	Washington, D.C.	3,933,920	3401
9	Detroit	3,903,377	3094
10	Houston	3,822,509	2951
11	Atlanta	3,499,840	1783
12	San Francisco	2,995,769	7004
13	**Phoenix**	**2,907,049**	**3638**
14	Seattle	2,712,205	2844
15	San Diego	2,674,436	3418
16	Minneapolis-St. Paul	2,388,593	2671
17	St. Louis	2,077,662	2506
18	Baltimore	2,076,354	3041
19	Denver	1,984,877	3979
20	Cleveland	1,786,647	1206

SOURCE: U.S. Census 2000, retrieved from www.census.gov/geo/www/ua/ua2k.txt.

now the nation's most densely populated *urbanized area*. Development in the Los Angeles area is limited by natural barriers, land is expensive, and the new immigrant households who populate the metropolitan core often contain several families and large numbers of people.

The penchant for compact development at the urban fringe in Phoenix has not prevented leapfrog development beyond the boundaries of the built-up area.[11] Developers have found creative ways to find water well beyond the urban fringe, as they are required by the 1980 Groundwater Management Act to demonstrate a 100-year water supply. For Anthem, a community designed for between 35,000 and 40,000 residents, 35 miles north of down-town Phoenix, Del Webb Corporation leased water rights from the Ak Chin Indian Community and built a pipe to the CAP aqueduct to get the water. Growth in Anthem, 12 miles beyond the built-up area, is seen by some as a welcome counterpoint to the one-lot-per-acre pattern that aggravates the problem of urban sprawl. Others see it as a classic example of disorderly growth that inter-feres with an organized and logical outward progression of the city because it is so far from the urban boundary. That cities agree to leapfrog development is obvious: Phoenix strip annexed land up to the boundaries of Anthem, including an outlet mall on the other side of the freeway. This act is an effort by the city to regu-late growth in an area that ultimately will be included in its terri-tory and to protect its northern growth corridor.

A second example of leapfrog development—one that illus-trates the inherent tension between creative urban design and compact urban form—is the new master-planned community of Verrado on the westside. Verrado is just now being developed; around 2,000 homes have been sold. Its built-out population is expected to be around 35,000. Verrado responds to the criticism that Phoenix's built environment is boring and homogeneous and does not foster community building or a sense of place. Its design follows the principles of New Urbanism, including a variety of vi-sually distinctive houses with front porches, tree-lined streets and shaded sidewalks, and a pedestrian-friendly main street. Em-phasis is on an outdoor lifestyle organized around a champion-ship golf course and three miles of paths and trails that are said to be "ideal for exploring the desert in bloom." Verrado answers migrants' need to quickly establish relationships with neighbors. It markets itself as a "small town" and "authentic," but it lacks the substance and history that are key to community. It presents the New Urbanism style of architecture, but the development is suburban, not urban in character. Few of Verrado's low-wage, service-oriented jobs are a good match for its affluent, professional residents. Moreover, employment opportunities in central Phoenix are more than 30 miles away.

As places like Anthem and Verrado draw affluent white residents to the urban fringe, existing communities brace for fundamental changes in their established ways of life. In a rapidly growing place like Phoenix, these changes often occur in the blink of an eye as the fringe passes through, giving established rural communities little time to respond to the growth forces enveloping them.[12] By the time the ramifications of growth are fully understood on the ground level, not just in theoretical terms on county planning maps, the peak phase of new development is past and there is little opportunity to shape its form and timing. In a study of urban growth policies, the ASU Morrison Institute of Public Policy evaluated the strictness of growth policy for valley communities and found that smaller, urban-fringe communities, particularly those on the westside, had less stringent growth management policies than the larger, more established eastside communities.[13] More than half of new home construction is now occurring on the westside and in communities with weak growth management standards.

Nowhere are pro-development forces more evident than in Buckeye. Buckeye has annexed so much land in anticipation of urban growth that it is now the region's largest municipality, having recently surpassed Phoenix. Named for the home state of the Ohioans who founded the settlement in the late 1880s, Buckeye maintained a rural, farming heritage on the outer margins of metropolitan Phoenix until recently. It was far from the city, and Phoenix-area growth spread northward and eastward before turning westward. Population in the Buckeye Municipal Planning Area, including the city and its surrounding area, is projected to grow from just over 18,000 in 2000 to 439,000 in 2050. The community's official response to growth is: "bring it on." Local developers extol the virtues of cooperative officials in Buckeye after working with much stricter East Valley communities. Says one local developer:

I don't mean this to be a negative term, but Buckeye wants development. They're not rolling over and letting us run rough-shod over them. But they're being very reasonable in asking for growth because they want their slice of the American pie.[14]

Inevitable growth is viewed with greater ambivalence by some long-term residents who correctly see fundamental change ahead for their rustic, close-knit community. One local resident puts it this way:

If you really want to see what any rural town is about, go to a funeral. You can have a neighbor die and have 400 people there. You don't have that in Phoenix.[15]

Another rural community in the path of urban-fringe development is Laveen, nestled into the foothills of South Mountain just east of the confluence of the Salt and Gila Rivers. Like many other valley communities, Laveen traces its roots to farming. In 1913, the settlement was marked by two general stores, a church, and a school. Subdivision began in the 1950s, but the community maintained a semirural way of life as the westside's industrial and minority reputations deterred large-scale residential developments. Horses are a common site munching on grass in people's front and side yards. Laveen's Del Monte Market, the oldest continually operating business south of the Salt River, has a horse tie-up in front that is not for decorative purposes. The market is a community institution where residents congregate to chew over local and national events. But all that now is changing as Laveen's attributes—magnificent views of the city's skyline to the north and of the jagged Sierra Estrella Mountains to the west, large lots for inexpensive home development, and easy access to downtown Phoenix—have been discovered by developers and suburbanites. For-sale signs dot the landscape, and ground is broken daily in new subdivisions. Local residents, some of whom moved to Laveen in the 1950s and 1960s to escape big-city life, lament the loss of the community's semirural character, neighborliness, and openness. Laveen is especially vulnerable to the pressures of homogeneous, anonymous, big-city development for it is not an autonomous jurisdiction with the ability to plan and zone for itself, but rather a small pocket of the City of Phoenix. Despite this, the community has seized every opportunity to have its say through the urban village structure of planning that the city put in place a few decades ago both to foster identity and public participation in the planning process. Few, if any, of the other urban villages in Phoenix have so fully taken advantage of the possibilities this structure affords, a fact acknowledged by the city in its 2004 planning awards in which Laveen led others for its participation in the planning process. Much is at stake in Laveen as urban growth occurs at full speed, but unlike many parts of the city, there is a critical mass of long-time residents who are interested in guiding the development process.

As urban growth here expands outward, it encounters, and in some ways is shaped by, conditions that are unique to Phoenix. Four large Indian communities serve as de facto growth boundaries to the south and northeast, and are becoming more fully integrated into the metropolitan sphere through casino gambling. In addition, farmers on the fringe shape the cultural landscape as they search for creative ways to retain the legacy of agriculture in suburban development, and an ephemeral, seasonal population of elderly snowbirds adds 250,000 to 300,000 people to the normal pressures of rapid urbanization during the winter months.

NATIVE AMERICAN COMMUNITIES

The prehistoric Hohokam did not completely disappear from the region upon the drastic decline of their settlements during the fifteenth century. Small bands of their descendants, known as the Pima (or their traditional name Akimel O'Odham) settled along the Gila River southeast of modern Phoenix in a place called the Pima Villages. Their livelihood was based on irrigation agriculture, growing corn, beans, tobacco, and squash, and cotton, first for their own consumption and later to trade with Anglo explorers and settlers.[16] Sometime in the mid to late eighteenth century, the Pima welcomed into their community a migrating tribe called the Pee Posh, known today as the Maricopas, for mutual protection from predatory Apaches to the north. The Pima and Maricopa farmers were forced to leave the Pima Villages in the 1860s when Mormon settlers upstream at Florence and Safford diverted the Gila River to irrigate their own fields. The Pima Villages became a parched and barren wasteland, unable to yield enough food to sustain community members let alone support trade with others.[17] In 1873, several hundred Pima and Maricopa moved to the Salt River Valley and settled among Jack Swilling's ditch diggers and John Y. T. Smith's hay camp. In addition to the sedentary Pima and Maricopa Indians, Yavapais occupied the area northeast of Phoenix between the McDowell Mountains and Four Peaks. They still consider the area to be their spiritual homeland.[18]

Intertribal warfare and conflicts between the region's Indians and the early miners, merchants, and settlers led to resettlement of the Indians onto four reservations: (1) the Gila River Indian Community established by executive order in 1859 for use by the Pimas and Maricopas; (2) the Salt River Indian Community founded in 1879, also for use by the Pimas and Maricopas; (3) the Fort McDowell Indian Community established in 1903 for use by Yavapais; and (4) the Ak Chin Community established in 1912 for use by the Maricopas (Figure 19). Reservations were situated along river courses because of the historic importance of water to the Pima's and Maricopa's sedentary, subsistence way of life and the Verde River Valley's spiritual significance for the Yavapai. Far

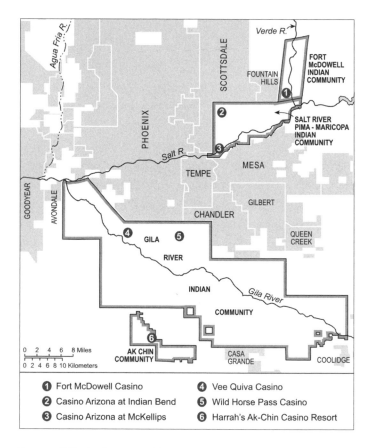

Figure 19. Native American communities.

① Fort McDowell Casino   ④ Vee Quiva Casino

② Casino Arizona at Indian Bend   ⑤ Wild Horse Pass Casino

③ Casino Arizona at McKellips   ⑥ Harrah's Ak-Chin Casino Resort

from early American and Mexican settlements, these reservations were largely self-sufficient, with economies based on agriculture, hunting and gathering, and grazing. The Yavapai of Fort McDowell, historically not a sedentary or farming people, also earned wages as cowboys and dam builders and worked in mines throughout the state.

The isolation and self-sufficiency of the reservations changed dramatically after World War II with the expansion of Phoenix. By the early 1970s, the Salt River Community was in the direct paths of fast-growing Scottsdale, Tempe, and Mesa. The Fort McDowell Indian Community today abuts Fountain Hills on its west side. Chandler and Phoenix adjoin the Gila River Community on its northern edge. The Ak Chin, although buffered by the Gila River Community, is less than twenty miles from Phoenix's southern edge. The Indian communities today act as de facto growth boundaries to the south and northeast and as are prime locations for commercial, industrial, and entertainment development. They are also precious open spaces in a rapidly growing urban environment, and meaningful reminders of the region's earliest inhabitants (Figure 19). Fewer than 20,000 people live on these reservations, but their land areas total more than 475,000 acres.

The Salt River Pima-Maricopa Community leases land for multiple purposes: the Pavilions, a 140-acre retail shopping center; an industrial park; stores, gas stations, and cafes; a country club and an 18-hole golf course; a mobile home park; and Scottsdale Community College. Development is complicated by the Pima tradition of passing land collectively to descendants. Development approval requires consent by a majority of landowners, a process that can entail a sizable number of people. The average five-acre tract, for example, has 88 owners.[19] In the case of the Pavilions, there were some 250 co-owners, necessitating a collective decision to allow development. In addition to the income generated from leasing land for urban development, Indian communities benefit from sales taxes collected by reservation enterprises, and from available jobs for community members. Notwithstanding its central location and new urban development at its edges, the core of the Salt River Community retains much of its historic agrarian character. Cotton fields are abundant, tractors stir up dust, farming equipment sits ready for harvest season, and homes are organized in a linear fashion along the old farming roads. Just three miles from the glitzy shops and upscale restaurants of central Scottsdale is an open and green landscape with magnificent views of the surrounding mountains reminiscent of the region's agricultural past.

The most obvious effects of urbanization are six Las Vegas-style casinos (Figure 19). In 1988, Congress passed the Indian Gaming Regulatory Act which permitted Native Americans to operate casinos if state laws allowed any form of gambling. State governors were obliged to negotiate agreements with Indians, and if they could not or would not, a mediator would be appointed. Phoenix-area Indian communities signed agreements with the State of Arizona in 1993 and subsequently opened gaming establishments. In contrast to Las Vegas, where casino-style entertainment is focused in the city center, Phoenix's casinos are at the urban fringe. Each day, tens of thousands of city dwellers, suburbanites, and tourists travel to the reservations to gamble, dine, and enjoy big-name entertainment. Along the way, they take in scenes of irrigation agriculture, and mountain vistas, and are reminded subtly of Phoenix's cultural history of Indian settlement and its agricultural heritage.

An increasingly important feature of the urban Indian communities is their legitimate and legal claim on some of the region's water. Under the 1908 legal doctrine of "federally reserved rights," Indian tribes are entitled to sufficient water to serve the purpose of their reservations, which in the case of the Gila River community, is irrigated agriculture. The community has been limited in water for farming and in economic resources to develop land for other purposes. Cities, farmers, businesses, Indian tribes, and the state have been haggling for decades over how much water the Indians are entitled to, causing great uncertainty about the region's future water supply and growth. The Groundwater Management Act of 1980 requires developers to identify an assured 100-year water supply. The Gila River Indian Community claims 1.5 million acre feet, equivalent to the average annual flow of the Central Arizona Project. Rather than face uncertainty over future litigation and perhaps jeopardize future growth, the interested parties have agreed to a solution brokered by Arizona Senator John Kyl. This solution provides 2.1 billion gallons of water to the Gila River Community, primarily for farming, but the tribe has the option of leasing back the water to Arizona cities. The agreement provides the community with roughly half of the Central Arizona Project's annual allotment to the Phoenix area and reinforces the Gila River Community's crucial role in regional land management and urban growth decisions.

As reservations come to be developed for non-Indian use, there is growing pressure to maintain and express Native American identity through the nature of Indian education and various public performances of ritual and ceremony.[19] In the case of the landscapes of the Salt River Community, Native American identity is expressed by striking earth-tone signs, replete with the community's seal of the Pima god, Seh-huh, and his spiritual home in a mountain maze at entrances to the community. The Pima Freeway, which runs north-south through the reservation, contains artfully decorated freeway overpasses with geometric designs and noise abatement walls adorned with desert cacti, lizards, and snakes. The latter, however, have prompted some community members to note that lizards and snakes have no particular meaning to the Pimas and to ask state highway engineers to use symbols more appropriate to Pima culture when decorating urban infrastructure on the reservation.

WHERE CITY AND FARM MEET

For most of the twentieth century, city and farm life coexisted agreeably in Phoenix. Irrigated agricultural lands were cooler and more comfortable than hot urban surfaces. Proximity to them offered views of the surrounding mountains. City dwellers purchased fresh produce at roadside stands, boarded their horses at nearby stables, and extolled the virtues of the sweet smell of springtime orange blossoms and the picturesque Japanese flower gardens lining Baseline Road in South Phoenix. As recently as 1975, there was still a significant agricultural presence in the area, although this would change dramatically due to the demographic pressures of urban growth described previously (Figure 20).

As the visceral connection between city and countryside was lost, some local farmers looked for innovative ways to preserve agricultural traditions in the face of large-scale urbanization. One example is the Morrison family of Gilbert who are making the transition from agriculture and ranching to urban through new land and home development with a farming spin. Like many Westerners of the early twentieth century, Howard and Leatha Morrison displayed the rolling-stones-gather-no-moss tendencies described by Wallace Stegner. Leatha's family moved to Arizona from Oklahoma to farm in 1918 when she was thirteen. Howard, five years her senior, followed on his own. When she was sixteen and he was twenty-one, they were married at the old courthouse in Florence, Arizona, and later returned to Oklahoma to farm. When Howard received letters from his brothers in California beckoning him to join them in the dairy business, he and Leatha moved to California. In the depths of the Depression in 1933, Howard and his brothers lost their businesses, and Howard and Leatha headed east in a Chevrolet truck with $1,000 in their pockets for a reclamation project in New Mexico. On the way, they stopped to spend Thanksgiving Day with Leatha's family in Gilbert. Her brother offered Howard work for $9 per week and a home. The three children, Marvin, Kenneth, and Betty, registered for school the next Monday morning, and the Morrison tradition in the East Valley was born.[20]

Howard and Leatha planted a garden and raised calves for meat and eventually acquired their own parcel of land, reclaiming

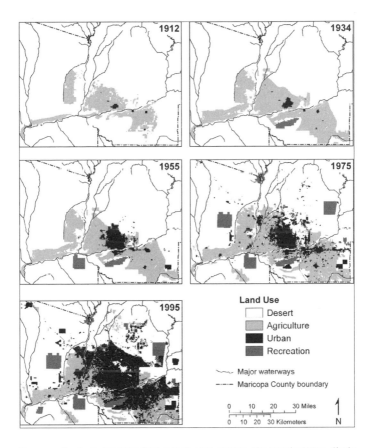

Figure 20. Land use transition from 1912 to 1995. Source: Kim Knowles-Yañez, Cherie Moritz, Jana Fry, Charles L. Redman, Matt Bucchin, and Peter H. McCartney, "Historic Land Use: Phase 1 Report on Generalized Land Use, Central Arizona—Phoenix Long Term Ecological Research Contribution, Center for Environmental Studies, Arizona State University. Courtesy of CAP-LTER, ASU.

it from the desert with an ax and a small tractor. They grew cotton and started a dairy. Marvin and Kenneth took over farming operations when they returned from World War II. The Morrison Ranch eventually grew to several square miles of crop land and became one of the state's largest ranching businesses. Kenneth died in 2004, but Marvin, along with Kenneth's son Glen and grandsons

Denton and Dustin, continue to manage the family's farming, dairy, and cattle operations.

Even though the family recognized that the city was coming and their ranch ultimately would be displaced by urbanization, brothers Marvin and Kenneth, because of their deep ties to the land and farming way of life, wanted to continue farming as long as possible. The children and grandchildren honored Marvin and Kenneth's wishes but understood that ranching would not be part of their future. Several of the grandchildren pursued careers in the ministry. By 1980, urban growth drew near the borders of the Morrison Ranch, and the family experienced typical problems of farming in the midst of new residential subdivisions. Neighbors complained about the aerial spraying of pesticides, the noise of plowing at night, and the odoriferous dairy. Tractors traveling at speeds of 22 miles per hour on urban thoroughfares bedeviled nearby suburbanites. Still, the family persisted in farming, as it was so much a part of Marvin's and Howard's lives and the family's identity.[21]

In the early 1990s, Scott Morrison, one of Marvin's sons and an ordained minister, returned from Colorado Springs and convened a family meeting to decide what to do about the family's land, which quickly was becoming more akin to urban infill rather than urban-fringe development. The family decided that, instead of selling off their land piecemeal to land developers, they would translate the family's legacy of farming into a master-planned community. The family eschews the label of land developer in favor of "land planners," "community developers," and "creators of master-planned communities." So Scott, his brother Howard, and Dawnie Stewart (Kenneth's daughter) are now transforming Morrison Ranch, the farming operation, into Morrison Ranch, the master-planned community with a farming theme.

In visualizing and implementing plans for the Morrison Ranch, the close-knit third-generation Morrisons describe their aspirations as wanting to be "as proud of this as our parents were of farming."²² What separates them from the typical Phoenix-area land developer is that their family personally worked this land for more than seventy years. The history of farming and family influence the look and feel of Morrison Ranch. The farming theme is captured in many ways. Straight streets evoke images of the straight lines of the farm field, in lieu of the typical suburban cul-de-sac. Grass everywhere conveys the greenness of oasis farming, and deciduous trees reflect the seasonality of farming. Plenty of open space conveys the wide vistas of farmland, and homes face the main roads as they would on a working agricultural landscape. Shady, tree-lined streets are reminders of the canal landscapes that dominated the valley during the first half of the twentieth century. The family theme draws upon the architecture and designs of New Urbanism, and is expressed in front porches, grassy front yards for children to play, bike paths, and open space for children to explore. The development of the Morrison Ranch reflects the relentless march of the urban fringe through what is left of the region's farmland, but it is also the unique adaptation of one family's personal experience. The Morrisons are, by no means, unusual as a farming family making the transition to land development. They are unique in imprinting their personal history to the project.

Farmers on the fringe who seek to retain agrarian lifestyles also adopt "agritainment," a blend of agriculture and entertainment, to supplement their incomes as land prices rise and the pressure to sell grows. Forms of agritainment in Phoenix include pick-your-own fields of broccoli, cabbage, and beets; sales of cookbooks, cooking classes, farm tours, and farmer's markets at suburban shopping centers. The Schnepf Farm in Queen Creek, 35 miles southeast of downtown Phoenix, has gone from a traditional family farm growing cotton, grain, and potatoes to a "suburban" farm featuring a store stocked with local produce and tee shirts. The farm offers pick-your-own peach orchards, a petting zoo, picnic area, and amusement park, and an assortment of annual events, including a peach festival in May. Country Thunder USA, a three-day music festival with more than 100,000 country music lovers, moved several years ago from the Schnepf Farm to the Canyon Moon Ranch in Florence.

RV RESORTS AND SNOWBIRDS

Adding to this odd assortment of new master-planned communities, agritainment, casino gambling, dairies, and irrigation agriculture are between 250,000 to 300,000 temporary residents, known as "snowbirds," who settle in outlying parts of Phoenix from January through April each winter. Although many snowbird communities are at the urban fringe, others have been passed by and now are firmly embedded into the urban fabric. Most snowbirds are Anglo, retired couples who come from the cold climes of Canada, the Midwest, and the Pacific Northwest; they return annually to take up residence in the same recreational vehicle (RV) campgrounds, hotels, apartments, and private residences, or to camp on the same parcels of federal land in the open desert. Depending upon the setting, their pastimes include playing cards, eating out, golfing, sightseeing, and visiting with friends from home. Entire communities reunite in the fall and early winter and then disband again like migrating birds in the spring as temperatures soar. Certain parks are known to be home to Canadians, while others cater to Illinoisans, Ohioans, and Oregonians. Cheap land at the urban fringe keeps the price of accommodation low. Outlying locations allow snowbirds to enjoy the desert and the outdoors, but avoid the hustle-bustle of big-city life. Moreover, it is possible to avoid engagement with non-Anglos except in packaged ways, as, for example, at the Heard Museum of Native Culture and Art or at ethnic festivals. Snowbirds stay close enough to the city to attend Cactus League spring training baseball games, go to dinner theaters, and pick up friends at Sky Harbor International Airport, but far enough away to engage life in Phoenix on their own terms.

About 85 percent of the Phoenix-area RV population is concentrated in the East Mesa and Apache Junction areas.[23] A majority are repeat visitors, having made five to six previous visits to the area. Luxurious RV resorts are quite different from the travel trailer courts that once dotted the landscape along America's highways. In a very real sense, these resorts are the snowbirds' equivalent of master-planned communities. RV resorts provide a sense of community and a leisure-oriented lifestyle. Activities include swimming, Jacuzzi, sauna, tennis, shuffleboard, lawn bowling, and horseshoes. Community centers feature arts and crafts, aerobics, dancing, libraries, and loads of entertainment activities. Security is tight, as many RV resorts are walled and gated, have security personnel, and use resident identification badges. The resorts create a small-town atmosphere in which the traditional main street is replaced by the community center, the population ranges from 500 to 3,000, and social life is organized around pancake breakfasts, special events, and holiday dinners. Although residents venture outside the resort, their lives are strongly focused on immediate neighbors and the community itself. Ironically, these resorts enable their residents to leave the frigid cold of the North during the winter, but still live among their northern friends and neighbors while in Phoenix. They experience Phoenix, but in a very programmed and familiar way.

Casinos and other urban-fringe businesses cater to snowbirds. It is estimated that they spend almost $1 billion annually in local establishments. While contributing to the local economy, they strain the local infrastructure already pressed to the limit by rapid growth. Hospitals, transportation networks, water delivery systems, and sewage treatment facilities must be built to handle win-

Figure 21. May 1987 cartoon spoofing the annual migration of snowbirds. Courtesy of the *Arizona Republic*.

ter maximums that are significantly larger than populations the rest of the year. Snowbirds are the butt of local jokes and angst because they sometimes do not know their way around, crowd popular restaurants, drive slowly, and clog already-busy roads (Figure 21).

URBAN GROWTH MANAGEMENT INITIATIVES

The people of Phoenix and Arizona more generally are uncomfortable with the idea of a government-mandated, one-size-fits all approach to planning and managing future growth. They are unwilling to sacrifice their personal piece of the American Dream for the larger regional good, a fact made abundantly clear in the public's reaction to a series of initiatives and proposed legislation between 1996 and 2000. The real estate boom of the 1990s spread new development beyond the boundaries of the 101 and 202 freeways and the Central Arizona Project canal. Local newspaper articles warned that growth was consuming the desert at a pace of "an acre an hour." Environmentalists announced that this was the time for action. In the words of Sandy Bahr of the local Sierra Club: "This could be the last battle for our future and our quality of life in Arizona. Air pollution and traffic congestion are bad, and our schools have deteriorated as a result of rapid and unchecked growth. In many areas, our water supply is overburdened and police and fire protection services are spread too thin."[24]

In early 1998, the local chapter of the Sierra Club started a petition drive to put a comprehensive package of growth management strategies, including strict growth boundaries, on the November 1998 ballot. Unsuccessful in getting the required number of signatures, and facing stiff opposition from the development community and political establishment, the drive was called off in the summer. In the meantime, pro-development groups and moderates joined forces with Republican Governor Jane Dee Hull to lobby the state legislature to pass Growing Smarter, a weak, voluntary, and locally based growth management program. The Growing Smarter Act, signed into law in May 1998, required cities to adopt general plans that incorporate open space preservation, growth management, environmental planning, and impact fees. Growing Smarter contained no provision for voter approval and no penalties for jurisdictions that failed to produce plans. Moreover, there was nothing in the law to prevent a pro-growth community like Buckeye from producing a plan that encouraged unrestrained growth and then following that plan.

Environmentalists cried foul. Citizens for Growth Management (CGM) renewed efforts to place their growth-management initiative on the ballot and collected 162,000 signatures statewide. The Citizens for Growth Management Initiative, designated as Propo-

[handwritten: Planning law]

[handwritten: Prop 202]

sition 202, was placed on the November 2000 ballot. Support was expected to come from the environmental community, as well as from long-term residents, and from recent arrivals concerned about quality-of-life issues like air pollution, congestion, and sprawl. The daunting 21-page proposal contained provisions that required communities to adopt and obtain voter approval for growth management plans by January 1, 2003. Plans would set boundaries to accommodate ten years of projected population growth, and would provide the framework for collecting fees to cover the full costs of new development. Land outside growth areas could not be rezoned to increase the number of dwellings, to increase the coverage of impervious surfaces, or to convert from residential to commercial or industrial use. Farmers would be prevented from subdividing their land for development purposes outside of growth boundaries. Local governments would be precluded from extending public services beyond their growth boundaries, and plans would need to be approved by public vote every ten years. The idea was to put growth into areas that were already developed and make the planning process more responsive to public input.

In anticipation of the face-off with environmentalists, the Republican-controlled Arizona Legislature passed Growing Smarter Plus in 2000 to put teeth into the earlier legislation. Declaring that the bill answered "many of the problems created by urban sprawl," and helped to win "a statewide battle against piecemeal planning, subsidized growth and irresponsible annexation," Governor Hull signed the bill into law. Growing Smarter Plus required cities and counties to submit their plans to voters for approval, authorized (but did not require) them to create infrastructure service boundaries, limited annexation without long-range planning, and created (but did not provide money for) a fund to purchase development rights from private owners. To confuse matters, pro-development forces put a second urban lands initiative on the

November 2000 ballot. Proposition 101 would set aside 3 percent of land held in trust for the state's schools for preservation purposes. Proponents argued that Proposition 101 would preserve highly visible and environmentally significant parcels of desert open space. Critics countered that it diverted attention from Proposition 202 and gave the impression that the state was taking action to manage urban growth when, in fact, it was not.

Proposition 202 enjoyed widespread public support throughout the summer of 2000 when supporters were able to frame the public debate around god-mother-and-apple-pie issues of open space, orderly growth, and clean air. An independent statewide poll in July showed that 68 percent of voters favored the initiative; only 17 percent were against it. As the discussion unfolded, however, it became clear that urban planners and environmentalists—supporters of Proposition 202—were no match for the local development industry. In addition, Phoenicians were not ready to sacrifice their personal best interests for the region's well-being. The defining image of the campaign was a television spot featuring a family stuck using a porta-potty on the site of their dream home in the middle of the desert. The young son in the advertisement whines, "its not fair!" as he is forced to use the portable latrine because, under Proposition 202, the city would be unable to supply services to his family's new home. Although the campaign was long on scare tactics and misinformation, it revealed deep-seated Phoenician values about growth and the sanctity of private property rights, local control, affordable housing, and a low-density lifestyle.

The opposition was led by the development industry, but attracted odd bedfellows. The AFL-CIO feared the loss of construction jobs. Advocates for the homeless and low-income families worried about higher housing prices. Farmers complained about infringement of their property rights, and the Arizona League of Cities objected to the loss of local control. The Governor tapped into public anxieties about high-density lifestyles and concerns about personal freedom, when she proclaimed that the measure "takes away fundamental rights and mandates the crowded life-style we all fled when we left other states in favor of Arizona."[25] In the end, voters were convinced that strict growth boundaries would lead to a blizzard of lawsuits, lost jobs, high housing costs, and dense communities. The initiative was defeated with more than 70 percent of the electorate voting no. Voters also rejected Proposition 101 to set aside 3 percent of the most distinctive state trust land for preservation. It is unclear whether the electorate was simply confused, worried about taking money away from public schools, thought that the 3-percent set aside was too little, or turned off by the contentious and sometimes silly growth-management debate.

OPEN SPACE PRESERVATION

Phoenix has a credible record of preserving open space, but the true test of the region's willingness to retain connections to its desert roots lies ahead. With more than 16,000 acres, Phoenix's South Mountain Park is the largest municipal park in the nation. Its land was acquired incrementally, beginning in 1924 when prominent local citizens, with the help of Senator Carl Hayden, bought 13,000 acres from the federal government for $17,000. In 1935, the National Park Service developed a master plan for the park, with riding and hiking trails, picnic areas and overlooks, all in rustic regional character. The Civil Conservation Corps built many of the park's facilities, based on this master plan. Visitation of the park has grown from 3,000 a month in 1924 to three million a year today.[26] In the late 1980s, city efforts to exchange private property for land within the park borders for use as a golf course led to a public outcry and a successful citizen's initiative to pro-hibit the city from trading away land in its mountain preserves.

Park
Space

Additional preservation efforts were led by housewife, writer, and environmental activist, Dorothy "Dottie" Gilbert. Gilbert was born and raised in Cleveland, Ohio. As a young girl, she had an affinity for horses and made every effort to ride and own a horse. As a young adult, she was a journalist who worked, first at *Newsweek* and then at *Time*. In 1941, she married Elbert Roy Gilbert, a chemical engineer, who had been born and raised in Phoenix. They had three sons within ten years, and decided in 1953 to relocate to Phoenix to raise their family. Dottie combined her love of horseback riding and the outdoors with her formidable journalistic and research skills to advocate for preserving Phoenix's mountain wildlands that were, at the time, in imminent danger of urban encroachment. She spearheaded a grassroots organization, the Phoenix Mountains Preservation Council, and through extensive correspondence over three decades, convinced the Phoenix City Council and state and federal officials to designate 7,000 acres of prime land as the Phoenix Mountain Preserves.[27]

The preservation stakes have been raised by rapid urbanization, and by the fact that today's growth is occurring on virgin desert. Until the 1980s, the lion's share of residential construction took place on retired farmland. While some of today's development is occurring on already disturbed desert (Verrado was a Caterpillar tractor proving grounds and a chunk of Ahwatukee played the same role for International Harvester), vast pieces of natural desert are being converted into new home developments. This process is hard on the desert because new home construction requires extensive scraping and grading of desert surfaces. The desert, in its natural state, requires a large area for flowing water. Desert soils are capable of absorbing moisture, but when they are replaced by impervious city surfaces, runoff must be channelized into central locations. Extensive grading leaves natural desert surfaces only in small patches of leftover spaces. The result is a profoundly artificial landscape. Homeowners and build-

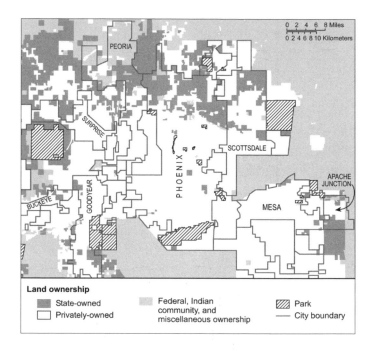

Figure 22. State trust land in the Greater Phoenix area.

ers often try to recreate the desert in their front yards by selectively planting desert shrubs and trees and then watering them to lush perfection, creating a landscape known as "designer desert."[28]

Given the significance of authentic desert landscapes to the identity of Phoenix and the rate at which these are being consumed, increasing attention is being directed toward a network of state-owned open spaces at the urban fringe (Figure 22). The problem is that current state law makes it difficult for these lands to be preserved. At the time of statehood, Arizona was granted some 11 million acres by the federal government. Rather than sell them off, as many other states did, Arizona put them in trust for the benefit of future generations, which included the state's school system. Historically, revenue from state trust lands came from livestock grazing leases. But more recently, urban expansion has dramatically increased the value of several hundred thousand acres of land adjacent to Phoenix and Tucson. Their sale and lease is now the major producer of revenue for the state land trust.

Large tracts of natural desert offer a unique opportunity to preserve, not only desert scenery, but also its wildlife. Their large size accurately conveys the vastness and openness of the desert. The fact that they are contiguous allows desert animals to roam freely from one parcel to another, affording a higher level of biological diversity than would be possible in the current, highly fragmented network of mountain preserves. Despite the obvious significance of these lands to the future of urban Arizona, the state has been slow to change its longstanding principle that they are economic commodities with value that is measured in the marketplace. The notion of state land as a public good with aesthetic, social, and environmental value, and of state land as the logical equivalent of California's coastline is not generally held. Traditionalists argue against tampering with the intentions of Arizona's constitution. Environmentalists counter that times have changed, Arizona is now highly urbanized, and the desert has ecological, spiritual, and aesthetic as well as economic value.

In 1996, the Arizona State Legislature passed a modest bill to *Arizona* encourage the preservation of select parcels of state trust land in *preserve* and around urban areas. The Arizona Preserve Initiative specified *initiative* that state trust land could be designated for conservation purposes, if this results in "protection of natural assets . . . for the long-term benefit of the land, the beneficiaries, lessees, and public, and unique resources such as open space, scenic beauty, protected plants, wildlife, archaeology, and multiple use values."[29] Only trust land within incorporated cities and towns or within three miles of a municipality with more than 100,000 residents could be reclassified for conservation purposes. Still, land set aside for conservation purposes would need to be leased or sold at a later date to meet the state's constitutional obligation to raise money for the beneficiaries of the original land trust. Amendments in 1997, 1998, and 1999 expanded the applicable area in metro Phoenix and Tucson up to an additional ten miles beyond the 1996 boundaries and set up a public-private matching grant program for acquisition or lease of state trust lands for conservation. Only $20 million per year was set aside beginning in 2000, a puny sum in light of the skyrocketing cost of prime urban land. Recently, a Tucson-based property-rights group challenged the legality of the program arguing that land sold for preservation may not garner the highest price, as the law requires. The entire program currently is stalled awaiting reform from the notoriously slow and conservative Arizona legislature. In the meantime, development continues apace on state land in the northern and western parts of Greater Phoenix.

State-owned lands sell for record-setting prices, and cities are unable to compete with private-sector buyers. In May 2004, the CHI Construction company paid $56 million for a 365-acre parcel in the Camino a Lago development of Peoria, and Pulte Homes paid $99 million for a 279-acre parcel in the Desert Ridge community of north Phoenix.[30] On May 27, 2004, the Gray Development Group made the final bid of $32 million to purchase 41 acres of state trust land in the Desert Ridge area. The price of $780,500 per acre shattered the previous record by nearly $300,000. With reform of the preservation program stalled in the state legislature, and a hot real estate market, cities have little opportunity to acquire and preserve strategic pieces of the network of state-owned open spaces.

Meaningful reform lies in efforts by the State Land Department to offer trust land for sale, in amounts of hundreds and even thousands of acres at a time. By planning and offering land on a large scale, the state would be able to foster more orderly growth, earn more money, and facilitate open space preservation. Supporters hoped the reforms would be placed on the November 2004 ballot, but the Arizona Legislature has more pressing items on its plate, and it appears more likely that the package will wait until the 2006 elections. The reforms were put together by a coalition of educators, business leaders, ranchers, developers, and environmental groups; the legislators were told that no changes were possible. When the legislature balked, the entire package was put on hold.

One example of a city obtaining state trust lands for preservation was Scottsdale's use of state trust land to expand its McDowell Mountain Preserve, a spectacular piece of desert along the community's northeastern border (Figure 23). Existing boundaries of the Preserve amounted to 9,825 acres, and another 9,975 had been previously classified as suitable for preservation through zoning, or planned for purchase. In 2001, the city sought immediate reclassification of almost 16,000 acres of state trust land that would not only enlarge the preserve, but also ensure a critical land bridge connecting the two major pieces. Scottsdale, an affluent and politically powerful community, mustered support from local environmental and citizens groups, and used its political muscle, in the form of state senator Russell Gnant, to advocate for the proposal. In August 2001, State Land Commissioner Michael Anable announced the immediate reclassification of 11,290 acres for conservation deed restriction to be used only as open space, the holding of 1,630 acres of noncontiguous parcels as suitable for conservation but not deed restricted to be purchased later by the City of Scottsdale. He also designated 3,543 acres as not suitable for conservation, but to be held for future purchase. Estimated costs to purchase the reclassified and nonreclassified parcels ranged from $700 million to $1 billion. Environmentalists applauded the agreement but worried that non-reclassified parcels might be snapped up by developers before they could be

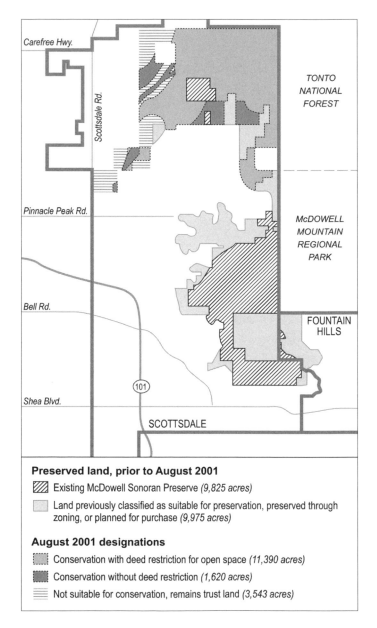

Carefree Hwy.

Scottsdale Rd.

TONTO
NATIONAL
FOREST

Pinnacle Peak Rd.

McDOWELL
MOUNTAIN
REGIONAL
PARK

Bell Rd.

FOUNTAIN
HILLS

101

Shea Blvd.

SCOTTSDALE

Preserved land, prior to August 2001

Existing McDowell Sonoran Preserve *(9,825 acres)*

Land previously classified as suitable for preservation, preserved through zoning, or planned for purchase *(9,975 acres)*

August 2001 designations

Conservation with deed restriction for open space *(11,390 acres)*

Conservation without deed restriction *(1,620 acres)*

Not suitable for conservation, remains trust land *(3,543 acres)*

Figure 23. Scottsdale's plan to acquire state trust land to enlarge its McDowell Mountain Preserve.

purchased by the city. Political officials were pleased but concerned about the high costs of the impending land purchases.[31] In 2004, Scottsdale passed a referendum to raise its sales tax for the purchase of state trust lands, but the city has backed away from new purchases hoping that the reform package would get back on track. With trust lands in the path of future growth, some developers are moving beyond the fringe, buying cheaper parcels for new development. The delay encourages leapfrog and uncoordinated development and jeopardizes municipal efforts to preserve open space.

ENVIRONMENTALLY SENSITIVE LAND ORDINANCES

Scottsdale also has led the way in developing policies to protect environmentally sensitive lands on a smaller, subdivision level. In 1974, the community passed a hillside ordinance that banned development on slopes of more than 25 degrees. The idea was to prevent drainage problems in mountainous areas as well as the development of mountaintops. Almost immediately, the ordinance was challenged by local liquor distributor Kemper Marley and his daughter, Joyce Corrigan, who owned some 8,000 acres in North Scottsdale. Marley and Corrigan argued that the ordinance impinged on their development rights, rendering 76 percent of their property unusable. They lost in trial court, but their claim was upheld in the state Court of Appeals and later in the Arizona Supreme Court in 1986. Scottsdale went back to the drawing board to find a way to limit development on fragile mountain slopes without illegally barring development. After extensive discussion with a broad range of interest groups and numerous drafts, the Scottsdale City Council passed the Environmentally Sensitive Lands Ordinance (ESLO) in 1991 to direct development in the northern part of the city.[32] To get around constitutional problems of the previous ordinance, ESLO allows development anywhere, but a parcel's density is determined by a formula based on the topographic and environmental features of the land including steep slopes, flood hazards, unstable soils, and rock and boulder outcroppings. ESLO allows density transfers from one portion of the property to another. Developers can receive a density incentive, allowing them to build more houses on the flatter parts of their properties if they agree to preserve open space on the steeper hillsides and other sensitive areas. Critics argue that Scottsdale and other cities with hillslope ordinances too often allow developers to take credit for vacant areas that are too steep to build on anyway, and they build at densities inappropriate for their fragile natural settings. Developers counter that creative enforcement allows more land to be protected from unsightly development than otherwise would be the case.[33]

Critics also charge that cities are negligent in enforcing existing guidelines. Ironically, many of these complaints come from well-heeled residents who live downslope from offending properties. In a 2002 case, residents of an exclusive Ahwatukee Foothills neighborhood pressured the City of Phoenix to stop construction temporarily on a home being built above their homes. "What used to be a pretty natural looking ridge line now looks like someone has taken a bulldozer across the top of it and flattened it," said one neighbor. Reflecting the every-man-for-himself attitude that governs land development in Phoenix, the homeowner retorted, "Maybe I'm just ignorant, but it never dawned on me that I was doing anything to the residents below me."[34] The city ultimately allowed the homeowner to proceed with construction.

The central paradox of new land development in Phoenix is how to protect the fundamental rights of individuals and corporations to use land as they see fit and for profit and, at the same time, to preserve the quality of life and desert open spaces for all Phoenicians. The city has a long history of cooperative action managing its water supply, and accepted and indeed solicited help from the federal government to build the Salt and Verde river dams and the Central Arizona Project. Federal pressure to protect the region's underground water reserves is generally accepted as good public policy. This mind set of cooperative action never translated to land development. As the region urbanized, growth at the fringe became the central driving force underlying the regional economy and prosperity. Focus on new land development satisfied the development industry's quest for profit, the individual's dream of homeownership, and the political establishment's understanding of the essence of Phoenix as a place of unbounded opportunity and a place of the future. The search for coherent land development policy has proven difficult because it pits two of Phoenix's most distinctive traits—growth at all costs and the love of the desert—squarely against each other. It also requires regional-level action at the time when, as we saw in the previous chapter, Phoenicians are defining their sense of place on ever smaller scales.

CHAPTER FIVE

Not Another LA!

Automobile travel goes hand in hand with Phoenix's low-density *law-density*
built environment, but the relationship is not unidirectional, nor *led to*
is it simple. Automobiles enable people and businesses to spread *increasing*
out, and the low-density built environment breeds further depen- *commuting*
dence on cars. Even Phoenix's planned light rail system assumes *times +*
that people will use cars to get to stations; park-and-ride is a *distances*
significant feature of the system. A low-density residential landscape would not, however, create demand for long-distance commuting if employment activities were logically decentralized
corresponding to residences. It is the uncoordinated nature of
residences and employment sites, in addition to the low-density
urban form, that has led to increasing commuting times and distances in Phoenix.

The car is very much part of Phoenix's built environment today,
just as the streetcar was 100 years ago when many of the city's *Streetcar*
distinctive residential districts were developed. The one-mile-
wide grid of old agricultural service roads provides drivers with
enormous flexibility in moving from place to place. Wide streets
are punctuated by businesses, such as fast food restaurants and
drive-in banks, automatic teller machines, dry cleaners, and liquor stores, laid out specifically to serve automobile users. Acres
of asphalt parking lots surround shopping centers, movie theaters,

and office buildings. Phoenicians expect to use their automobiles to travel to most destinations, and they expect free and available parking when they get there.

Despite the early embrace of the automobile and a built environment designed around automobile travel, Phoenix was one of the last major metropolitan areas in the nation to assemble a comprehensive freeway system, in part, because of a well cultivated "we-don't-want-to-be-another-Los-Angeles" mentality. Public discourse is riddled with an obsession about LA-style development patterns and LA-style traffic problems, as if doing things differently from Los Angeles constitutes a road map for Phoenix's future.[1] As recently as 1985, metropolitan Phoenix's 42 miles of freeways ranked dead last in number of miles among large metropolitan areas.[2] Recently, the freeway system has been upgraded, but the region will likely never rival the metropolises of San Diego, Los Angeles, or San Francisco in using freeways for daily travel. Plans for densification lie in a light rail system planned to begin operation in 2008, ironically serving some of the same neighborhoods established when streetcars were in vogue some 100 years ago.

TRANSPORTATION TECHNOLOGY, URBAN FORM, AND BUILDING STYLES

Growth patterns in American cities have been shaped by prevailing modes of intra-metropolitan travel defined by four eras: (1) pedestrian and horsecar travel from 1800 to 1890, (2) electric streetcars between 1890 and 1920, (3) recreational automobiles between 1920 and 1945, and (4) freeways from 1945 to present.[3] A distinctive spatial structure characterized each era with rapid geographical reorganization accompanying each transition in technology. American cities today are the evolutionary composite of the growth patterns and architectural styles of these transportation eras. Because Phoenix grew so rapidly after World War II when automobile travel prevailed, the city has a spatial structure designed for the automobile. In 1880, as the pedestrian era was drawing to an end, Phoenix was but a speck on the map with fewer than 2,000 residents, compared to New York City's population of 1.9 million. In 1900, during the heyday of the streetcar era, New York's population exceeded 3 million, Chicago's reached 1.7 million, and Phoenix's barely topped 5,000. It is no wonder then that Phoenix's built environment, urban form, and transportation needs are different from cities that grew during earlier eras of transportation technology. *urbanform*

In 1880, Phoenix was a pedestrian city, but unlike New York or Boston, little physical evidence of this era remains today. The city was tightly clustered along Washington Street from Fourth Street to Fourth Avenue, and along Central Avenue from Jefferson to Monroe. Buildings were flush with the street, and smaller houses faced back alleys. Early settlers constructed vernacular structures of adobe, sun-dried bricks made of local soil. Adobe had long been used for building by inhabitants of the desert Southwest, given its ability to keep interiors cool during the summer and warm during the winter. This material was easily available, and lumber, glass and other building materials were expensive to import. The best remaining example of this early architecture is Charles Trumbell Hayden's home and store. Currently occupied by Monti's La Casa Vieja Restaurant in downtown Tempe, this structure is the oldest surviving Anglo building in the Salt River Valley. Built like a typical Spanish hacienda around a large patio (now enclosed), "the old house" is a low-slung, flat-roofed, one-story building at First Street and Mill Avenue. It was Hayden's home, general store, and headquarters for his ferry services across the Salt River. Hayden's daughters opened a tearoom there early in the twentieth century, but the family lost the building during the Depression. In 1956, it was bought by Leonard Monti, a Minnesota native, who moved to the area after his wartime military service. Monti cleaned up the old building, retained much of its historical integrity, and opened a restaurant that is still owned by his family.[4] Monti's La Casa Vieja's simple but functional architecture conveys the rough-hewn appearance common to western towns of this era.

The arrival of the railroad in 1887, and turn-of-the-century notions of modernity and prosperity, led to a fleeting period of Victorian construction between 1885 and 1900. The railroad allowed local architects to import building supplies, including glass, pressed and cast metal, prefabricated elements, and a variety of woods. Phoenix-area Victorian buildings reflected the influence of California as an economic partner, source of early migrants, and model of future development. Elegant Victorian homes on tree-lined streets served by electricity, streetcars, and telephones allowed boosters to portray Phoenix as a refined, progressive, and modern American town. Lawns and cast-iron lawn ornaments and fences replaced the earlier adobe walls that ran along the sidewalk. The crown jewel of Phoenix's Victorians is the Rosson House at Sixth Street and Monroe, built in 1895 by a local physician and his wife at a cost of $7,525. The neighborhood was, at the time, the most desirable and fashionable in Phoenix. The Rossons owned the house from 1895 to 1897, when it was sold to a Phoenix merchant. The property changed hands many times and was converted to a rooming house, until it was acquired in 1970 by the City of Phoenix for $80,000. Eventually, it was renovated by the Phoenix Junior League and stands today as centerpiece of the city's Heritage Square Restoration Project. Unfortunately, many Victorians were demolished to make way for later growth; fewer than 50 remain in the city today.[5]

The Phoenix Railway Company was begun by General Moses Hazeltine Sherman, an entrepreneur, real estate developer, and member of the city's early elite. Born in 1853 in New York State,

Sherman was the town school teacher and administrator in Prescott, and was later appointed territorial superintendent of education. In 1883, the governor named him adjunct general of Arizona and he helped to organize the state's militia. He liked the title "general," using it later in his business life. After moving to Phoenix in the early 1880s, Sherman took an active role in the Arizona Canal Company, and in 1884, became a founding officer of Valley Bank of Phoenix. He purchased land and sold real estate in Phoenix, and began operating mule-driven streetcars along 14 blocks of Washington Street in 1887. An 1888 extension ran out Grand Avenue; and by 1892, there were eight miles of track and five cars in operation (Figure 24). At the end of the Walking-Horsecar Era, the scale of Phoenix had expanded only slightly. Looking back, it is clear that horsecars were only a stopgap measure and brought only a small amount of new land into the city. Horses were prone to disease and unable to move fast enough to significantly expand the city's geographic limits.

After General Sherman installed the first electric cars in 1893, residential development spread swiftly from the historic downtown into the adjacent countryside. The *Phoenix Gazette* declared that "Phoenix is ever on the forward march and no sooner does she secure one great achievement than she seeks to get another. . . . No wonder people are coming here by the hundreds, filling every house in this beautiful city."[6] Use of electric cars tripled the speed of the railway up to 15 miles per hour, allowing new residential neighborhoods to push beyond the original townsite. Northern routes were initiated and extended, and by 1916, there was an extensive network of public transportation serving the city. The form of the streetcar city generally corresponded to the network of public transit lines, with extensions northward along Third Street to Freemont, just south of Indian School Road. No lines developed in the low-lying areas south of the downtown

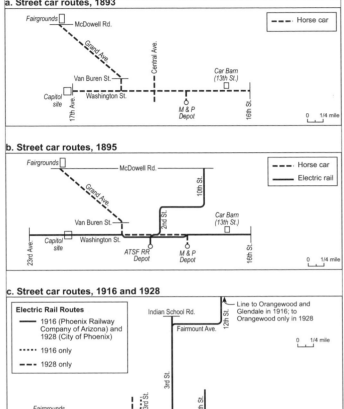

a. Street car routes, 1893

Fairgrounds — McDowell Rd.

- - - Horse car

Grand Ave.

Central Ave.

Van Buren St.

Capitol site

17th Ave.

Washington St.

Car Barn (13th St.)

M & P Depot

16th St.

0   1/4 mile

b. Street car routes, 1895

Fairgrounds — McDowell Rd.

- - - Horse car
— Electric rail

Grand Ave.

10th St.

Van Buren St.

2nd St.

Car Barn (13th St.)

23rd Ave.

Capitol site

Washington St.

ATSF RR Depot

M & P Depot

16th St.

0   1/4 mile

c. Street car routes, 1916 and 1928

Electric Rail Routes

— 1916 (Phoenix Railway Company of Arizona) and 1928 (City of Phoenix)

····· 1916 only

- - - 1928 only

Indian School Rd.

12th St.

Line to Orangewood and Glendale in 1916; to Orangewood only in 1928

Fairmount Ave.

0   1/4 mile

3rd St.

3rd St.

Fairgrounds — McDowell Rd.

10th St.

Grand Ave.

5th Ave.

2nd Ave.

2nd St.

Car Barn (13th St.)

Adams St.

State Capitol

Washington St.

22nd Ave.

Arizona Eastern RR Depot

ATSF RR Depot

ATSF RR Connection

Arizona Eastern RR Transfer

24th St.

Figure 24. Phoenix Street Railway in 1893, 1895, 1916, and 1928. After Jerry W. Abbitt, *History of Transit in the Valley of the Sun* (Phoenix: City of Phoenix Transit System, 1990), 12, 14.

that were prone to flooding, and inhabited by the city's minority residents.[7]

Dwight Bancroft Heard epitomized the aggressive land baron of this era. Heard moved to Chicago from Wayland, Massachusetts after finishing high school. He began work at Hibbard, Spencer and Bartlett Company, one of the largest wholesale hardware companies in the country, and precursor of True-Value Hardware. Heard became the protégé of Adolphus Bartlett and eventually married Bartlett's daughter Maie in 1893. A year later, the couple headed west in the hope that the warm, dry climate would cure Dwight Heard's lung ailment. In 1895, Dwight and Maie Heard settled in Phoenix, where Maie began a lifelong interest in the arts and culture. Dwight, with backing from his father-in-law, invested heavily in Phoenix-area land. In 1900, the Bartlett-Heard Land and Cattle Company purchased 7,500 acres in South Phoenix, where they raised prime cattle, grew cotton and alfalfa, and cultivated orange and grapefruit trees.[8] They also purchased 160 acres north of the downtown and developed it into an exclusive subdivision, named Los Olivos, where Dwight and Maie built their home, Casa Blanca. Many wealthy and influential investors stayed at Casa Blanca during their visits to Phoenix. Heard was a personal friend of President Theodore Roosevelt, and was influential in convincing him that Phoenix was the ideal site for the large reclamation project that would become Roosevelt Dam and the Salt River Project. Heard's biography fits nicely with the previously mentioned characterization of Chicagoans as empire builders and agents for bringing western landscapes into the Windy City's commercial sphere.

General Sherman's streetcars facilitated the development of new residential neighborhoods, with the direction of growth primarily to the north. Higher ground protected the land there from sporadic Salt River flooding, local circulation brought cool evening breezes down the slopes away from Camelback Mountain, and the Phoenix Indian School had opened at Central Avenue and Indian School Road in 1892. The Phoenix Indian School was a source of cheap labor and provided band concerts, plays, and other entertainment of the era. The attractiveness of the northern additions was enhanced by the large number of shade trees planted along the irrigation ditches.[9]

Today, the gems of Phoenix's historic residential districts date to this era, when the city's elite and middle classes moved away from the congested, culturally diverse, and flood-prone areas of downtown into subdivisions on adjacent farmland to the north. The first subdivision in the Willow Neighborhood between Mc-Dowell and Thomas Avenues west of Central Avenue was filed in 1901, and the neighborhood grew quickly after the Phoenix Railway Company added the Kenilworth line in 1910 to serve residents on the west side of Central Avenue. The Kenilworth line ran from Third Avenue and Encanto Boulevard, south to Palm Lane, west to Fifth Avenue, east to Second Avenue and then south and east to Second Avenue and Washington (see Figure 21, p. 124). The 4.07 mile round trip took about 30 minutes.[10] The F. Q. Story Neighborhood west of Seventh Avenue between Roosevelt and McDowell was conceived as a retreat for professionals working downtown. Many of the homes were built in the Period Revival style popular during the 1920s. Neighborhood streetscapes retain the wide sidewalks, palm trees, and broad vistas between homes designed by early twentieth century architects.[11]

Much of what is now the Coronado Neighborhood, north of McDowell and west of Seventh Street, was a dairy farm until housing construction began during the early years of the century, extending to the 1930s. Because of its proximity to downtown, Coronado provided modest working-class houses for Phoenicians. In the 1920s, developers built a trolley line along Tenth Street to encourage rapid growth. One early neighborhood association, Hurley Heights, was very restrictive, excluding nonwhites and requiring that all homes have a value of at least $4,000. Residential construction flourished during the 1920s, and after a brief lull during the early Depression, residential lots for semi-custom homes were still being sold. Pattern or style books were available from which to choose the components of each home. This explains why many homes in the subdivision have a similar size and floor plan but look quite different on the outside. The use of rear-yard guest houses became popular during the Depression, as homeowners who fell on hard times moved into the guest houses and rented the main houses until their finances improved. Although bungalows are the prevalent style in Coronado, the neighborhood also contains excellent examples of the Spanish Colonial Revival, English Cottage Style, and Early Western Ranch styles of architecture.[12] Coronado and other historic neighborhoods fell on hard times during the 1950s and 1960s as suburban living became more popular. They recently made a comeback as proximity to the downtown and their old-fashioned qualities, unique architecture, and noteworthy place in Phoenix's history are valued by the new creative class of urban professionals.

The arrival of the automobile was enthusiastically embraced by Phoenicians. The first cars appeared in the summer of 1900. By 1913, there were ten automobile dealers in town and 646 cars. By 1920, there were 11,539 cars and 53,064 by 1930—a ratio of one car for every three persons.[13] Automobiles were ideally suited to the flat terrain and hard-packed soils of the valley floor. They enabled rural farmers, who still constituted two-thirds of the county's population, to circulate easily between the city and countryside, even before the roads were paved. City leaders accepted automobiles immediately because they dovetailed nicely with the image of Phoenix as a fashionable and progressive place, as a place of the future. As part of the City Beautiful movement, Mayor Lloyd B. Christy organized the Phoenix's Street Paving Association in 1910. Two years later, 19 blocks of dusty downtown streets were paved, and by March of the following year, all the streets in the original town site were paved. By 1929, there were 86 miles of paved roads connecting virtually every neighborhood in Phoenix.[14]

The automobile was formidable competition for General Sherman's trolleys, and eventually he sold out to the city. Constructed for short-term real estate profit, the system was badly in need of repairs by the mid-1920s. Sherman was pressured by the local regulatory agency, Arizona Corporation Commission, to pave the spaces between the tracks. In addition, the Commission restricted his ability to abandon unprofitable lines and to raise rates. As a private business, the railway was required to pay taxes. Sherman announced in April 1925 that service would end in October. The city considered Sherman's offer to sell in May 1925 and countered with their own proposal to buy the system at its "junk value" of $20,000. Sherman stunned city officials by accepting the offer, forcing the city to scramble to maintain service after the October 1925 takeover date.[15] Phoenix quickly passed a public bond issue to rehabilitate the dilapidated railways and to purchase new 40-passenger Brill streetcars from the American Car Company of Saint Louis. Profitability returned, and in 1929, the system carried 6.7 million passengers at five cents each, and showed a gross revenue of $298,000.[16]

Streetcar lines carried many workers to the downtown, but more affluent Phoenicians chose to drive from their homes in outlying areas. Dwight Heard developed a prestigious new neighborhood outside the built-up area called Palmcroft during the 1930s, incorporating many aspects of the City Beautiful movement. Palmcroft later assimilated the Encanto Neighborhood bordering Encanto Park, on the edge of what was then Phoenix. The park had waterways, boats, and Venetian atmosphere. The Encanto-Palmcroft area became the most fashionable neighborhood in Phoenix with plentiful greenery and Spanish and Mediterranean architecture.[17] It is still the inner city's most prestigious address, home to downtown lawyers, business executives, and community leaders.

After a rocky period early in the Depression, trolleys rebounded as many Phoenicians still relied on public transportation to get to work. To accommodate dwindling ridership due to high unemployment, the city raised fares in 1931 from five to seven cents and cut back service. Patronage plummeted to 3.5 million in 1932, and revenues fell to $156,000.[18] A fare rollback from seven to five cents increased ridership, and an upturn in the economy restored the system to profitability in 1933. Buses were introduced as feeders into the street railway system, because they were less noisy than trolleys, and better able to serve the new suburban territory. For the remaining years of the Depression and World War II, the integrated public transportation system of buses and trolleys carried Phoenicians to work and pumped money into badly depleted city coffers. The system carried 7.6 million passengers in 1938 and 18 million in 1943. While cars had begun to fill in the gaps between trolley and bus lines, the city remained quite compact.

The prosperous postwar period brought an extensive highway network to Maricopa County with boosters claiming that no farm was more than two miles from a paved road. Urban development extended further out and filled in the spaces between the old trolley lines. The ranch-style homes that dominated this architectural era originated in California during the lean years of the Depression. Their simplicity and low cost were popular among veterans. The style incorporated design and construction standards under the newly available VA/FHA loan programs. Veterans could purchase a ranch house with no down payment. Subdivisions of ranch-style homes developed by John F. Long and others pushed the city rapidly outward, and dependence upon the automobile grew.

As the city grew, patronage of the streetcars declined, a process common in most American cities. Public transportation suffered nationwide as automobiles became more available, suburbanization flourished, and people demanded more convenient, private, and flexible means of transportation. Public transportation carried 35 percent of the nation's urban passenger miles in 1945, 18 percent in 1950, 10 percent in 1955, seven percent in 1960, and less than two percent today.[19] In Phoenix, ridership fell more than 50 percent from 19 million to 9 million between 1947 and 1954. Trolley service was discontinued in 1948. Regulatory pressure further undermined Phoenix's bus system as the Arizona legislature in 1947 denied it the right to extend into areas already served by private carriers, thus cutting off access to potentially profitable routes.[20] Ridership continued to decline, profits evaporated, and the system lost money in 1953–54.

Public officials, community leaders, and the local newspaper had little sympathy for the floundering public transportation system. At the urging of Eugene Pulliam, publisher of the *Arizona Republican*, the system was sold to L. A. Tanner, owner of Valley Transit, a private bus company, in March 1959 for the bargain-basement price of $400,000.[21] Facing the same structural problems as the city—increased competition from the automobile, a sprawling urban form, and changing tastes regarding personal transportation—neither Valley Transit nor its successor, American Transit Corporation, could manage the bus system profitably. Pleas for public subsidies fell on deaf ears at City Hall, and in 1971 the privatized transit company announced it would discontinue service. The city searched for a solution and agreed to assume ownership, with American Transit in charge of management.

Freeway construction began quite late in Phoenix, with the opening of the Black Canyon Freeway in 1960, running seven miles north from the downtown and the 1968 Maricopa Freeway running east. Local opposition to freeways was led by Eugene Pulliam, the same man who earlier lobbied for the city's divestiture of the bus company. A longtime winter visitor to Phoenix, Pulliam in 1946 purchased Phoenix's two daily newspapers, the *Arizona Republic* and *Phoenix Gazette*, and relocated from Indiana to Paradise Valley, an exclusive suburban community, to advocate for political conservatism and business growth. When, in the early 1970s, city officials and the downtown business establishment proposed construction of an inner loop from the southern end of the Black Canyon Freeway through central Phoenix, Pulliam's newspapers opposed the idea on the grounds that it would cost too much, give too much control to Washington, and divide the city needlessly. Calling the Los Angeles freeway system a mess, Pulliam cautioned readers that the experience should not be repeated in Phoenix. Early versions of the freeway called for a nightmarish eight-story elevated structure crossing at Central Avenue, but later versions were scaled down. Funding for the proposed freeway was rejected by local voters on May 8, 1973, but the idea of an inner loop lived on. Recast as a below-ground structure, the inner loop eventually was approved by voters in 1975, Pulliam having died before the campaign got started.[22]

Although desperately needed to improve inner-city circulation, the inner loop proved catastrophic for the city's historic neighborhoods. The proposed alignment ran through the city's residential core. More than 600 historic residences and two archeological sites were demolished between 1974 and 1975. Phoenix's future-oriented business community and population was more concerned about relieving congestion and preserving economic growth than in protecting the city's collective memory and historic continuity. The destruction of such a large chunk of the city's heritage, and devaluation of more of it with a noisy and unsightly freeway, did however, raise local awareness of the importance of historical preservation. In 1979, the State Historic Preservation Office and the Arizona Department of Transportation classified several prominent structures and parts of neighborhoods as eligi-

inner loop / destroyed early history of neighborhoods

ble for inclusion on the National Registry of Historic Places. This demanded a change in the alignment of the freeway to protect Kenilworth school and several other significant historical landmarks.[23]

In postponing freeway construction, Phoenix missed the window of opportunity for generous federal interstate highway support during the 1950s and 1960s, and had to seek local funding for new freeways. By the early 1980s, the business community was solidly behind freeway construction, viewing traffic congestion as a danger to future growth. In October, 1985, the Phoenix Metropolitan Chamber of Commerce proposed a public initiative to fund a 233-mile network of freeways, parkways, and public transit improvements, using a one-half cent sales tax starting in 1985 and ending in 2005. Additional sales tax revenues were estimated at $5.8 billion. The initiative, known as Proposition 300, passed overwhelmingly.

By the early 1990s, it was clear that Proposition 300 funds would be inadequate to fund the proposed system. A poor economy during the late 1980s and early 1990s generated lower-than-expected sales tax revenues, and public demands for an upgraded design increased costs significantly. The original concept stressed parkways, that would improve traffic flow but would have traffic lights. As the proposal unfolded, the public demanded full-freeway designs that required more right-of-way and 14 full freeway-to-freeway interchanges. Maricopa County went back to its voters in November 1994, asking approval to raise sales taxes an additional one-half cent, and to extend Proposition 300's funding from 2005 to 2015. This time the public said "no." Debate centered on broken promises of the 1985 initiative and on the widespread perception that land speculators were profiting excessively from right-of-way acquisition. Meanwhile, business leaders and public officials worried openly that inadequate mobility would hamper the region's future development.

Help came from then-Governor Fife Symington, a former real estate developer, who understood and embraced Phoenix's growth imperative. Symington called for additional funding from higher sales tax forecasts, a larger allocation of Maricopa Association of Governments (MAG) federal funds earmarked for freeways, and Arizona Department of Transportation budget savings. In 1999, the state legislature provided additional funds to accelerate construction of the 233-mile system by the end of 2007. Now (2005) almost completely funded and built, the freeway system has a long overdue outer belt, an inner loop surrounding the downtown core, and multiple east-west and north-south thoroughfares transecting the metropolitan area (Figure 25). In November 2004, county voters approved the extension of the sales tax for another 20 years, helping to fund a regional transportation plan that includes new and expanded freeway development, plus improvements on arterial streets, and expansion of an already in-the-works light rail system.

Politicos enable freeways

Freeway construction significantly affected local travel patterns, primarily in moving traffic from arterial streets to high-speed freeways. The number of daily vehicular miles traveled (DVMT) on freeways increased from three million in 1982 to almost 17 million in 1999, with steep gains from the late 1980s to the late 1990s when new freeways came on line. The percent of DVMT on Phoenix-area freeways increased from just over 10 percent in 1982 to 31.8 percent in 1999. Even with the recent flurry of freeway construction, however, Phoenix continues to lag behind its peers. In 1999, Phoenix had fewer freeway miles than any major city except Miami, and its freeway system carried a smaller proportion of the DVMT than any major city except Chicago. Freeways in the urban West tend to carry a much higher proportion of travel—55.1 percent in San Diego, 53.8 percent in San Francisco, 47.7 percent in Seattle, 45.1 percent in Los Angeles, 44.5 percent in Dallas, 40.2 percent in Denver, and 40.1 percent in Houston.[24]

effect of freeways

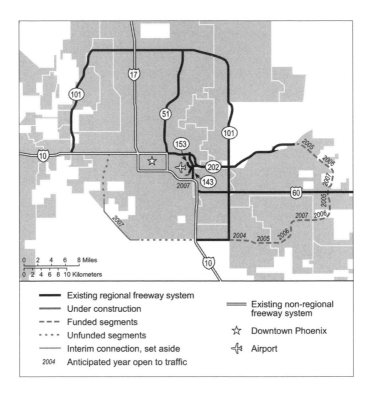

Existing regional freeway system
Under construction
— — — Funded segments
· · · · Unfunded segments
Interim connection, set aside
2004 Anticipated year open to traffic

==== Existing non-regional
freeway system
☆ Downtown Phoenix
⊰⊱ Airport

Figure 25. Current and planned freeway system.

What matters most to people in their everyday lives is not how many miles of freeways exist, or how much of the traffic they carry, but how long it takes them to get from place to place. Phoenicians, like other American big-city dwellers, face increasing traffic delays and congestion. One important measure of this is the ratio of minutes it takes to travel during peak and non-peak hours. In 2002, it took 35 percent longer to travel a given distance in rush hour than in non-rush hour traffic in the nation's metropolitan areas, up from 12 percent in 1982.[25] In Phoenix the index rose at the national average from 12 to 35 percent, despite massive freeway construction. New freeways did not lower congestion in Phoenix as drivers shifted from surface streets to freeways. Free-

Freeway
congestion
construction
did not
lever freeway
congestion
just made
it worse
than it could
have been.

{ 154 }

way construction did, however, keep congestion from being worse than it would have been, had the new freeways not been built. In cities where infrastructure construction did not keep pace with population growth, congestion grew more dramatically than in Phoenix. In San Diego and Portland, for example, the index rose by 33 points, and in Seattle by 28 points. In Los Angeles, by far the most congested metropolitan area in the nation, it took more than 77 percent longer to travel during peak than off-peak hours in 2002.[26]

URBAN VILLAGES AND EMPLOYMENT PATTERNS

A sprawling residential pattern does not, in and of itself, dictate long travel distances and high levels of traffic congestion. Even a decentralized population could live near jobs if employment decentralized accordingly. The problem of long travel times and distances arises from a pattern of jobs that does not mesh well with the distribution of residences. This is what the City of Phoenix had in mind in 1979 when it adopted an urban village model of future growth. Implicitly, it gave up on building a single city with downtown jobs and suburban residential areas. Instead, Phoenix would be divided into smaller geographic communities to achieve a desirable jobs-and-housing balance within these units, to increase the density at their cores, and to satisfy residents' need to connect with an identifiable place. Village centers would concentrate shopping, recreation, and entertainment, and job-producing activities, and people would live nearby. Since the 1985 adoption of Phoenix's general plan, with nine original villages, six more villages have been created (Figure 26). Village planning committees are appointed by the City Council, and they advise the Planning Commission on the density and character of village subareas and help to define future directions.

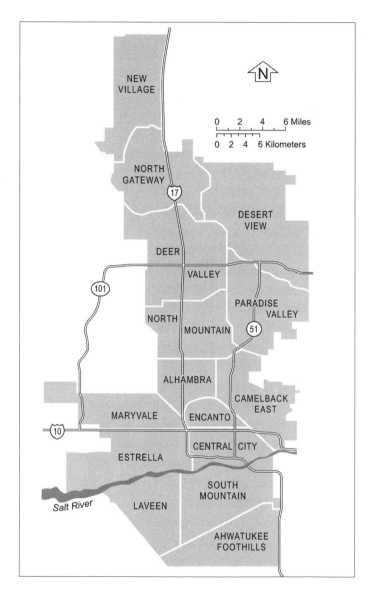

Figure 26. The city of Phoenix's urban villages.

The idea sounds great, but urban villages exist more in the minds and on the maps of City Hall planners than in the behaviors of the people who live and work in them. The vast majority of Phoenicians do not know what village they live in, and they cross village boundaries regularly to work, shop, recreate, visit the doctor, and go to church.[27] Only 17 percent of city residents work in their home village, and only 14 percent of village jobs are held by people who live in that village. Even in inner-city neighborhoods, where jobs are plentiful, the connection between jobs and housing is weak. Only 15 percent of Central City and South Mountain Village jobs are held by people who live in either one of these communities; people who live elsewhere in the City of Phoenix hold 39 percent of these jobs; and 45 percent go to suburbanites.[28] This imbalance is reflected in the job and housing patterns of Phoenix's new immigrants. Mexican immigrants are, for the most part, segregated in inner-city and near westside neighborhoods. But they work at the urban perimeter as laborers at construction sites, housekeepers, groundskeepers, and cooks in the hospitality industry, agricultural workers on farms, and as maids, babysitters, and gardeners in affluent homes. At the same time, the executive, legal, and government jobs in the city center are held by people from outlying areas, except for the few professionals who live in nearby historic neighborhoods and in the few downtown residential developments.

Although uptown and downtown Phoenix retain a critical mass of the region's jobs, there has been significant decentralization in several corridors: eastward along the prestigious Camelback Corridor, eastward past Sky Harbor International Airport into Tempe, along the I-10 freeway to Tucson, and northward along the I-17 corridor to Flagstaff (Figure 27). A new office and retail complex is growing, in classic edge-city fashion, at the intersection of the I-17 and 101 loop freeways. Although Central Scottsdale re-

[handwritten margin note: urban villages are just an idea]

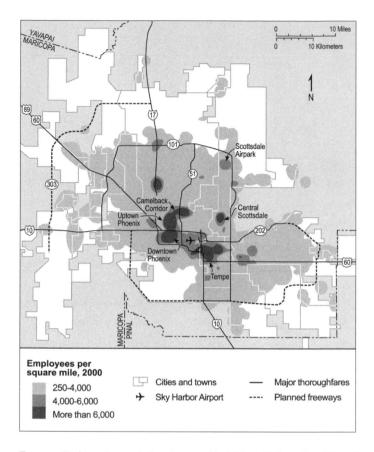

Figure 27. Employment concentrations in 2000. Adapted from Maricopa Association of Governments.

mains an important employment site, the city's center of gravity is shifting northward to the Scottsdale Airpark area.

Development of the Scottsdale Airpark is a cautionary tale about edge-city development and its ability to bring jobs closer to residences, and reduce the need for long-distance commuting. Far from shrinking the average journey to work, growth at the Scottsdale Airpark had led instead to long-distance commuting, because it is poorly coordinated with nearby residential development. The airport itself dates to War II when then-Thunderbird Field II was a training facility for Army Air Corps pilots. Subsequent owners included Arizona State Teachers College (now Arizona State University), the Arizona Conference of Seventh Day Adventists, and now the City of Scottsdale. The airport, which affords busy executives easy national and international access, was the stimulus for developing the surrounding business park, and retail and resort development. Today, Scottsdale Airport/Airpark area is the third largest concentration of jobs in the metropolitan area, after downtown Phoenix and the Sky Harbor Airport areas.[29] It is the site of 25 national or regional corporate headquarters and 1,800 small and medium-sized businesses. Two of the region's largest resorts are nearby, and Kierland Commons, an open-air shopping mall with over 400,000 square feet of high-end retail and office space, further enhances the area's attractiveness.

When businesses at the Airpark were asked in 2002 why they chose the Airpark as a site for their business, more than 60 percent said that owners and top management lived in the area. Another 27 percent wanted to be close to their customer base, and only two percent cited the convenience of the labor force.[30] The location is, indeed, ideal for corporate executives who live nearby and shuttle to and from New York and other cities for business via the airport. But Scottsdale's stratospheric housing prices are unaffordable for many middle- and low-income workers. The median price of a new single-family home in Scottsdale is $267,000.[31] According to a commonly used measure of affordability, the typical Scottsdale resident can only afford 53 percent of the mortgage payment for a new home and 78 percent for an existing home. Many Airpark workers live in central Phoenix and make the cross-town commute to north Scottsdale for work.[32] Air quality problems and congestion are exacerbated by the fact that cross-town bus travel is cumbersome, and the Airpark's physical

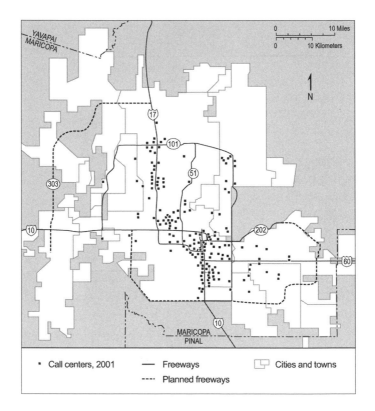

Call centers, 2001   —— Freeways   ⌐⌐ Cities and towns
                  ---- Planned freeways

Figure 28. Customer contact centers.

layout, bisected by the airport's runway, impedes through-traffic and creates troublesome bottlenecks at key intersections.

Long-distance commuting in Phoenix also stems from the locational tendencies of certain types of businesses. One example is the telephone call industry's affinity for freeway locations (Figure 28). Call centers are back-office operations for banks, insurance companies, health care providers, airlines, hotels and other businesses that have a customer-service component. Back-office activities began to separate from command-and-control functions and to move away from high-profile, high-rent, main-street locations some 30 years ago, with advances in computer technology, data management, electronic data exchange, and telephone call routing. Initially, they moved to specialized office space in inexpensive suburban locations, finding large pools of educated, married women who were willing to work part-time. Eventually, they moved to low-wage, networked cities with affordable housing such as Phoenix, Salt Lake City, Tulsa, Oklahoma City, and Sioux City. In positioning itself as a national center for the consumer contact industry, Phoenix touts its "advanced telecommunications infrastructure, large and growing labor pool, relatively low business and labor costs, neutral-accent population, excellent weather without natural disasters, and high quality lifestyle."[33] Call centers are tightly clustered along the Interstate Highway system for easy access to the widest pool of workers. But, in drawing workers from affordable residential areas on the urban fringe, call centers almost assure long-distance commuting. Although the industry is maligned locally for its footloose nature, lack of highly-paid jobs, and lack of career advancement, its negative effects on local transportation patterns and air quality largely are ignored.

Employment-housing imbalances also arise from poor planning, as in the case of the Ahwatukee Urban Village nestled along the foothills of South Mountain just north of the Gila River Indian Community. The city-owned South Mountain Park gives the area character and a sense of place. When the City of Phoenix annexed the area, it was never the plan for Ahwatukee to develop into a bedroom community. It slowly developed on its own out of a conglomeration of large master-planned communities. Home building south of South Mountain began in 1971 when Presley Development, a California firm, built 17 model homes near Fiftieth Street and Elliot Road. This initial development was followed by the construction of custom homes with horse privileges. The area was seen as appropriate for semirural development because it was isolated from the heart of Phoenix south of South Mountain.

Eventually, the population outgrew the transportation infrastructure and the area became known as "the world's largest cul-de-sac," because access to the village is limited to a narrow passage to the northeast at Forty-Eighth Street, and east-west streets that cross I-10, all of which experience severe peak-hour congestion.

Today, Ahwatukee's geographic isolation creates a severe jobs-housing imbalance. Only 13 percent of village commuters work inside the village itself, 44 percent work in other East Valley communities like Tempe and Chandler, 32 percent in central Phoenix, and the rest throughout the metropolitan area.[34] What jobs there are in Ahwatukee are a poor match for affluent residents of the village's expensive housing. The median price of an Ahwatukee home in 2003 was $202,500, compared to $127,500 for the City of Phoenix and $155,000 for metropolitan area as a whole.[35] Recent transportation improvements eased traffic congestion somewhat, but cannot overcome the geographic isolation and inadequate employment opportunities for local residents. The population of Ahwatukee is projected to reach 120,000 by 2020.

WHAT GOES AROUND COMES AROUND

After a century of watching public transportation wither, and promoting a built environment oriented toward the automobile, Phoenix now has a plan to develop a light rail system to connect employment centers in central Phoenix to the East Valley, and to expand bus use. Prior to the 2000 passage of a voter referendum supporting light rail and expanding bus service, the city's public transportation service was inferior to that of cities of comparable size. There was no Sunday bus service, and service ended at 8 P.M. on other days of the week. There was no dedicated funding source for transit, and no light rail lines had been authorized.[36] In pushing hard for light rail, city officials and the business commu-

nity acknowledged Phoenix's need for greater density and continued growth. With light rail, Phoenix can grow, but in a way that
stresses urban infill, density, and downtown development.

The idea of light rail first appeared in the mid-1980s, as the
region searched for ways to supplement its underdeveloped freeway system. The 1985 referendum approving highway construction provided for $5 million per year to create a regional public
transportation authority (RPTA) and to develop a long-range transit plan for Maricopa County. With little public input, the RPTA
proposed a 103-mile light rail system funded by a .005 sales tax.
Voters rejected this by a wide margin of 40 to 60 percent in 1989.
Transit proponents went back to the voters in 1994, as part of a
larger effort to extend the sales tax beyond 2005 for new freeway
construction. Again, the effort was defeated, although this rejec-
tion probably had more to do with the public's distrust of the
freeway-construction process than with disapproval of transit.
The voters were also being asked to support regional transportation at a time when public attention was directed toward smaller-
scale community and neighborhood concerns.

In both the 1989 and 1994 county-level elections, only the
landlocked, inner suburb of Tempe supported the tax increases.
Decision makers in Tempe abandoned the county-wide approach
and presented residents with a city-level transit funding measure
involving a .005 percent sales tax with no sunset clause. This
measure, which included light-rail funding, was approved by voters in 1996. Encouraged by Tempe's success, the City of Phoenix
proposed a .005 percent sales tax increase, with the money to be
used largely to improve both local and express bus services,
along with improvements in dial-a-ride service, beginning in 1997.
Light rail would be phased in, with construction beginning in
2007. Despite public support for the initiative in the weeks prior
to the election, it was defeated by 122 votes out of a total of
111,000 cast. Only a week before the election, Republican gover-

nor Fife Symington, the former real estate developer who championed freeway construction, intervened and ordered the Director of the Arizona Department of Transportation and the Chief of the Arizona Department of Environmental Quality to hold a press conference to encourage a "no" vote. These were influential voices in a campaign designed to convince voters that public transportation would reduce congestion and improve air quality. Although Symington resigned from office later that day, after being convicted on seven charges of bank fraud, his effort to discredit transit probably turned the tide in a very close election.

Finally in 2000, Phoenix voters supported an amended public transportation initiative. This time, the initiative had widespread and unequivocal support from the business community and political leadership, and was framed to address the public's earlier concerns. The sales tax rate was reduced to 0.4 percent, a 20-year sunset date was established, and local bus service improvements were added to the light rail component to provide greater geographic equity. A map sent to residents with the proposed improvements in local bus service did, in fact, show improvements throughout the city.[37] The mayor and his appointed steering committee, who were strongly supportive of light rail, used the bus option to garner widespread support and to get around public skepticism about light rail viability in Phoenix. Only 33 percent of the proposed funds would to be devoted to light rail, and the system would be phased in. The route would run through the heart of the city's employment core, turn east and pass the basketball arena, baseball stadium, and Sky Harbor International Airport, and connect with Tempe's light rail system before heading to downtown Mesa. A well-financed advertising campaign invoked the well-worn argument that, without improvements in transit, population growth would worsen traffic congestion and air quality problems. The opposition was weak, disorganized, and underfunded, and the initiative passed by a wide margin of 65 to 35 percent.

Light rail has emerged as the most well publicized and charismatic portion of Phoenix's public transportation initiative. The current plan calls for the opening of a 20.3-mile starter segment in 2008 connecting the employment cores of Phoenix, Tempe, and Mesa (see Figure 27, p. 158). In November 2001, the Federal Transit Administration officially endorsed Phoenix's light rail project, making it eligible for a half-billion dollars in federal matching funds. Also in November 2001, Glendale voters approved a half-cent sales tax for increased bus service and an extension of the light-rail system west three miles to the Glendale boundary. In November 2004, voters approved an extension of the city's transportation sales tax to fund freeway construction and an ambitious extension in the light-rail plan to connect suburban communities with the Phoenix-Tempe-Mesa line. The initiative featured a rancorous debate between a coalition of regional mayors and business leaders on one side and Dave Thompson, a Gilbert businessman, determined to defeat light rail development. The result was announced as the beginning of a new era of regional cooperation and as an indication that Phoenicians are finally ready for alternatives to freeway and automobile-related transportation.

Light rail will operate in its own lane on street level separated from auto traffic by a small curb, roadway bumps, or other divider, and will be powered by electricity from overhead wires. Traveling the length of the initial 20.3 mile starter segment is expected to take about an hour because in-street light rail operates at posted speed limits and obeys traffic signals. Light rail will have difficulty competing with the automobile, given that local commuting times now average only about 25 minutes. Limited geographic coverage means that the new system will need to be integrated with more flexible modes of transportation, such as the automobile, buses, and bicycles.

A major concern about transit in Phoenix is whether it can meet the growing need for trip linking, the tendency for people to combine the work trip with shopping, personal business, and recreational trips. Multi-purpose trips now constitute between 30 and 50 percent of all urban travel nationwide.[38] In the long run, Phoenix's light rail stations will need to be convenient to grocery stores, drug stores, dry cleaners, child care facilities, restaurants, doctor's offices, and the other places people routinely visit on their way to and from work. The traditional transit model oriented toward the single-purpose work trip is a poor fit with the way Phoenicians now live and work.

Critics of the proposed system argue that light rail will not attract a critical mass of riders because Phoenix's spread-out urban form lacks sufficient employment concentrations to sustain light rail. Indeed, the system was sold to the public under the false pretenses that it would reduce congestion, improve air quality, and mitigate the effects of population growth. Estimates of initial ridership are high and assume population and employment densities around transit stations that do not exist, nor are likely to exist in the foreseeable future.[39] Light rail in Phoenix is more about the nature of growth and economic development than it is about transportation per se. Light rail development is a mechanism to achieve a new form of growth for cities like Phoenix, Tempe, and Mesa whose geographic circumstances have changed during the past 20 years. As access to new development at the urban fringe becomes more difficult for these communities, they naturally look to stimulate more mature forms of growth that emphasize density and that play to their inherent strengths of centrality, historical significance, and distinctiveness.

MOBILITY TRENDS

Despite the popular stereotype of Phoenix as the penultimate sprawling, automobile city, the region is not significantly more car crazy than urban America as a whole. Fewer Phoenicians drive alone to work (73.9 percent in Phoenix versus 76.3 percent nationwide) and more carpool (20.2 versus 14.7 percent). Fewer use public transportation (2.4 percent versus 5.2 percent, but more use "other means," notably the bicycle, to get to work (3.1 versus 1.4 percent). It takes the typical Phoenician 25.0 minutes to commute to work, up two minutes from 1990 (23.0 minutes) and three minutes from 1980 (21.7 minutes). Phoenix's commuting times are slightly longer than the national average of 24.3 but shorter than in San Francisco (28.4 minutes), Los Angeles (27.7 minutes), and Dallas (26.1 minutes). Nationally, the longest travel times occur in highly populated, dense metropolitan areas like New York, where it takes the average commuter 38.1 minutes to get to work, and in Chicago, where the average commute is 30.5 minutes.[40]

The history of transportation technology and residential development in Phoenix suggests that automobile travel, in conjunction with the city's growth ethic, love of newness, and disdain for regional-scale action, has spawned a built environment that requires more automobile travel, which encourages more sprawl, which leads to more automobiles, and on and on. Poor planning creates residential developments that lack nearby employment opportunities, and employment sites that cannot be sustained by the residents of nearby housing. Travel times will likely double in the next 40 years. Light rail presents an opportunity to break out of the cycle of auto-oriented development at the urban fringe and promote a denser, more walkable urban form that integrates remnants of the city's past into its plans for its future.

CHAPTER SIX

Downtown Redevelopment: A Tale of Two Cities

The overwhelming dominance of suburbanizing forces after World War II undercut the viability of historic city centers in metropolitan Phoenix. Retail was first to go, followed by industrial activities and personal services. By the early 1960s, many downtown buildings were taken over by marginal businesses like pawn shops, storefront meeting rooms, sleazy bars, and thrift stores, or had been abandoned altogether. City leaders watched in dismay as new investment and the region's tax base moved to outlying areas. To remedy this, they launched downtown-revitalization efforts. By the early 1980s, demographic, cultural, and economic forces improved the position of city centers vis à vis outlying areas. Phoenix and Tempe, the most urban and centrally located of the region's cities, invested heavily in their downtown districts, but followed different paths to downtown revitalization.

Phoenix bulldozed historic buildings and emphasized large infrastructure developments, including a science and history museum, convention center, several performing arts venues, city hall, a major league baseball park, and a basketball arena. Phoenix created a downtown filled with impressive new buildings, befitting its self image as a dynamic new city at the heart of the metropolitan region. But there are weak functional connections among the downtown's various parts, and residences are in short supply. The built environment is inhospitable to pedestrians, and linkages to surrounding neighborhoods are weak. Downtown Phoenix lacks "fine-grained" activities that draw people onto the street and connect spatially dispersed activities.

In contrast, Tempe's downtown is small in scale and is built upon its past, preserving historic buildings, even creating new buildings that look old to evoke the nostalgia of bygone days. Its strategy of emphasizing small shops and restaurants pulls people onto the street, encourages pedestrian travel, and serves as a draw for new economy firms. Tempe's newly constructed Town Lake, in the once-dry bed of the Salt River, builds upon a past when water was crucial to the agricultural society and an integral part of people's daily lives. It was designed as a magnet for further economic development, but thus far, private development has progressed much slower than expected. Downtown Tempe risks becoming a victim of its own success, as high-rise development undercuts its small-scale, intimate atmosphere, and national franchises like Urban Outfitters, Abercrombe and Fitch, Borders, and Starbucks replace more distinctive mom-and-pop stores. City efforts to sanitize the downtown for middle-class shoppers led to strict "anti-slacker" regulations designed to keep the homeless out of sight and to export them to surrounding communities. Having traded on distinctiveness, diversity, and edginess to create a unique and successful experience, downtown Tempe risks becoming a generic shopping and entertainment district.

The whole idea of rehabilitating old buildings cuts across the grain of a metropolis that is programmed to grow at the margins and is inhabited by people with special memories of theaters, ballparks, and restaurants in downtown Chicago, Detroit, Cleveland, Pittsburgh, and St. Louis. Tempe's downtown has achieved a critical mass of profitable activities, but it remains unclear

Figure 29. Military parade down the main street of Phoenix in 1889. National Archives.

whether Phoenix's downtown will achieve a size and stature appropriate for one of the nation's largest cities. The tale of downtown redevelopment in Phoenix and Tempe offers lessons about the importance of history, geography, leadership, persistence, and luck in redirecting growth inward in one of the nation's fastest growing metropolises.

RISE AND FALL OF THE HISTORIC DOWNTOWN

City centers played a crucial role in the mercantile history of Greater Phoenix. Prosperous farmers went downtown in search of goods and services for both personal use and for agricultural operations. In the downtown, they obtained everything from clothing, jewelry, household goods, drugs and sundries to saddles, harnesses, feed, hardware, and credit. Downtown Phoenix was unquestionably the pinnacle of the region's urban hierarchy in the early twentieth century. Three- and four-story brick buildings lined Washington Street in the center of town (Figure 29).

Retail activity was on the ground floor, and upper floors were devoted to offices, furnished rooms, and hotels. The high cost of land near Central Avenue and Washington excluded activities such as lumberyards, warehouses, liveries, and other activities that demanded a great deal of space but produced less profit. Liveries were close to the hotels and were the nineteenth-century version of parking lots. Clerks, shopkeepers, dressmakers, and other downtown workers lived in boarding houses just north of the compact downtown within easy walking distance of their jobs.[1] Chinese laundries served the town's boarders and visitors. Streetcars ran up and down Washington Street drawing people to the central business district from the new residential subdivisions. Horse-drawn buggies brought shoppers from neighboring towns and outlying rural villages. Downtown Phoenix's position as the region's dominant retail and service center was reinforced by its status as state capital and county seat.

City centers of the outlying communities such as Glendale, Peoria, Scottsdale, Mesa, Gilbert, Chandler, and Tempe offered more everyday items for local consumption. Mesa emerged early in the twentieth century as the trading center of the East Valley, and Glendale occupied a similar position for the West Valley. Tempe was the site of the Arizona Territorial Normal School, founded in 1885 through the aggressive lobbying and delicate negotiations of former schoolteacher and Tempe booster, Charles Trumbell Hayden. Hayden and his intermediaries in the territorial legislature agreed to a deal that gave the state's research university to Tucson, and the insane asylum, the biggest institutional plum, to Phoenix. Tempe would be the site of the territory's teacher's college. Tempe Normal School opened with 21 students in January 1886. It would eventually become Arizona State University and play a central role in defining Tempe's identity as a college town and in influencing its downtown development and redevelopment efforts. This status as a college town, combined with the city's commercial success, translated into an especially active downtown. There were nine mercantile stores, two drug stores, two grocery stores, two lumberyards, five physicians, one hotel, and four saloons.[2] Known for its intellectual bent and support for the arts, Tempe had something extra, even then. The popular Goodwin Opera House packed in Tempeans for dramatic events and talent programs. During the summer season, the Goodwin moved outdoors to the so-called Goodwin Airdome on Fifth Street and Mill Avenue to show motion pictures. Years later, Betty Gregg Adams recalled "sitting on a blanket at the Airdome with my friends, eating popcorn watching 'The Perils of Pauline,' and swatting mosquitoes."[3]

The region's historic downtown districts were viable retail and service hubs and centers of social life until the 1950s. Going downtown for Saturday shopping was still a big event in people's lives. Downtown Phoenix contained all the Valley's high-rise development, most of it having been constructed during the 1924 to 1931 building boom.[4] The 10-story Luhrs Building (1924) and 13-story Luhrs Tower (1929) originally held medical offices, then lost them, as hospitals dispersed during the 1930s and 1940s, pulling away related services. Doctors' offices were replaced by insurance agencies and law offices, seeking proximity to the county courthouse.[5] During the first half of the twentieth century, downtown Phoenix had no rival regionally as a place to shop and do business. It contained department stores, banks, automobile dealers, jewelry stores, architects, accountants, real estate brokers, and insurance agents.[6] Downtown Phoenix accounted for 52 percent of the city's total retail sales in 1948, led by general merchandise with 28 percent of the total, automobiles with 22 percent, and apparel and accessories with 14 percent.[7] A trip downtown at the time might include shopping at Montgomery Ward, Sears and Roebuck, Diamonds, Goldwaters, or Porter's Saddle and Harness Company. A visit to one of the auto dealerships along Van Buren from Fifth Street to Fifth Avenue and lunch at one of the downtown's three premier hotels, the Westward Ho, San Carlos, or Adams, could also be on the agenda.

Tempe's downtown remained an important business center and focus of community life until 1960. Businesses stretched along Mill Avenue from the Salt River to University Drive. People bought groceries at the Safeway, Rundle's and Jim Shelley's. They shopped for automobiles at Dana Brothers and purchased drugs and sundries at Laird and Dines. At the end of a busy day, they could see a movie at the Valley Art Theater (originally called the College Theater), constructed in 1938 by Dwight "Red" Harkins. Harkins and his son Dan would later establish a successful chain of movie theaters throughout the Valley, but in the early years he and his young family lived above the Valley Art in downtown Tempe. The downtown also contained the local post office, city hall, newspaper plant, and library.[8] The end of World War II bought many veterans to attend Arizona State College, where the enrollment surged from 553 in 1946 to 11,128 in 1961.[9] Despite this rapid growth, Tempe retained a small-town character with Mill Avenue as its main street throughout the 1950s.

Postwar growth and new land development at the fringe undercut the viability of the region's downtown business districts. Quick to respond to the changing geography of markets, retailers opened new stores in suburban strip malls and shopping centers. The new stores were larger and more modern, selection was wider, and parking was plentiful. Park Central, the first major shopping center opened 2.5 miles north of downtown Phoenix in 1957. Goldwaters and Diamonds department stores relocated there from downtown. Tower Plaza opened in 1958 followed by Christown Mall and Scottsdale Fashion Square in 1961, Thomas Mall in 1963, and Tri City Mall in Mesa in 1969. Not only did the new malls draw retail activity from the downtowns, they also attracted new offices, hotels, and apartment buildings. The defense plants also were drawn to the suburbs where land was cheaper and more plentiful than in the downtown. Producing low-weight, high-value goods that could be transported by truck, they no longer needed to locate in the railroad yards south of the downtown. What is astounding is the speed at which downtown Phoenix declined! After almost 100 years of retail dominance, it sank in a mere decade. Downtown Phoenix's share of the city's retail sales plummeted from 52 percent in 1948 to 38 percent in 1954, and 28 percent in 1958.[10] At its worst moment in 1972, downtown retail sales accounted for only 3 percent of the city's total of $1.6 billion, and new private investment had all but halted. Phoenix became two distinct cities with suburban areas spreading outward, and the commercial core contracting. With retailing gone and services on the wane, all that remained downtown were banks and government and legal offices whose workers left promptly at 5 P.M. for their suburban homes.

Downtown decline dealt a fatal blow to the "Deuce," a skid row district from First Avenue to Sixth Street and from Washington Street south to the railroad tracks. The name came from its focus on Second Street.[11] Through the 1930s and 1940s, the Deuce contained Chinatown, Hispanic residential and commercial areas, a produce market, and a lively but racy entertainment district featuring nightclubs, bars, and a thriving red light district. Until the 1950s, the Deuce's residents were working men.[12] Chinatown moved during the 1930s and 1940s, and downtown jobs declined during the 1950s. As seasonal agricultural work declined with large-scale urbanization, the Deuce became a derelict region of flop houses, honky tonks, missions, pawn shops, thrift stores, blood banks, and disreputable bars frequented by drug dealers, prostitutes, and people down on their luck. As major businesses left the downtown, retailers catering to transients moved in. The area's physical deterioration reinforced its undesirability in the eyes of many Phoenicians. In a classic, blame-the-victim response, city leaders and downtown merchants pinned the shortage of downtown shopping on the Deuce.[13] The development of outlying residential subdivisions also weakened the economic position of downtown Tempe, but the city's unique status as a college town enabled the downtown to stay afloat during the difficult years of the 1960s and 1970s.

NATIONAL TRENDS IN DOWNTOWN REVITALIZATION

Trends in downtown Phoenix and Tempe were not unusual, as cities across the nation struggled with declining downtown commercial districts. City leaders experimented, first with federal urban renewal programs during the 1950s and 1960s, and later with shopping malls, museums and entertainment venues. Early federally-funded renewal projects aimed to replace unprofitable inner-city businesses and blighted residential areas with high-end housing, museums, galleries, concert halls, and convention centers. They offered desperate cities a much-needed economic boost, and gave them flexibility in deciding how to redefine their downtown districts.

Municipal efforts at downtown redevelopment were boosted by changing demographics. The 1950s Leave-It-to-Beaver household of male breadwinner, his nonworking wife, and their children gave way to a more diverse mixture of living arrangements, including dinks (dual income no kids), empty-nesters, persons living alone, and gay couples, many of whom valued the centrality, openness, diversity, character, and amenities of the downtown and inner-city neighborhoods. The economic shift from manufacturing to services favored more central locations as did the growing willingness of corporations to separate divisions such as headquarters, marketing and media, research and development, advertising and design from production. Added to these demographic and economic forces was the Starbucks Phenomenon: the emergence of a deep longing for neighborhood-scale places to connect with other people, socially and professionally. Downtown districts that were able to create a distinctive sense of place and coherent identity as centers of entertainment, business, and culture began to give the monotonous suburban strip malls, shopping centers, and edge-city developments a run for their money.

Within this national context of downtown redevelopment, it is remarkable that the revitalization of downtown Phoenix took so long. The city holds the dubious honor of having the least interesting and profitable downtown area of any major city in America. The reasons are many. First, Phoenix's obsession with annexation, and its penchant to look outward for investment opportunities and growth, led it to undervalue downtown opportunities. Second, the city used desert imagery and mountain scenery, not historically and architecturally significant buildings, to evoke a sense of place. Third, downtown Phoenix at its zenith was never more than the service center for an agricultural hinterland. It lacked a critical mass of historically important landmarks. Fourth, Phoenix's migrant population has only weak ties to the downtown and its rich and colorful history. Phoenician family narratives rarely include a trip downtown to attend the World Series, a visit to the art museum, or Easter brunch with grandma and grandpa at a favorite restaurant. These memorable events occurred in Chicago, St. Louis, Kansas City, and Milwaukee. And finally, Phoenix gave up on the notion of a single dominant core when it adopted its urban villages, each with a separate village center.

PHOENIX'S BIG BOX APPROACH

The concept for a performing arts center in downtown Phoenix originated in 1959, when cultural and theatrical events were held in outdated school auditoriums. It was decided then that the city needed an entertainment venue, and also a facility to accommodate regional and national conventions. A citizen's group was formed in the early 1960s, led by Newton Rosenzweig, jewelry store owner, member of an old and respected Phoenix family, and promoter of growth. The committee obtained land in the old Phoenix town site and commissioned a local architect to design a building that would complement several soon-to-be constructed hotels and a new 40-story bank center (Figure 30). Civic Plaza, funded through the sale of revenue bonds, opened in 1972 and featured a large convention hall and Symphony Hall rising above a spacious plaza with fountains and sculpture overlooking St. Mary's Basilica, the downtown's most significant and enduring historical landmark. Two convention hotels opened shortly thereafter: the Crowne Plaza (then the Adams and later the Hilton) in 1975 and the Hyatt Regency in 1976.

Civic Plaza failed miserably as a vehicle of public architecture and mechanism of downtown redevelopment because it embodied all the classic flaws of early downtown redevelopment.[14] When the Deuce was demolished to make way for Civic Plaza and subsequent expansion in 1984, a substantial number of the city's single-room occupany hotels were razed, creating a net loss in low-income housing. The Deuce's drug dealers, prostitutes, gangs, and homeless did not evaporate in the dry desert air, as city leaders seemed to expect; they hung around the nooks and crannies of the downtown and eventually drifted westward to the Capitol Mall neighborhood, where they destabilized an already declining area.[15] Symphony Hall, designed for high arts and culture and the city's elite, did little to bring the middle and working classes back to the downtown. And then there was the issue of poor design. Civic Plaza was structured explicitly to separate visitors from the rest of the downtown. Surrounded by austere concrete ramps, access is via an underground parking garage. Walkways are uninviting and hot during the summer months and do not encourage

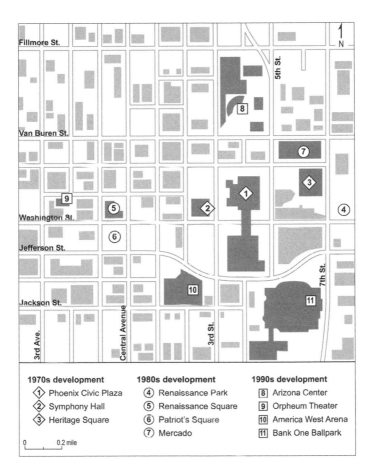

1970s development
⟨1⟩ Phoenix Civic Plaza
⟨2⟩ Symphony Hall
⟨3⟩ Heritage Square

0   0.2 mile

1980s development
④ Renaissance Park
⑤ Renaissance Square
⑥ Patriot's Square
⑦ Mercado

1990s development
8 Arizona Center
9 Orpheum Theater
10 America West Arena
11 Bank One Ballpark

Figure 30. Development in downtown Phoenix.

entry from the street or surrounding businesses. Only now after more than 30 years of isolation is Civic Plaza being redesigned to include more street-level activity, access to surrounding businesses, and open vistas of the downtown streetscape.

The second downtown-redevelopment effort several blocks to the east was smaller, more tradition bound, and pedestrian friendly. Unfortunately, it too was unable to stimulate significant private-sector investment. In 1974, Phoenix obtained a federal grant to acquire the historic Rosson House, a classic Victorian home at the corner of Sixth Street and Monroe. When it became clear that the restoration of the house would be successful, the city acquired adjacent residential structures and christened the only remaining residential complex from its original town site as "Heritage Square." The Lath House, a 22,200-square-foot open-air pavilion was commissioned to provide architectural cohesiveness for the historical buildings and to serve as a public gathering place. Although attractive and well designed, Heritage Square is a quiet, off-the-beaten-path hideaway from the hub of downtown business and governmental activity. It is not, as envisioned, an energetic public gathering place. Its tea room, gift shop, restaurant, and toy museum are better known to history buffs than to the general public. The one exception is Pizzeria Bianco, a small restaurant in an old machine shop that has developed a reputation for outstanding brick-oven baked pizzas with homemade mozzarella cheese and locally grown vegetables. Phoenicians gather in line daily at 4:30 P.M. to wait for the restaurant to open at 5 P.M. Customers spill over onto the porch of the wine bar next door and play bocci ball in a neighboring courtyard. The spectacular success of this establishment speaks both to the incipient demand for unique, human-scale businesses and to their scarcity in downtown Phoenix.

Many of downtown Phoenix's significant public buildings date to the Goddard era of city leadership between 1983 and 1990. Terry Goddard, a young local lawyer with degrees from Harvard College (1969) and Arizona State University College of Law (1976), came from an influential Arizona family, his father having served as the state's governor between 1965 and 1967. In 1982 Goddard co-chaired the Citizens for District Elections initiative to replace Phoenix's at-large method of electing city council members with district elections. Outspent by opponents, and opposed by the sitting mayor, local business organizations, the city's newspapers, and all but one city council member, the referendum passed. Goddard became the boy wonder of city politics. When incumbent Mayor Margaret Hance declined to seek reelection the following year, the thirty-six-year-old political newcomer entered the race against the establishment's hand-picked candidate, Peter Dunn, a local businessman and former state legislator. Goddard won, and four new members were elected to the city council, signaling a new era in city government.

Goddard was unabashedly pro-downtown. In 1984 he urged the city council to authorize development of Square One, a retail marketplace, and of Renaissance Park, the first downtown housing development in more than forty years. In addition, the council purchased and promised to renovate the Orpheum Theater, a Spanish Revival building, constructed in 1929. The Orpheum was intended to be used for film festivals, performing arts performances, and community activities. The mayor and council appointed a committee to lay the groundwork for a new downtown baseball park. Renaissance Park was completed in 1986, and work began on Renaissance Square, a high-rise office building with shops and restaurants on the ground floor. A five-level underground parking garage was completed at Washington Street and Central Avenue. Patriot's Square was refurbished, with a laser system shooting light into the night sky from a 115-foot spire. Amid all this activity, the city council approved tax abatements and other incentives to entice Rouse, a large national developer, to build a hotel, office, and retail complex on a "superblock" between Van Buren and Fillmore Streets and Third and Fifth Streets.[16] Arizona Center opened in 1990 with 20- and 18-story office towers and 150,000 square feet of retail space for specialty stores. Quickly, it was apparent that retail would not survive, and a multiplex cinema was added. The Arizona Center moved away from shopping and became an entertainment hub with restaurants, clubs, and specialty stores designed for tourists and downtown diners.

Arguably, the most meaningful achievement of the Goddard era was a 1988 bond initiative to build new downtown infrastructure. Goddard's idea was to develop a critical mass of architecturally significant public buildings close enough together to function actively.[17] In the late 1980s, downtown Phoenix was poised to attract substantial private investment and draw people to the new cultural and entertainment sites. Unfortunately, the city fell into a deep recession driven by real estate speculation and the collapse of its home lending institutions. Goddard resigned in 1990 to run unsuccessfully for governor against real estate developer Fife Symington. His successors at city hall, while supportive of downtown redevelopment, have not presented and implemented a coherent vision of what the heart of a desert city should look like. The downtown has languished, despite construction of the Phoenix Museum of History in 1995, the Arizona Science Center in 1997, Bank One Ballpark, a 48,000-seat baseball facility in 1998, Phoenix Municipal Courthouse in 1999, Sandra Day O'Connor Federal Courthouse and the Dodge Theater in 2001. The streets of downtown Phoenix are dead after 5 P.M. if there is no major event, and even then, most people make a beeline for their cars when the event ends.

The large pieces of civic infrastructure in downtown Phoenix are desperately in need of investments and activities with fine-grained, pedestrian-scale development like bookstores, coffee houses, novelty shops, and outdoor bars and restaurants that draw people out of their cars and onto the streets. The current physical design offers few places were such activities could occur as the downtown is, with a few notable exceptions, dominated by big buildings separated by hot, harsh, uninviting walkways; wide, difficult-to-cross streets; and large, hulking parking garages. Even the Arizona Center, with its semi-circular design oriented around an attractive sunken courtyard, faces inward. Most people arrive by car and emerge from the parking garage rather than from the street. Goddard's plan to build a "solar oasis" with giant cooling towers in the plaza in front of Symphony Hall at Civic Plaza, to create an inviting public space unique to the desert city, was replaced by an ugly, utilitarian tent that serves as a pavilion for public events.

The Mercado was perhaps the most disappointing downtown failure. The brightly colored, festive office and retail complex was inspired by the Mexican market town of Guanajuato and was developed jointly by Chicanos Por La Causa and the Symington Co. (the same Symington who defeated Terry Goddard in the 1990 Arizona governor's race.) The Mercado opened to much fanfare in November 1989. Intended as a shopping center with a Latin flavor, the Mercado offered shops and restaurants organized around a central plaza, and seemed to provide the type of retail and restaurants that downtown Phoenix sorely needed. It failed in part because of poor timing, opening at the start of a serious recession. In addition, it had inadequate on-site parking in a city where parking is viewed as an entitlement, and there were too few middle-class neighbors to support the restaurants and shops on evenings when there were no major events. The Mercado fell into bankruptcy, was taken over by its lender, and eventually sold to Arizona State University for its downtown campus. Fife Symington was convicted of financial improprieties connected with the Mercado's loans, and resigned from the governorship, although his case was later overturned on appeal. In a peculiar—but quintessential Phoenician—twist of fate, Symington reinvented himself by going to cooking school and is now part-owner and dessert chef at one of the valley's leading eateries. The Mercado also was reinvented as an office park and university campus. The building was repainted to tone down its distinctive color. The former retail spaces are all but empty, and the Mercado's charming, winding streets are deserted.

City boosters again proclaim that the success of downtown Phoenix is imminent. Today's optimism stems first from the fact that Phoenicians are by nature positive about the future, and secondly, from what boosters are calling the "perfect storm" of emerging private and public projects downtown. The current buzzword for downtown redevelopment is research. In February 2002, more than 50 leaders gathered at the Arizona State Capitol to coordinate an effort to attract an important genomics research institute to the state. The institute was led by Dr. Jeffrey Trent, a Phoenix native who holds a Ph.D. in genetics from the University of Arizona. Trent, formerly the Scientific Director of the National Human Genome Research Institute at the National Institutes of Health, was looking for a site to develop an institute to translate breakthroughs in genetic research into medical advances. Within five months, the team secured $90 million in commitments from the State of Arizona, City of Phoenix, the Salt River Pima-Maricopa Indian Community (where the incidence of diabetes is astonishingly high), the state's universities, and various private foundations. Trent agreed to move the headquarters of the International Genomics Consortium (IGC) and a companion research institute, the Translational Research Institute (TGen) to downtown Phoenix. The city promised to develop the Phoenix Biotech Campus on a 13-acre site as the permanent home for IGC and TGen. Groundbreaking occurred on June 13, 2003.

This event was noteworthy both because of its speed—downtown leaders have been talking about a third downtown hotel for more than 20 years—and because TGen was spawned from a regional collaboration. Then-Phoenix Mayor Skip Rimsza likened the process to the effort of building the Central Arizona Project to bring water from the Colorado River to Phoenix and Tucson. "We drank from that fountain this summer and this (biotech) is the same kind of fountain."[18] The biotech campus promises to bring highly-paid knowledge workers to the downtown and to attract spin-off and related businesses. TGen offers the potential to transform downtown Phoenix into a place where new knowledge is created and translated into products and services, where highly-paid and creative people work and want to live, and where businesses form to serve their needs.

When the new light rail system begins operations in 2008, it will bring more people to downtown Phoenix on foot, reinforcing the pedestrian potential of downtown. Currently, a large majority of those who attend cultural events, baseball games, and downtown museums arrive by car, proceed across the street to their venues, and then return to their suburban homes without eating, shopping, or taking in the downtown sights. Light rail can contribute to the downtown's dynamic in a way that automobiles cannot. Also, the Phoenix City Council recently agreed to public financing for a third downtown hotel. After more than 20 years of fruitless effort to cajole private investors to build a third hotel, the city finally recognized the reality that public funding would be needed to support hotel development. Without the third hotel, the benefits of the publicly funded $600 million expansion of Civic Plaza would be compromised.

Yet another piece of this rapidly evolving picture of downtown Phoenix is a recent decision by Michael Crow, President of Arizona State University, to move a substantial portion of the university to downtown Phoenix. The first programs will move in August 2005, and the downtown campus is expected to enroll 15,000 students by 2015. City officials are positively giddy about the prospect of adding a lively, youthful profile to their downtown mix. The University challenged local architectural firms to prepare "pie-in-the-sky" designs of how the new Capital Center should look, requiring only that the campus be within five minutes walking distance of a light-rail stop and integrated into the downtown environment, rather than being walled off from it. Headed downtown are programs in nursing, public policy, social work, communications, health management, extended education.

After more than 40 years of fits and starts, the city seems finally to "get it," and larger societal and metropolitan forces are working in favor of downtown redevelopment. There is more support and enthusiasm now for the downtown than at any time in the past 30 years, save perhaps during the period of Goddard's tenure as mayor during the 1980s. There is a vision and coherence to the plan for a knowledge-driven downtown economy. Even the most cynical of downtown critics are guardedly optimistic that the long awaited turnaround finally is at hand.[19] Private spin-offs from the planned public initiatives are, however, more promise than reality at this point. In addition, there appears to be little serious thinking about the place-making aspects of the new development. It is not clear whether existing museums, sport facilities, and theaters and the planned genetics institute will meld to create a distinctive place, and whether this place will become the economic engine and spiritual heart of the region.

TEMPE'S MAIN STREET

When Comedy Central's "Insomniac with Dave Attell" came to Phoenix in 2002 to profile the hot spots of urban nightlife, it picked downtown Tempe, not downtown Phoenix, for the site of its show. The historic downtown of this landlocked suburb has emerged as a vibrant public space, lively entertainment district, and magnet for new economy firms. It is animated in the evenings, especially on the weekends, and has gained national attention through shows like Insomiac, its local music and comedy scene, and the annual New Year's Eve Block Party and New Year's Day Fiesta Bowl at Sun Devil Stadium on the ASU campus. Downtown Tempe is an accessible and inviting public gathering place and shopping district. If Phoenix developed its downtown from the top down with emphasis on public infrastructure, Tempe's approach was to build from the bottom up and create a critical mass of fine-grained activity from which large-scale development would emerge.

Tempe had formidable geographic advantages for downtown redevelopment. The city is centrally located and at a transportation crossroads. Unlike Phoenix, Tempe became landlocked early in its development. By the mid-1970s, it was clear that Tempe's economic development would be based on infill and would be vertical not horizontal development. Proximity to the Arizona State University (ASU) campus offered a sizable pedestrian-oriented market. The ASU connection also enabled downtown Tempe to frame a new self image and established the basis for later redevelopment at a time when historic downtown districts across the valley were failing miserably. As mainline businesses fled to strip malls and outlying shopping centers after 1960, downtown Tempe's historical buildings attracted counterculture businesses. The counterculture movement had its genesis in generational conflict over civil rights, free speech, the Vietnam War and the draft, sexual behavior, and lifestyle choices. "Hipness" was manifest in the use of illegal drugs, rock music, long hair, avant garde clothing styles, and political radicalism. Markets emerged to serve the needs of this community, often around college campuses.[20] Downtown Tempe, just two blocks from the heart of the rapidly growing ASU campus, was an ideal location for the counterculture businesses. These businesses included a food cooperative; arts and crafts stores selling hand-made leather sandals and boots, art glass, candles, and clothing; a used bookstore, record shop, and establishments specializing in drug paraphernalia. Circus Circus, one of the downtown's signature establishments, sold tie-dyed shirts, candles and incense, and beaded wall dividers. Many of the young entrepreneurs were art school dropouts from ASU. A small printing press, the Little Wonder Press, published a bi-weekly newspaper.[21]

An unsavory spinoff of the drug scene, sexual freedom, and laissez-faire lifestyles of the Mill Avenue counterculture was a biker element that frequented several local bars. A notorious motorcycle gang claimed Mill Avenue as its turf.[22] Many middle-class Tempeans looked unfavorably on the bikers and hippies. In 1971, the *Tempe Daily News* decried the downtown district as "a festering sore on the community."[23] There was serious talk of moving city hall two miles south. Wiser heads prevailed, however, and the counterculture era turned out to be a transitional phase in the downtown's path from small town main street to a successful entertainment district and magnet for new economy firms.

The young merchants, many of whom had little experience as small business owners, formed the Mill Avenue Merchants Association (MAMA) in 1968 to promote the interests of downtown merchants, and to make downtown Tempe the focal point for the region's hip life. MAMA wanted better street lighting, less traffic, and the elimination of on-street parking. MAMA also wanted better control over the bikers, who detracted from their nonviolent, socially and politically-conscious lifestyles. One of MAMA's first activities was to sponsor an arts and crafts festival to display hand-crafted merchandise, bring people to the downtown, and raise money for charitable purposes. Over the years, the semi-annual MAMA festivals grew from 50 booths to 500 and from a local to a regional event. MAMA began to advertise in hotel magazines and on local radio stations, and by 1994, was earning in excess of $1 million per festival. More significantly, each festival drew some 250,000 people to the downtown, popularized it as accessible and safe, and forged an image of downtown Tempe as playful, colorful, youthful, edgy, and different.[24]

MAMA and the merchants lobbied for historical preservation at a time when the city's establishment was inclined to tear down unsightly old buildings to help eliminate the downtown's disreputable population. The city hoped initially that downtown Tempe would become an upscale shopping district along the lines of Scottsdale's swank Fifth Avenue shops. To the hippies and MAMA merchants, the turn-of-the-century commercial buildings were aesthetically pleasing and reminiscent of Tempe's colorful past. They vehemently opposed the city's plan for urban renewal.[25] The election of Harry Mitchell, a Tempe native and local history teacher, as mayor in 1978 solidified support for historical preservation, and pushed the balance of power in this direction. His vision of downtown redevelopment was to create an authentic, distinctive, and historically significant place. In his words: "You don't try to recreate the Main Street of Disneyland, I really believe that."[26] Mayor Mitchell also understood the symbolic importance of a thriving downtown for a city's image. Reflecting on the status of Mill Avenue in the 1970s, he said:

Mill Avenue . . . was still the main gateway to the city. There was no other river crossing but Mill Avenue when the river flooded. It is the entryway to the university and to many people, what they saw of Tempe was what they saw of the downtown.[27]

Downtown Tempe got a boost when it became the corporate headquarters of America West Airlines, the state's eleventh largest private sector employer with 7,280 employees, and the nation's eighth largest air carrier. Founded in 1983 with three aircraft and 280 employees, the airline expanded quickly to develop routes to Hawaii and Japan and many U.S. cities. Overexpansion during the 1980s thrust the airline into bankruptcy in 1991 from which it emerged in 1994 leaner and more cost-conscious. Initially, America West occupied space in an old shopping center on the northern edge of the downtown, and later moved into a headquarters building that was part of one of the city's early rede-

velopment efforts. Eventually, America West built its own headquarters west of the main commercial district. The multiplier
effects of the airline are quite large in the sense that payments to
employees and suppliers generate new cycles of consumer
spending.[28] The psychological and practical effects of headquar-
tering the nation's eighth largest airline in downtown Tempe are
even more significant. America West employees increase the
number of people who want to live downtown, and put people on
the streets.

While Tempe's downtown combines both old and new, critics
argue that developers were given too much leeway, and that more
of the historic buildings should have been preserved. An early
developer broke his promise to preserve original facades, and
several historically significant buildings were lost. Also controver-
sial is the loss of the mom-and-pop businesses that defined the
downtown during its early years of redevelopment. Changing
Hands, a second-hand bookstore, moved to a suburban strip mall.
The proliferation of national chains and loss of signature businesses like Circus Circus and Changing Hands Bookstore detracted from the charm and funkiness of the downtown, but in
classic Phoenician fashion, change is accepted as making way for
future development.

The physical fabric of Tempe's downtown is anchored by eight
historically significant turn-of-the-century buildings. At the north
end and at the gateway to the city are the bookends of Hayden's
Flour Mill and Hayden House, now Monti's La Casa Vieja. (Figure
31). Other historical buildings are Hackett House (1888), the Casa
Loma Hotel (1899), the Andre Building (1899), Vienna Bakery
(1893), the Laird and Dines Building (1893) and Tempe Hardware
(1898). The city employs aesthetics and design features to integrate new buildings with old ones, using brick building materials
and sidewalks, neoterritorial architecture, and dense greenery.

The Laird and Dines Building represents the stylistic evolution
of downtown Tempe as well as the importance of historical build-

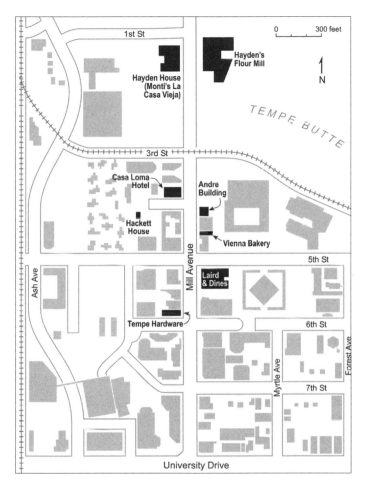

Figure 31. Historical buildings in downtown Tempe.

ings to postmodern sensibilities, even to the point of constructing
new buildings to look old. The original Laird and Dines Building
at the corner of Mill Avenue and Fifth Street, historically called
the "busy corner" was constructed in 1893 and purchased in 1897
by the family of Hillary Laird (Figure 32). Laird had previously
owned the Lone Star Saloon on Fourth Street, but his wife, Clara,
did not want their children brought up in the saloon business, so
she bought the dry goods store at Fifth and Mill. In 1902, Laird

Figure 32. The Laird and Dines Building in downtown Tempe, circa 1900, 1972, and 2004. Top two photos courtesy of Tempe Historical Museum; bottom photo by the author.

added Dr. James Dines as a partner, changed the business to a drugstore, and called it Laird and Dines, a name that is still used to describe the building at Tempe's busy corner. The building was constructed in the Victorian architecture that was in vogue at the time with natural brick bearing walls, corner turret, pressed metal cornice, and decorative woodwork on the second floor and veranda. Over the next 63 years, the drugstore provided Tempeans with prescription drugs, remedies, and sundries, and also served as the unofficial town hall, political campaign headquarters, and place to meet members of the opposite sex. Both owners, Laird and Dines, served terms as mayor of Tempe. Early in 1929, the wooden veranda was stuccoed as an arcade in keeping with the Spanish Colonial Revival movement in construction, the body of the building was stuccoed, and the turret and bay window were removed. In 1994, the Spanish Colonial features were removed, and the building was reconstructed to mimic its original Victorian origins with construction of a new turret and second-floor veranda. In this case, the drive for historical preservation and architectural authenticity involved tearing down much of the historical building to construct a new structure that would look old (Figure 32).

The most ambitious attempt to link Tempe's future with its past and to promote downtown development, is Town Lake at the northern edge of the downtown district in the bed of the Salt River (Figure 33). For some, the development of Town Lake was merely an opportunity for real estate profit; for others it was a once-in-a-lifetime chance to reconnect with the Salt River as the lifeblood of the city's early agriculture and as a cool escape from the desert's heat. Life in early Tempe was closely tied to the river. Charles Hayden's wooden boat ferried people, animals, and buggies back and forth across the river. The adjacent grist mill was powered by water diverted from the river. Canals ran through the city, bringing irrigation water to the farm fields. After Roosevelt

Figure 33. Aerial view of Tempe Town Lake.

Dam was completed in 1911, regular flow in the river ended. But the connection to the river remained, as Tempeans swam in a lake at the base of the Mill Avenue Bridge. On at least three occasions, in 1916, 1923, and around 1940, there was a lake—the remnant of flood waters—for swimming, boating, and fishing. While swimming in the lake was popular, civic groups worried about public safety and encouraged people to use the nearby Tempe Beach Park instead. The park opened in 1923 with an Olympic-sized swimming pool which served as a social gathering spot in the hot, dry, summer heat for young people until it closed in the mid-1970s. The pool was seen by many urban parents as being a safer environment for their children than the canals, but the pool charged admissions, which many could not afford.[29]

During the long dry spell from the 1940s through the mid-1960s, Tempe, like the rest of Phoenix, lost its historic connection with the river. The lakes dried up, and the derelict river bed became home to land fills, quarry mining, and industrial businesses. Flights into and out of Sky Harbor International used the riverbed as a flight path, and the noise made conversation difficult.

The idea of reclaiming the river originated in 1966 when Dean James Elmore of the ASU College of Architecture challenged his students to design concepts that used the dry river bed. Students came back with what has come to be known as the Rio Salado Project, calling for a series of locks and channels and creating an inland seaport in the desert for flood control, recreation, and economic development. The concept perked along for years, with on-again-off-again local interest. The original seaport idea was abandoned in favor of a long green belt with a series of lakes and braided streams. In 1979, Tempe Mayor Harry Mitchell formed the Tempe Rio Salado Citizen Advisory Commission to provide citizen input and publicity for the project. In 1987 Maricopa County voters were asked to support a property tax increase to finance a valley-wide green belt version of the Rio Salado Project; it was defeated, with heavy opposition coming from the socially isolated, urban-fringe retirement communities. Citizens of Tempe supported the concept, and Mayor Mitchell announced that Tempe would move ahead to reclaim its portion of the river.

On June 2, 1999, water from the Central Arizona Project flowed into Tempe Town Lake, and the two-mile lake was declared full some five weeks later (Figure 33). The lake is held in place with inflatable bladder dams at either end that are designed to deflate in case of river flow and then inflate again when the flow subsides. The lake provides a spectacular backdrop for city festivals, fireworks, rock concerts, and sporting competitions and magnet for sailors, canoers, joggers, cyclists, walkers, and nearby workers who picnic along the lake and serves as a reminder that a dryland river once flowed through Phoenix.

Private development has been slow. The promised bevy of restaurants, hotels, and entertainment sites have yet to materialize. Two current developments are Hayden Ferry Lakeside, a nine-story office complex on the south bank close to Mill Avenue, and Regatta Point Condominiums on the south side of the lake with 136 luxury units. The biggest disappointment was the city's inability to attract the planned $220-million Peabody Hotel. The hope was that the Peabody would allow Tempe to compete for small, but high-end conventions. Although the lake has yet to realize its potential as a stimulus for economic growth, it has emerged as a significant public space, and a symbol of downtown Tempe's attempt to link the past with future. As then-Mayor Mitchell noted in 1988, the downtown and lake are the city's entrance. They brand the city as young, hip, and athletically oriented.

Downtown Tempe also contains a cluster of software and design-oriented businesses. Increasingly, it is recognized that there are two sides to the high technology revolution: the hard side involving sophisticated gadgets such as laptop computers, and cell phones and the soft side focused on creative fields such as media, fashion, advertising, and design. Lively, 24/7 downtown districts are attractive to members of this new creative class, and downtown Tempe has emerged with one of the region's strongest concentrations of new economy firms.[30]

OTHER VALLEY DOWNTOWNS

Downtown redevelopment in other parts of the valley is an uphill battle. Although just about every city has some sort of downtown redevelopment plan, they are faced with daunting competition from growth at the fringe. Rarely, does the downtown win this contest. A current example is Glendale's downtown, which features a charming cluster of antique and specialty shops. The city's image has been as a quaint, family-oriented bedroom community. Recently, the city orchestrated a sports-centered economic growth plan, securing a new $220 million arena for the National Hockey League's Phoenix Coyotes and a $355-million stadium for the National Football League's Arizona Cardinals, all surrounded by six million square feet of planned restaurants, retail, commercial, upscale residential, and convention facilities. A factor that enabled development of this scale and gave Glendale a competitive advantage over other cities vying for these projects was its ability to secure large tracts of land. The site of this development is four miles west of the current downtown. It is unclear at this point whether the sports venues will suck the life out of downtown Glendale or whether the city is capable of supporting two contrasting nodes of economic development.

Downtown Scottsdale has had trouble deciding whether it wants to be the "West's Most Western Town," a center for arts and culture, or a shopping district catering to tourists. In the late 1980s, Scottsdale floated the idea of a canal bank project along the Arizona Canal, just north of the current downtown. The project was intended as a mixed-use development that would unite the newer commercial district around Scottsdale Fashion Square to the north with the older one to the south. Using San Antonio's Riverwalk as a model, the city viewed canal development as a mechanism for enhancing its tourism-based economy. The Salt River Project agreed to alter its management and maintenance procedures to accommodate this vision. In 1993, the City declared 91 acres along the canal as "a slum" in order to acquire land and then resell it to developers.[31] The city would ultimately pay a stiff price for this move when negative public reaction derailed the project.

Throughout the 1990s, the go-ahead for development of the north bank was imminent, but never occurred. In 1997, the city turned its attention to the south bank and issued a request for proposals for mixed-use development. The successful bidder, the Scottsdale Waterfront South Associates, a partnership of local and California developers, envisioned a group of villages linked by navigable canals, retail-oriented pedestrian walkways, bridges, trolley and cart paths and other linkages. Hoping to augment local funding sources, the city lobbied for use of an obscure State of Arizona theme-park statute to help pay for the planned cultural district. This legislation required public participation, which ultimately led to the project's undoing. Existing merchants in the Fifth Avenue retail district feared that their buildings would be condemned and they would be forced to move to make way for the new waterfront development. They ultimately forced a public vote in 1999. The project was depicted as an effort by private developers to use public funds to put small, established Scottsdale retailers out of business. After more than 20 years of discussion and development, the waterfront project has not yet materialized, and the center of gravity for Scottsdale's economic life is migrating northward.

Mesa began a downtown revitalization effort in 1998, including a $10.5 million streetscape improvement project, to attract retail and commercial businesses to the downtown. It was, however distracted by an ill-fated attempt to lure the region's new professional football team to its border with Tempe. Downtown Mesa continues to languish. Chandler seeks to develop its downtown, but continues to represent itself as the "high-tech oasis of the Silicon Desert," reflecting the concentration of high-tech firms, including Intel, in newer parts of the city.

The region's historic city centers followed a predictable course of early growth and prosperity followed by sudden collapse after 1950. Suburbanization sent retailing and then manufacturing and services to outlying areas. Cities were slow to revitalize their downtown districts, in large part, because they were diverted by continued rapid growth at the fringe. Landlocked Tempe aggressively redeveloped Its downtown because it had little alternative but to emphasize vertical over horizontal development. As Phoenix and suburban communities like Mesa reach the limits of their available land, they too are becoming more serious about downtown revitalization, and there is a gradual shift toward more mature forms of growth and economic development.

Thinking Small and Living Big

The story of modern Phoenix is about growth and dynamism, the uncertainty of the desert, place making, and community building in the face of continual turnover and rapid social change. Phoenix has never known a period of sustained economic decline. There have been brief times of hardships, for example, when the cotton market failed after World War I, in the early years of the Depression, and more recently with the savings-and-loan collapse of the late-1980s and early-1990s, but the region has always bounced back. Periodic floods and droughts threatened public safety and derailed growth briefly, but Phoenix moves inexorably forward, doing away with the desert, with a collective sense of optimism and deep faith that, despite occasional setbacks, the city's destiny is to grow.

The traditional model of growth as new land development on the urban fringe is deeply ingrained in the vision of Phoenix as a place of renewal. For many, the starting-over process meant a new home in a new subdivision at the city's edge and new friendships with new neighbors. This was true of the sick who moved to Sunnyslope during the early twentieth century, of the World War II veterans drawn to John F. Long's new community of Maryvale, of the retirees who saw the original Sun City as a place to discover new pursuits and make new friends, up to today's retirees looking for active lifestyles in Sun City Grand, Sun Lakes, and Rio Verde, and today's migrants gravitating to new master-planned communities like Verrado and Anthem. Mexican migrants continue this tradition, although not at the urban fringe, but in the neighborhoods they are remaking and rebuilding in central Phoenix. For them, the urban core is Phoenix's new frontier.

Phoenix is not a nostalgic or romantic city; continual growth means change, dynamism, continual adjustment, and a fair bit of uncertainty. It is, in the words of a local author, "a shambling, unfocused, optimistic, indifferent, imaginative, energetic, cafeteria-style heaping of possibilities."[1] Growth is so rapid that the migrants of twenty years ago, indeed the migrants of five years ago, have difficulty recognizing the place they moved to. In 2003, Greater Phoenix added more than 140,000 new people, the equivalent of Pasadena, California or Syracuse, New York.[2] The labor force grew by almost 40,000.[3] More than 41,000 building permits for single-family homes were approved.[4] Home sales set a new record of 123,000 units.[5] During the first eight months of 2004, Phoenix was the nation's top home-building market in the nation, edging out Atlanta for this position. Pretty much everyone in Phoenix either became a new neighbor, or got a new neighbor. And this does not include renters, who are three times more likely than homeowners to move. A new hockey arena opened in Glendale, and construction began on a new football stadium. Arizona State University announced a new plan to expand its downtown campus. Light rail construction began, and Scottsdale passed a new sales tax to support open space preservation in its McDowell Mountain Preserve. Ground was broken for Tempe's new Fine Arts Center. In short, it was business as usual in the nation's fastest growing large metropolis.

Phoenicians traditionally have measured the city's stature and growth in physical terms: as numbers of people, homes, businesses, and urban land. This view of growth is old fashioned in an era when wealth generation is linked to the knowledge economy of ideas, scientific discoveries, computing power, and communications and information technology, and personal aspirations are tied to amenities, aesthetics, quality of life, and a sense of place. The nature of the new economy and Phoenix's larger size require a more sophisticated and resourceful approach to growth, with fresh attitudes about what form it takes, where it occurs, and how people and jobs come together. The search for more mature growth requires an eye for complexity, not the usual, simple-minded approach of building new homes on cheap land in the desert to attract new people from California, Illinois, Ohio, and Kansas.

Dolores Hayden regards sprawl as a process rather than as a physical form and adopts the *Merriam-Webster's Collegiate Dictionary* definition of the verb sprawl, "to cause to spread out carelessly or awkwardly."[6] It is useful to think about sprawl as something other than low-density development, because much of Phoenix's new residential construction would not fit the model of low-density, one-house-per-acre development. It would, however, fit Hayden's definition of careless and awkward development. New master-planned communities leapfrog the boundaries of the built-up area, and there is little forethought to logical relation- *Fierce* ships between jobs and housing. Despite good intentions, Phoenix's urban villages are but lines on a map, not the functional alternative to long-distance commuting and urban sprawl they were originally envisioned to be. The nature of the urban form makes it difficult for the residents of Ahwatukee to work nearby or for the workers at Scottsdale Airpark to live nearby.

The urban geography of Phoenix, although built on the old-fashioned model of land development at the fringe, now shows glimmers of maturity, with an emphasis on the urban core, historic downtowns and neighborhoods, densification, and alternative forms of transportation. Serious attempts are afoot to remake downtown Phoenix into a pedestrian-oriented district geared towards biotechnology research and higher education. The planned light rail system makes no sense whatsoever as a way to support travel in the built environment as it currently exists but does offer an alternative of more mature, higher density forms of urban growth. Tempe's Town Lake promotes density and vertical development. It is also a powerful symbol of the region's attempt to reconnect with the river that gave life to large-scale development of the desert. In the past five years, Glendale has morphed from bedroom suburb to the economic heart of the rapidly growing West Valley. While the future of these projects and places is in no way assured, together they represent a fresh way of thinking about and defining growth in a region that has rarely done so in the past. It is no coincidence that Tempe, the region's only landlocked major city, was the first to seriously pursue downtown redevelopment, mass transit, and reclamation of the riverbed. Phoenix, now cut off from new development on all sides but a slim corridor to the north, is moving in a similar direction.

A second theme in the history and geography of Phoenix is the monumental struggle to overcome the harshness and uncertainty of desert life, and the role of desert iconography, in creating a sense of place. Early Phoenicians built the world's largest and most sophisticated water storage and delivery system, and created a productive and prosperous agricultural society. With a stable water supply and greatly reduced risk of flooding, they transformed the wild, vast, and uneven beauty of the desert into an agrarian landscape of straight rows and green fields interspersed with shady, tree-lined canals. City leaders in the 1920s began a campaign of extensive tree planting to "do away with the desert." Luckily, visionary leaders, dating from the 1920s, saw the need to protect remnants of the natural desert, and so began the creation of South Mountain Park and the rest of the Phoenix Mountain Preserves. The desert's scorching heat was made livable for the masses, first with evaporative cooling and later with air conditioning, allowing Phoenix to function pretty much like other cities in the summer. The result of these engineering feats, however, is that many of today's residents have only the vaguest notion of what it means to live in a desert. For them, the desert consists of the faux designer landscapes in their yards and the few icons of the natural desert left in and around the city. The latter play a crucial role in defining sense of place and in sustaining the outdoor and athletic lifestyle that is vital to Phoenix's identity.

Despite the fact that many do not identify with the "desert" part of their desert oasis, Phoenix still receives only eight inches of rainfall a year, with huge fluctuations from one year to the next. The rapidly urbanizing desert of central Arizona depends for its water, not only on the watersheds of the Salt and Verde Rivers in central Arizona, but on underground aquifers and the vast Colorado River Basin. This makes the city vulnerable to shortages from any one of these sources. The West is in a six-year drought, and it is increasingly clear that the Colorado River will be unable to supply water in the quantities mandated by the 1922 Colorado River Compact.

As the city grew and was able to shield itself from the vagaries of desert life, Phoenicians grew both arrogant and complacent about the limitations of their dryland setting and the precariousness of its water supply. The jig is now up; the day of reckoning with the desert is at hand. The city faces growing climatic uncertainty stemming from global climate change, episodic droughts and floods, and an urban heat island that threatens human comfort. Scientists are concerned that large-scale urbanization was based on assumptions of higher-than-normal precipitation. The Intergovernmental Panel on Climate Change predicts a two-to-three degree rise in temperature and a 5 percent reduction in precipitation, potentially substantial changes for a city that already functions at the edge of habitability.[7] The heat island raised summer nighttime temperatures in some parts of the valley by as much as 12° in the past 50 years, with more change on the horizon as the urbanized area grows. Warmer temperatures increase demand for water as outdoor plants require larger applications due to increased evaporation. Approximately half of the region's municipal water is used for outdoor purposes. The demand for electrical power grows as air conditioning units must work harder on hot summer nights due to the heat-island effect. Responsible and thoughtful people are asking whether the environment of Phoenix, and the vast lands and underground aquifers upon which it depends for water, are capable of sustaining a population that is double the current size during prolonged periods of environmental stress. The public also asks whether human-induced environmental change is altering the physical and natural systems that support life, economic development, and the basic human need to connect with place.

Given the aesthetic significance and intensive use of desert open spaces that are interwoven into the built environment, it is surprising that so little progress has been made to change state laws regarding the sale and lease of state trust lands at the urban fringe. There is little glue to hold Phoenicians together, but their outdoor lifestyles and the significance of their desert icons are critical ingredients of that glue. Constitutional mandates to use profits from mining and ranching leases on state lands to support public schools are a vestige of Arizona's rural past, and no longer appropriate to its urban present. More than 82 percent of the state's population now lives in metropolitan Phoenix or Tucson. These mandates are a foil used by the development industry to preserve the status quo of new land development at the fringe. As described in Chapter 4, the sale of public land facilitates the traditional model of growth.

One of the great charms of Phoenix is that, despite its large size, gangly shape, and cultural diversity, it exudes a small-town feel. People are open, friendly, and polite. The economic and political establishment is surprisingly small and cohesive. Phoenicians are strongly motivated to bond with immediate neighbors and neighborhoods, and to do it quickly. This gives them a safe harbor from which to navigate the shambling, unfocused, cafeteria-style heaping of possibilities that are Phoenix. Retirement communities popularized the place-within-a-place concept. Success in insulating themselves from responsibility for the larger Phoenix community set the stage for numerous master-planned communities, selling lifestyles to increasingly diverse populations, seeking to surround themselves with people pretty much like themselves, and separating themselves from those who are different. Lifestyle communities are, on the one hand, logical adaptions to a large, sprawling urban environment of migrants who need to connect with others quickly—to fast forward a sense of belonging and community. On the other hand, they breed an ethos of exclusivity and isolation that make it difficult to see, feel, and experience Greater Phoenix in its entirety. Phoenicians tend to think small, but to live big. They feel connected to small places but drive further to get to work, feel the effects of the regional heat island and air quality problems, and depend for their water on snow pack in Wyoming.

The future of Phoenix is about confronting the impossibility of thinking small and living big. When residents voted down the unwieldy urban growth initiative in 2000, they said they were not yet ready to confront this dilemma. The essence of this issue has been debated on and off for the past thirty years by local residents, academics, and the media. Hopeful signs of regional thinking are the passage of the recent transportation initiative, efforts to create a biotechnology incubator in downtown Phoenix, and growing publicity about water shortages and the need for a regional response.

Phoenix is now at a crossroads. One path to the future is continuing to think small and to live big. This path promises more of the same: greater social fragmentation, mismatched workplaces and residences, precarious water supplies, increasing congestion, and declining environmental quality. The alternative is to live smaller and to think bigger. Living smaller involves a built environment that allows, and indeed encourages, people to live close to their workplaces and greater balance between urban-fringe development and urban infill. This view of the future would provide housing options that encourage affluent whites to return to the urban core. Thinking bigger involves more attention to regional-level environmental and social issues, including transportation, water supply and quality, air quality, the urban heat island, urban growth, and the preservation of desert open spaces. Phoenicians ignore these issues at great peril, given the fragility of their natural setting, the importance of that environment to their quality of life, and the growing importance of quality-of-life issues to economic growth. Given its dramatic population growth and enormous capacity for change, Phoenix can become a prototype for twenty-first-century urbanization if it is able to adapt to more mature forms of growth, reconnect with its desert setting, and build a multicultural sense of belonging and identity that transcends the entire metropolitan community.

NOTES

Chapter 1. Desert Urbanization

1. E. J. Montini, "Pittsburgh Colors Views of Phoenix," *Arizona Republic*, January 23, 1996.

2. Philip VanderMeer, *Phoenix Rising: The Making of a Desert Metropolis* (Carlsbad, Calif.: Heritage Media Corp., 2002), 66.

3. Jane Freeman and Glenn Sanberg, *Jubilee: The 25th Anniversary of Sun City, Arizona* (Phoenix: Sun City Historical Society, 1984), 35–52.

4. The U.S. Census defines an urbanized area as a densely settled area containing more than 50,000 people.

5. As cited in Yvonne Wingett, "County Official Under Fire for Razing History," *Arizona Republic* (September 17, 2004), B1.

6. Thomas A. Heinz, *The Life and Works of Frank Lloyd Wright* (New York: Barnes & Noble, 2002).

7. U.S. Bureau of the Census, "Population Estimates," Population Estimates Program, Population Division, retrieved October 21, 2004 from http://www.census.gov/popest.

Chapter 2. Building a Desert City

1. David Abbott, *Ceramics and Community Organization Among the Hohokam* (Tucson: University of Arizona Press, 2000).

2. Alfred Simon, "Mixing Water and Culture: Making the Canal Landscape in Phoenix," Ph.D. dissertation, Arizona State University, 2002, 31.

3. Abbott, *Ceramics and Community Organization*, 195.

4. Charles L. Redman, *Human Impact on Ancient Environments* (Tucson: University of Arizona Press, 1999), 148–56.

5. Jane Freeman and Glenn Sanberg, *Jubilee: The 25th Anniversary of Sun City, Arizona* (Phoenix: Sun City Historical Society), 1.

6. Peter Russell, "Downtown's Downturn: A Historical Geography of the Phoenix, Ariz., Central Business District, 1890–1986," master's thesis, Arizona State University, 1986, 29.

7. Ernest J. Hopkins and Alfred Thomas, Jr., *The Arizona State University Story* (Phoenix: Arizona Southwest Publishing, 1960), 34–45.

8. As cited in Dean Smith, *Tempe: Arizona Crossroads* (Chatsworth, Calif.: Windsor Publications, 1990), 24.

9. Hopkins and Thomas, *The Arizona State University Story*, 38.

10. Simon, "Mixing Water and Culture," 39.

11. Simon, "Mixing Water and Culture," 40.

12. Charles Sargent ed., *Metro Arizona* (Scottsdale, Ariz.: Biffington Books, 1988), 47.

13. D. T. Patten, "Present Vegetation-Environmental Conditions at Orme, Buttes, Charleston and Hooker Dam Locations," report prepared for the Bureau of Reclamation, 1972.

14. W. M. Pierce and W. Ingalls, *Plat Map Field Notes* (Phoenix: Bureau of Land Management, 1868).

15. Janie Chase Michaels, *A Natural Sequence: A Story of Phoenix, Arizona* (Bangor, Maine: C. H. Glass, 1895), 46.

16. Simon, "Mixing Water and Culture," 61–66.

17. Sargent, *Metro Arizona*, 88–89.

18. As cited in Smith, *Tempe: Arizona Crossroads*, 53.

19. Courtland L. Smith, *The Salt River Project: A Case Study in Cultural Adaption to an Urbanizing Community* (Tucson: University of Arizona Press, 1972), 10.

20. Smith, *The Salt River Project*, 11–12.

21. Bradford Luckingham, *Phoenix: The History of a Southwestern Metropolis* (Tucson: University of Arizona Press, 1989), 47.

22. Salt River Project. "Arizona Falls Showcases Art, History and Technology, retrieved on September 19, 2004 from http://www.srpnet.com/water/canals/azfalls.asp.

23. Luckingham, *Phoenix*, 74–76.

24. James H. Gordon, "Temperature Survey of the Salt River Valley, Arizona," *Monthly Weather Review* 49 (1921): 273.

25. Luckingham, *Phoenix*, 56.

26. Pete R. Dimas, *Progress and a Mexican American Community's Struggle for Existence: Phoenix's Golden Gate Barrio.* American University Studies Regional Studies 10 (New York: Peter Lang, 1999), 45.

27. As cited in Luckingham, *Phoenix*, 109.

28. Dimas, *Progress*, 49.

29. Sargent, *Metro Arizona*.

30. Gail Cooper, *Air-Conditioning America: Engineers and the Controlled Environment, 1900–1960* (Baltimore: Johns Hopkins University Press, 1998), 177.

31. Robert J. Schmidli, "Climate of Phoenix," NOAA Technical Memorandum NWS WR-177. (Phoenix: National Weather Service, 1993).

32. Luckingham, *Phoenix*, 139.

33. Michael Konig, "Phoenix in the 1950s: Urban Growth in the Sunbelt," *Arizona and the West* 24 (1982): 19–38.

34. Matthew Gann McCoy, "Desert Metropolis: Image Building and the Growth of Phoenix, 1940–1965," Ph.D. dissertation, Arizona State University, 2000, 46–47.

35. G. Wesley Johnson, Jr., *Phoenix: Valley of the Sun* (Tulsa, Okla.: Centennial Heritage Press, 1982), 208.

36. Sargent, *Metro Arizona*, 116.

37. Cooper, *Air-Conditioning America*, 166.

38. John F. Long Biography, retrieved on September 17, 2004 from http://www .jflong.com/about.html.

39. David Majure, Arizona Memories video, a production of KAET-TV, 1995.

40. Konig, "Phoenix in the 1950s," 32.

41. Abby Bussel, "Report from Phoenix: City or Supersuburb?" *Progressive Architecture* 75 (1994): 58–63.

42. Edward H. Peplow, Jr.,"You'll Like Living in Phoenix," *Arizona Highways* (April 1957).

43. Simon, *Mixing Water and Culture*, 89–94.

44. P. Schafer, "Ben Schliefer's Vision of Youngtown," *Youngtown Reflections: A Special Supplement in the News-Sun*, November 5, 1979.

45. Youngtown Land and Development Company, *Fifth Anniversary of Youngtown, Arizona* (Phoenix: Youngtown Land and Development Company, 1959), 5.

46. Youngtown Land and Development Company, *Fifth Anniversary*, 5.

47. Youngtown Land and Development Company, *Fifth Anniversary*, 21.

48. Freeman and Sanberg, *Jubilee*, 19–20.

49. Freeman and Sanberg, *Jubilee*, 32.

50. Patricia Gober, "The Sun Cities of Metropolitan Phoenix: No Children Allowed." In Tom L. McKnight, ed., *The Regional Geography of the United States and Canada* (Upper Saddle River, N.J.: Prentice-Hall, 2001), 373–75.

51. U.S. Army Corps of Engineers, *Study of Flood Damage Reduction for Allenville, Arizona* (Los Angeles: U.S. Army Corps of Engineers, District of Los Angeles, 1980), 9.

52. Craig Martin Roberge, "Physical Interactions Between Phoenix and the Salt River, Arizona," Ph.D. dissertation, Arizona State University, 1999.

53. Stephen E. Lee, "Indian Bend Wash"; William L. Graf ed., *The Salt and Gila Rivers in Central Arizona*, Department of Geography Publication 3 (Tempe: Arizona State University, Department of Geography, 1988), 93–104.

54. City of Scottsdale, *Indian Bend Wash* (Scottsdale, Ariz.: City of Scottsdale, Communications and Public Affairs, 1985).

55. Lee, "Indian Bend Wash."

56. City of Scottsdale, *Indian Bend Wash*, 97–100.

57. Desmond D. Connall, Jr., "A History of the Arizona Groundwater Management Act," *State Land Journal* 2 (1982): 313–44.

58. Connall, "A History of the Arizona Groundwater Management Act," 315.

59. Connall, "A History of the Arizona Groundwater Management Act," 343–44.

60. Katharine L. Jacobs and James M. Holway, "Managing for Sustainability in an Arid Climate: Lessons learned from 20 years of Groundwater Management in Arizona, USA," *Hydrology Journal* 12 (2002): 52–65.

61. Jacobs and Holway, "Managing for Sustainability in an Arid Climate," 56.

62. Arizona Department of Environmental Quality, *Air Quality Report, FY2003* (Phoenix: Arizona Department of Environmental Quality, A.R.S. 49-424.10, 2004), 24.

63. Weathersmith, "Phoenix Metropolitan Area Air Quality Summary 1990–2002,"

retrieved on August 28, 2004 from http://www.weathersmith.com/WsAq Phoenix.html.

64. Andrew W. Ellis, Mark L. Hildebrandt, Wendy M. Thomas, and H. J. S. Fernando, "Analysis of the Climatic Mechanisms Contributing to the Summertime Transport of Lower Atmospheric Ozone Across Metropolitan Phoenix, Arizona, USA," *Climate Research* 15 (2000): 13–31.

65. Weathersmith, "Phoenix Metropolitan Area Air Quality Summary 1990–2002."

66. Arizona Department of Environmental Quality, *Air Quality Report*, 31.

67. Anthony J. Brazel, "Future Climate in Central Arizona: Heat and the Role of Urbanization," Arizona State University, Consortium for the Study of Rapidly Growing Regions, Research Vignette No. 2, September 2003.

68. Lawrence A. Baker, Anthony J. Brazel, Nancy Selover, Chris Martin, Nancy McIntyre, Frederick R. Steiner, Amy Nelson, and Laura Musacchio, "Urbanization and Warming of Phoenix (Arizona, USA): Impacts, Feedbacks and Mitigation," *Urban Ecosystems* 6 (2002): 183–203.

69. Donna A. Hartz, Anthony J. Brazel, and Gordon M. Heisler, "A Case Study in Resort Climatology of Phoenix, Arizona, USA," paper, Department of Geography, Arizona State University, 2004.

70. Hartz et al., "A Case Study in Resort Climatology."

Chapter 3. An Ever-Changing Social Dynamic

1. "Neighborhood Crafting," *Verrado Home Town Arizona* 1 (2004): 16.

2. As cited in Shirley Roberts, "Minority-Group Poverty in Phoenix: A Socio-Economic Survey," *Journal of Arizona History* 14 (1973): 350.

3. As cited in Roberts, "Minority-Group Poverty in Phoenix," 348.

4. Roberts, "Minority-Group Poverty in Phoenix," 328.

5. Roberts, "Minority-Group Poverty in Phoenix," 357–58.

6. Arthur G. Horton, *An Economic, Political and Social Survey of Phoenix and the Valley of the Sun* (Tempe, Ariz.: Southside Progress, 1941), 27.

7. Robert A. Trennert, *The Phoenix Indian School: Forced Assimilation in Arizona 1891–1935*. (Norman: University of Oklahoma Press, 1988), 72, 168.

8. Edward B. Liebow, "A Sense of Place: Urban Indians and the History of Pan-

Tribal Institutions in Phoenix, Arizona," Ph.D. dissertation, Arizona State University, 1986.

9. Helena Paivi Noikkala, "Native American Women and Community Work in Phoenix, 1965–1980," Ph.D. dissertation, Arizona State University, 1995.

10. U.S. Bureau of the Census, "Census 2000 Summary File 1," retrieved October 22, 2004 from http://factfinder.census.gov.

11. Leah S. Glaser, "The Story of Guadalupe, Arizona: The Survival and Preservation of a Yaqui Community," Ph.D. dissertation, Arizona State University, 1996.

12. Leah S. Glaser, "Working for Community: The Yaqui Indians at the Salt River Project," *Journal of Arizona History* 37 (1996): 337–57.

13. Glaser, "Working for Community," 347.

14. Glaser, "Working for Community," 347, 353.

15. Pete R. Dimas, *Progress and a Mexican American Community's Struggle for Existence: Phoenix's Golden Gate Barrio*, American University Studies Regional Studies, 10 (New York: Peter Lang, 1999), 22.

16. Bradford Luckingham, *Minorities in Phoenix* (Tucson: University of Arizona Press, 1994).

17. Simon, "Mixing Water and Culture," 63.

18. Luckingham, *Minorities in Phoenix*, 96.

19. Dimas, *Progress*, 61–62.

20. Dimas, *Progress*, 83–84.

21. Dimas, *Progress*, 50.

22. Dimas, *Progress*, 101–12.

23. U. S. Bureau of the Census, "Census 2000 Summary File 1."

24. Luckingham, *Minorities in Phoenix*, 110, 117.

25. Melissa Keane, A. E. Rogge, and Bradford Luckingham, *The Chinese in Arizona, 1870–1950: A Component of the Arizona Historic Preservation Plan* (Phoenix: Arizona State Historic Preservation Office, 1992), 6.

26. Keane et al., *The Chinese in Arizona*, 35.

27. Luckingham, *Minorities in Phoenix*, 82.

28. Keane et al., *The Chinese in Arizona*, 36.

29. Luckingham, *Minorities in Phoenix*, 82.

30. Luckingham, *Minorities in Phoenix*, 103.

31. U.S. Bureau of the Census, "Census 2000 Summary File 1."

32. Matthew C. Whiteaker, "In Search of Black Phoenicians: African American Culture and Community, 1868 to 1940," Master's thesis, Department of History, Arizona State University, 1997.

33. Whitaker, "In Search of Black Phoenicians."

34. Whitaker, "In Search of Black Phoenicians," 59.

35. Luckingham, *Minorities in Phoenix*, 133–34.

36. As cited in Whitaker, "In Search of Black Phoenicians," 56.

37. As cited in Whitaker, "In Search of Black Phoenicians," 63–64.

38. Luckingham, *Minorities in Phoenix*, 144.

39. Dolores Hayden, *A Field Guide to Sprawl* (New York: W.W. Norton, 2004).

40. American Religion Data Archive, "Religious Congregations & Memberships Maps and Reports," retrieved October 13, 2004 from www.thearda.com.

41. Mesa Public Schools, *Our Town: The Story of Mesa, Arizona, 1878–1991* (Mesa, Arizona: Mesa Public Schools, 1991), 50.

42. Mesa Historical Museum, "A Brief History of Mesa, Arizona," retrieved July 31, 2004 from http://www.mesaar.org/mesa/index.htm.

43. American Religion Data Archive, "Religious Congregations & Memberships."

44. U. S. Bureau of the Census, "Census 2000 Summary File 1."

45. U.S. Bureau of the Census, "Population Estimates."

46. *Philadelphia Inquirer*, "Phoenix Sprawls Past Philadelphia in Population," May 18, 2004, B1; *Philadelphia Inquirer*, "Philadelphia Still One on Phoenix," June 25, 2004. B1; John Talton, "Lucky Friday the 13th—Now the Real Work Begins," *Arizona Republic*, June 15, 2003, B1.

47. U.S. Bureau of the Census, "Population Estimates."

48. Arizona Department of Economic Security, "July 1, 1997 to July 1, 2050 Arizona County Population Projections," retrieved on September 20, 2004 from http://www.de.state.us/population.

49. U.S. Bureau of the Census, "Census 2000 County-to-County Migration Flows," retrieved September 19, 2004 from http://www.census.gov/population/www/cen2000/ctytoctyflow.html.

50. G. Wesley Johnson, Jr., *Phoenix: Valley of the Sun* (Tulsa, Okla.: Centennial Heritage Press, 1982.

51. William Cronon, *Nature's Metropolis: Chicago and the Great West* (New York: W.W. Norton, 1991).

52. Tom R. Rex, "Chicago and Phoenix Are Major Migration Partners," *Arizona Business* 49 (2002): 1–5.

53. U.S. Bureau of the Census, "Census 2000 Summary File 1."

54. U.S. Bureau of the Census, "Census 2000 Summary File 3."

55. William F. Frey, "Metropolitan Magnets for International and Domestic Migrants," 2003, retrieved September 22, 2004 from http://www.brookings.edu/metro/publications/200310_frey.htm.

56. U.S. Bureau of the Census. "Census 2000 Summary File 3."

57. John Harner, "The Mexican Community in Scottsdale, Arizona," *Yearbook, Conference of Latin Americanist Geographers* 26 (2000): 29–46.

58. U.S. Bureau of the Census. "Census 2000 Summary File 3."

59. Arizona Department of Economic Security, Refugee Resettlement Program, "Refugee Arrivals by Nationality and Year of Resettlement," March 8, 2001.

60. Neel Battacharjee and Patricia Gober, "Bosnian Refugee Resettlement in Phoenix," paper presented at the annual meeting of the Association of American Geographers, Los Angeles, March 2002.

61. Battacharjee and Gober, "Bosnian Refugee Resettlement in Phoenix."

62. Battacharjee and Gober, "Bosnian Refugee Resettlement in Phoenix."

63. Battacharjee and Gober, "Bosnian Refugee Resettlement in Phoenix."

64. Battacharjee and Gober, "Bosnian Refugee Resettlement in Phoenix."

65. Arizona Department of Health Services, "Advanced Arizona Vital Statistics for 2000," Section 1, Births by Mother's Age, Race/Ethnicity, and County of Residence.

66. Population Reference Bureau, *2004 World Population Data Sheet* (Washington, D.C.: Population Reference Bureau, 2004).

67. Kevin E. McHugh, Patricia Gober, and Daniel Borough, "The Sun City Wars: Chapter 3," *Urban Geography* 23 (2002): 627–48.

68. Maricopa County, "Seniors in Maricopa County: Background Report" (Phoenix: Maricopa County, 1997).

69. McHugh et al., "The Sun City Wars: Chapter 3," 633–35.

70. McHugh et al., "The Sun City Wars: Chapter 3," 639–40.

71. McHugh et al., "The Sun City Wars: Chapter 3," 644.

72. As cited in L. Baker and C. Elias, "Reactions Mixed to Dysart Turmoil Resignations over Luke: Jets has Foes, Friends," *Arizona Republic*, July 4, 2001, 1.

73. Patricia Gober, "Phoenix: A City of Migrants," unpublished report for the Morrison Institute of Public Policy, Arizona State University, 2000.

74. Motoko Rich, "Bring the Family," *Wall Street Journal*, June 25, 2001.

75. Anthem Activities Guide & Information, "A Message for You," Winter 2001/02: 4.

76. "Anthem Country Club," retrieved November 17, 2004 from http://www.del webb.com/homefinder/Community.aspx?ID = 100024.

77. Sarah JoAnne Brinegar, "Emergency Shelter Location and Homeless Family Displacement in the Phoenix Area," Ph.D. dissertation, Arizona State University, 2000.

78. Herberger Center for Design Excellence, Renaissance of the Capitol District, *Proceedings of the Capital Mall Charrette* (Tempe: Arizona State University, College of Architecture and Environmental Design, Herberger Center for Design Excellence Publications, 1996).

79. Sarah JoAnne Brinegar, "The Social Construction of Homeless Shelters in the Phoenix Area," *Urban Geography* 24 (January 2003): 61–74.

80. Brinegar, "Emergency Shelter Location," 33–35.

81. Brinegar, "Emergency Shelter Location," 36.

82. Brinegar, "Emergency Shelter Location," 38.

83. Don Mitchell, "Anti-homeless Laws and Public Space: I. Begging and the First Amendment," *Urban Geography* 19 (1998): 6–11; Don Mitchell, "Anti-homeless Laws and Public Space: II. Further Constitutional Issues,"*Urban Geography* 19 (1998): 98–104.

Chapter 4. You Can Never Get Hurt in Dirt

1. Jonathon Laing, "Phoenix Descending: Is Boomtown Going Bust?" *Barron's* (8 December 19, 1988).

2. "Banking on Growth," *Arizona Republic*, November 21, 2004, A1, A24.

3. "Philly vs. Phoenix," *Arizona Republic*, June 20, 2004, A1.

4. U.S. Bureau of the Census, "Census 2000 Summary File 1"; U.S. Bureau of the Census, "General Social Characteristics, Arizona, 1980."

5. Mary Jo Waits, Rebecca L. Gau, Mark Muro, Tina Valdecanas, Tom R. Rex, Leonard G. Bower, Elizabeth Burns, Lisa DeLorenzo, William Fulton, Patricia Gober, John Hall, Alicia Harrison, Kent Hill, Glen Krutz, and Scott Smith, *Hits and Misses: Fast Growth in Metropolitan Phoenix* (Tempe: Morrison Institute for Public Policy, Arizona State University, 2000), 19.

6. National Association of Realtors, "Median Sales Price of Existing Single-Family Homes for Metropolitan Areas," retrieved September 19, 2004 from http://www.realtor.org/publicaffairsweb.nsf/Pages/2QtrMetroPrices04?OpenDocument.

7. Bussel, Abby, "Report from Phoenix: City or Supersuburb?" *Progressive Architecture* 75 (1994): 58–63.

8. Arizona Department of Economic Security, "July 1, 1997 to July 1, 2050 Arizona County Population Projections," retrieved September 20, 2004 from http://www.de.state.us/population.

9. Maricopa Association of Governments, "View of the Valley in 2040: What Are We Leaving Our Grandchildren?" retrieved August 16, 2002 from http://www.mag.maricopa.gov/archive/PUB/PRESENT/Fullpresentation.pdf.

10. Grady Gammage, *Phoenix in Perspective: Reflections on Developing the Desert* (Tempe: Herberger Center for Design Excellence, College of Architecture and Environmental Design, Arizona State University, 1999), 68.

11. Carol E. Heim, "Leapfrogging, Urban Sprawl, and Growth Management: Phoenix, 1950–2000," *American Journal of Economics and Sociology* 60 (2001): 245–83.

12. Patricia Gober and Elizabeth K. Burns, "The Size and Shape of Phoenix's Urban Fringe," *Journal of Planning Research and Education* 21 (2002): 379–390.

13. Waits et al., *Hits and Misses*, 33.

14. As cited in Marty Sauerzopf, "Tiny Town Quietly Arranges a Boom," *Arizona Republic*, August 18, 2001, 1, 14.

15. As cited in Sauerzopf, "Tiny Town Quietly Arranges a Boom," 14.

16. Donna Benge, *Know Your Neighbor: The Salt River Pima and Maricopa Indians* (Mesa, Ariz.: Mesa Public Schools, 1974).

17. Gregory McNamee, *Gila: The Life and Death of an American River* (New York: Orion Books, 1994), 113.

18. Dick Glenn Winchell, "Space and Place of the Yavapai," Ph.D. dissertation., Arizona State University, 1982, 101.

19. Kenneth Madsen, "Edge City in Progress: The Case of the Salt River Pima-Maricopa Indian Community," report, Department of Geography, Arizona State University, 1997.

20. Gilbert Oral History Project, "Interviewee: Marvin Morrision," interviewed by Carol Shepard on July 9, 1992 at the Morrison Home, 12930 E. Elliot Road, Gilbert, Arizona.

21. Howard Morrison, personal communication, Morrison Ranch, August 4, 2004.

22. Morrison, personal communication.

23. Kevin E. McHugh and Robert C. Mings, "On the Road Again: Seasonal Migration to a Sunbelt Metropolis," *Urban Geography* 12 (1991): 1–18.

24. Sandy Bahr, "Proposition 202, the Citizen's Growth Management Initiative," Greater Phoenix Net, retrieved July 9, 2004 from http://www.greaterphoenix.net/work/opinions.htm.

25. Engineering News Record, "Desert Debate: Ballot Initiative Could Box in Arizona's Growth," July 3, 2000, 9.

26. City of Phoenix. "South Mountain Facts," retrieved September 19, 2004 from http://www.ci,phoenix.az.us/PARKS/hiksofac.html.

27. Arizona State University. "Dottie Gilbert and the Phoenix Mountain Preserves," retrieved September 19, 2004 from http://www.asu.edu/lib/archives/gilbert/index.html.

28. Gammage, *Phoenix in Perspective*, 99

29. Arizona State Land Department, "State Land Department Programs: Arizona Preserve Initiative Program," retrieved May 28, 2002 from http://www.land.state.az.us/programs/operations/api.htm.

30. Arizona State Land Department, "Public Auction Held by the State Land Department," retrieved September 17, 2004 from www.land.state.az.us/programs/realestate/auctions/results.htm.

31. Thomas Ropp and Lesley Wright, "Scottsdale Preserves Land," *Arizona Republic*, August 31, 2001, A1.

32. City of Scottsdale, *ESLO Users' Manual* (Scottsdale, Ariz.: Planning and Zoning Department, 1991).

33. K. Ingley, "Loopholes for Hillsides Upset Critics," *Arizona Republic*, July 29, 1996, A1, A5.

34. C. I. Provencio, "Hillside House Angers Residents," *Arizona Republic*, April 24, 2002.

Chapter 5. Not Another LA!

1. Peter Alshire, "LA-2," *Phoenix Magazine* 31 (December 1996): 62–94.

2. Bradford Luckingham, *Phoenix: The History of a Southwestern Metropolis* (Tucson: University of Arizona Press, 1989), 241.

3. Peter O. Muller, "Transportation and Urban Form: Stages in the Spatial Evolution of the American Metropolis," and Susan Hanson, ed., *The Geography of Urban Transportation* (New York: Guilford Press, 1995), 26–52.

4. Dean Smith, *Tempe: Arizona Crossroads* (Chatsworth, Calif.: Windsor Publications, 1990), 163.

5. Allen Roberts, Thomas Graham, and Claudia Anderson, *Historic Homes of Phoenix: An Architectural & Preservation Guide* (Phoenix: City of Phoenix Publication, 1992), 34–43.

6. As cited in Jerry W. Abbitt, *History of Transit in the Valley of the Sun* (Phoenix: City of Phoenix Transit System, 1990), 10.

7. Abbitt, *History of Transit*, 11–12.

8. Luckingham, *Phoenix: The History of a Southwestern Metropolis*, 91.

9. Charles Sargent, ed., *Metro Arizona* (Scottsdale, Ariz.: Biffington Books, 1988).

10. City of Phoenix, *Willow Neighborhood Conservation Plan* (Phoenix: City of Phoenix Planning Department, 1991), 3.

11. City of Phoenix, *Story Neighborhood Conservation Plan* (Phoenix: City of Phoenix Planning Department, 1991), 3.

12. City of Phoenix, *Neighborhood Conservation Plan for the Coronado Neighborhood* (Phoenix: City of Phoenix Planning Department, 1991), 4–7.

13. Roberts et al., *Historic Homes of Phoenix*, 44.

14. Roberts et al., *Historic Homes of Phoenix*, 45.

15. Abbitt, *History of Transit*, 13–15.

16. Lawrence J. Fleming, *Ride a Mile and Smile the While: A History of the Phoenix Street Railway, 1887–1948* (Phoenix: Swaine Publications, 1977), 122.

17. G. Wesley Johnson Jr., *Phoenix: Valley of the Sun* (Tulsa: Centennial Heritage Press, 1982), 95–97.

18. As cited in Abbitt, *History of Transit*, 36.

19. *Urban Transport Fact Book*, "Personal Vehicle & Public Transport Market Share from 1945" retrieved on November 19, 2001 from www.publicpurpose.com/ ut-usptshare45.htm.

20. Abbitt, *History of Transit*, 89.

21. Abbitt, *History of Transit*, 133.

22. Luckingham, *Phoenix: The History of a Southwestern Metropolis*, 200–201.

23. Roberts et al., *Historic Homes of Phoenix*, 10.

24. Texas Transportation Institute, "Mobility Data 2001," retrieved December 4, 2001 from

    http://mobility.tamu.edu/2001/study/cities/tables/complete data.xls.

25. Texas Transportation Institute, "Mobility Data 2004," retrieved October 20, 2004 from http://mobility.tamu.edu/ums/congestion_data/tables/national/ table_1.pdf.

26. Texas Transportation Institute, "Mobility Data 2004."

27. John Pickus and Patricia Gober, "Urban Villages and Activity Patterns in Phoenix," *Urban Geography* 9 (1988): 85–97.

28. Elizabeth K. Burns and Patricia Gober, "Job Linkages in Inner-City Phoenix,"*Urban Geography* 19 (1998): 12–23.

29. Scottsdale Chamber of Commerce, "Business Areas," retrieved March 16, 2005 from http://www.scottsdalechamber.com/economic/index.html#Business.

30. City of Scottsdale, *City of Scottsdale 2002–2004 Economic Vitality Strategy Plan* (Scottsdale, Ariz.: Economic Vitality Department, 2002).

31. Jay Q. Butler, "Home Sales, Appreciation Rates at All-time High in 2003," *Arizona Business* 51 (2004): 1–11.

32. Gene Slechta, "Scottsdale Airpark Employment/Housing Study," report, Department of Geography, Arizona State University, 2003.

33. Greater Phoenix Economic Council, "Greater Phoenix Call Center Listing and Map," Retrieved July 16, 2004 from http://www.gpec.org/InfoCenter/Reports/ callcenter.html.

34. Lima & Associates, "Transportation Needs Study for the Ahwatukee Foothills Village," Prepared for the City of Phoenix, December 2000.

35. Butler, "Home Sales, Appreciation Rates at All-time High in 2003," 9.

36. Richard Werbal and Peter Haas, "Factors Influencing Voting Results of Local Transportation Funding Initiatives with a Substantial Transit Component: Case Studies of Ballot Measures in Eleven Communities," Mineta Transportation Institute (San Jose, Calif.: San Jose State University College of Business, 2001), retrieved July 2, 2004 from http://transweb.sjsu.edu/publications/ BallotMeasures.htm.

37. Werbal and Haas, "Factors Influencing Voting Results," 72–82.

38. John S. Pipkin, "Disaggregate Models of Travel Behavior," in Susan Hanson, ed., *The Geography of Urban Transportation* (New York: Guilford Press, 1995), 188–239.

39. Carol Atkinson-Palombo, "How Much TOD Is Needed to Make Light Rail Work? Phoenix—A Case Study," report, Department of Geography, Arizona State University, 2003.

40. U.S. Bureau of the Census, "Census 2000 Summary File 3."

Chapter 6. Downtown Redevelopment: A Tale of Two Cities

1. Peter Russell, "Downtown's Downturn: A Historical Geography of the Phoenix, Ariz., Central Business District, 1890–1986," master's thesis, Arizona State University, 1986, 37–40.

2. Dean Smith, *Tempe: Arizona Crossroads* (Chatsworth, Calif.: Windsor Publications, 1990), 50.

3. As cited in Smith, *Tempe: Arizona Crossroads*, 46.

4. Russell, "Downtown's Downturn," 92.

5. Russell, "Downtown's Downturn," 67.

6. Charles Sargent, ed., *Metro Arizona* (Scottsdale, Ariz.: Biffington Books, 1988), 47.

7. Russell, "Downtown's Downturn," 77.

8. Smith, *Tempe, Arizona Crossroads*, 88.

9. Ernest J. Hopkins and Alfred Thomas, Jr., *The Arizona State University Story* (Phoenix: Arizona Southwest Publishing, 1960), 263.

10. Russell, "Downtown's Downturn," 21.

11. Michael H. Bernstein, "Geographical Perspectives on Skid Row in Phoenix, Arizona," masters thesis, Arizona State University, 1972, 31.

12. Bernstein, "Geographical Perspectives on Skid Row," 57–63.

13. Bernstein, "Geographical Perspectives on Skid Row," 71–72; Russell, "Downtown's Downturn," 118–120.

14. Bernard J. Frieden and Lynne B. Sagalyn, *Downtown, Inc.: How America Rebuilds Cities.* (Cambridge, Mass.: MIT Press, 1990), 39.

15. Herberger Center for Design Excellence, *Renaissance of the Capitol District, Proceedings of the Capital Mall Charrette* (Tempe: Arizona State University, College of Architecture and Environmental Design, Herberger Center for Design Excellence Publications, 1996), 7–8.

16. Bradford Luckingham, *Phoenix: The History of a Southwestern Metropolis* (Tucson: University of Arizona Press, 1989), 240.

17. Karrie Jacobs, "Public Space: Can an Ambitious Program of Public Buildings, Including a Dramatic New Library, Turn a Sprawling Urban Area into a Real City?" *Metropolis* (March 1996): 56–69.

18. Jodie Snyder, "State's 'Big Ambitions' Seen in TGen Center," *Arizona Republic* (June 13, 2003).

19. John Talton, "Lucky Friday the 13th—Now the Real Work Begins," *Arizona Republic* (June 15, 2003), B1.

20. Gerald Ray Stricklin, "Transition in the Tempe, Arizona Central Business District," master's thesis, Arizona State University, 1976, 105.

21. Matthew R. Holochwost, "Changing Perceptions About the Role of the Central Business District: Downtown Tempe, 1968–1997." master's thesis, Arizona State University, 1997, 25–31.

22. Holochwost, "Changing Perceptions About the Role of the Central Business District," 34–35.

23. As cited in Stricklin, "Transition in the Tempe, Arizona Central Business District," 123.

24. Holochwost, "Changing Perceptions About the Role of the Central Business District," 82.

25. Holochwost, "Changing Perceptions About the Role of the Central Business District," 52–53.

26. Harry Mitchell, personal communication, June 3, 2002 at State Office Building, 1700 West Washington Street, Phoenix.

27. H. E. Mitchell, "Mill Avenue Oral History Project," interview conducted by Ron McCoy in 1988. Tempe: Arizona State University, Department of Archives and Manuscripts.

28. Lee McPheters, "The Economic Impact of America West Airlines on Arizona," report prepared for America West Airlines, 2001.

29. City of Tempe, "Tempe Town Lake: Historic Timeline," retrieved July 31, 2004 from http://www.tempe.gov/rio/LakeHistory/timlin.htm.

30. Mary Jo Waits and Chi Nguyen, *The Downtowns of the Future: Opportunities for Regional Stewards* (Tempe: Morrison Institute for Public Policy, Arizona State University, 2001).

31. Alfred Simon, "Mixing Water and Culture: Making the Canal Landscape in Phoenix," Ph.D. dissertation, Arizona State University, 2002, 127–141.

Chapter 7. Thinking Small and Living Big

1. Peter Alshire, "L.A. 2," *Phoenix Magazine* 31 (December 1996): 62–94.

2. Arizona Department of Economic Security, "Population Estimates for Arizona Counties, Incorporated Places, and Balance of County Areas," retrieved March 23, 2005 from http://www.workforce.az.gov/admin/uploadedPublications/ 1468_EEC04.pdf.

3. Arizona Department of Economic Security, "Phoenix, Mesa, Scottsdale Metropolitan Area Labor Force and Nonfarm Employment," retrieved March 23, 2005 from http://www.workforce.az.gov/admin/uploadedPublications/635_phxnaics.exl.

4. Butler, Jay Q., "Single Family Construction Increases in Third Quarter," *Arizona Business* 51 (January 2004): 6; Butler, Jay Q., "Single-Family Commercial Construction Up in First Quarter," *Arizona Business* 51 (July 2004): 5.

5. Butler, Jay Q., "Housing Affordability Faces Uncertain Future," *Arizona Business* 51 (December 2004): 5.

6. Dolores Hayden, *A Field Guide to Sprawl* (New York: W. W. Norton, 2004), 7–8.

7. J. T Houghton, et al., eds., *Climate Change 2001: The Scientific Basis* (Cambridge: Cambridge University Press, 2001).

INDEX

Active Management Areas (AMA), 47–48

Adams, Betty Gregg, 173

Adams Hotel, 27, 79, 174

Adams, John C., 79

African Americans, 29, 54, 70–74

African Methodist Episcopal Church, 71

Age restrictions, 88–90

Agritainment, 121–22

Ahwatukee, 74, 129, 161–62, 203

Ahwatukee Foothills, 136

Ahwatukee Urban Village, 161–62

Air conditioning, 32–33, 205

Air quality, 48–50

Ak Chin Indian Community, 109, 113, 115

Albuquerque, 13, 30

Allen, John, 41

Allenville, 41–42

Alluvial fans, 13

America West Airlines, 189–90

Andre Building, 190

Andres, Cecil, 46

Annexation, 34–35, 126

Anthem, 88, 94–95, 108–10, 202

Apache Indians, 16–17, 59, 113

Apache Junction, 3, 105, 123

Aquifers, 12–13, 45, 205

Arizona Biltmore Hotel, 7, 79

Arizona Canal, 20, 25, 26, 42, 43, 59–60, 197

Arizona Center, 181–83

Arizona Falls, 21, 25

Arizona Groundwater Code, 47

Arizona monsoon, 33

Arizona Preserve Initiative, 131–32

Arizona Science Center, 182

Arizona State College, 159, 174

Arizona State Hospital, 28

Arizona State University (ASU), 159, 172, 183, 185–87, 195, 202

Arizona Territorial Normal School, 172

Arizona Water Banking Authority, 48

Army Corps of Engineers, 42

Asians, 69–70, 84

Atlanta, 78, 83, 107, 202

Austin, 78

Automobile city, 139–41, 147–48, 164, 166–67

Avondale, 105

Babbitt, Bruce, 41, 46–47

Bank One Ballpark, 182

Barrios, 62, 63, 66

Bartlett, Adolphus, 79

Bartlett-Heard Land and Cattle Company, 145

Bartlett, Maie, 79

Basin and Range Physiographic Province, 11

Beatty, Elizabeth, 27
Bedrock pediments, 13
Black Canyon Freeway, 150
Boomburbs, 78
Bosnians, 85–86
Boston, 107
Bradshaw Mountains, 13, 16
Braun, Father Albert, 64–65
Buckeye, 3, 41, 105, 110–11, 125

Camelback Mountain, 6, 13, 25, 125
Camp Hyder, 30–31
Capitol Mall District, 96, 178
Carefree, 3, 105
Carter, Jimmy, 46
Casa Blanca, 143
Casa Loma Hotel, 190–91
Casinos, 112, 116, 123
Catholic Social Services, 85
Cave Creek, 3, 105
Central Arizona Groundwater Replenish-
    ment District (CAGRD), 48
Central Arizona Project (CAP), 11, 39–40,
    45, 46, 109, 116, 137, 184, 195
Chandler, 27, 60, 78, 107, 115, 172, 198
Chavez, Cesar, 65
Chicago, 5, 28, 30, 53–54, 79–80, 85,
    90, 141, 145, 153, 167, 170, 177
Chinatown, 68–69, 175
Chinese, 54, 67–70
Christown Mall, 174
Christy, Lloyd B., 147
Church of Jesus Christ of Latter-Day
    Saints (LDS; Mormons), 54, 74–77,
    113
Citizens for Growth Management Initia-
    tive, 125

Citizens for Tax Equity, 91–92
City of Zion town plan, 76
Climate change, 205
Colangelo, Jerry, 80–81
Colley, Marguerite, 27
Colorado Plateau, 11
Colorado River Basin, 11
Colorado River Compact, 39–40, 205
Commuting, 167
Considine, Bob, 37
Coronado Neighborhood, 146–47
Corrigan, Joyce, 135
Cotton production, 25–26
Counterculture, 187–88
Cronon, William, 80
Crosscut Canal, 59
Crow, Michael, 185

Dallas, 35, 153, 167
Davis, Arthur P., 24
Davis, Sallie Calvert, 20
Deer Valley School District, 95
Del Monte Market, 111
Del Webb Corporation, 37
Densification, 140, 203
Density transfer, 136
Denver, 30, 153
Desert landscaping, 95, 129–30
Desert Mission, 27
Detroit, 107, 170
Deuce, 96, 97, 175, 176, 178
Díaz, Porfirio, 58
Dines, James, 193
Dodge Theater, 182
Downtown: history, 171–75; (re)develop-
    ment, 163, 169–99
Dreamy Draw, 6
Drought, 13, 23, 205

Duppa, Darrell, 17, 20
Dysart School District, 88, 91–93

Early Western Ranch architecture, 146
East Mesa, 123
El Paso, 13
Elmore, James, 195
Employment-housing imbalance,
    161–62
Encanto-Palmcroft Neighborhood, 148
English Cottage architecture, 146
Environmentally Sensitive Lands Ordi-
    nance (ESLO), 135–36
Evaporative cooling, 7, 29, 32, 205

F. Q. Story Neighborhood, 146
Farming, 12–13, 16–17, 19–22, 25–26,
    46, 103, 111, 115–22
Floods, 17, 23, 40–43, 62, 145, 205
Fort McDowell, 16–17, 61
Fort McDowell Indian Community, 115
Fort Whipple, 18
Fountain Hills, 74
Frank Lloyd Wright School of Architec-
    ture, 7
Frederick Douglass Elementary School,
    72
Freeways, 140, 150–55, 163
Fresno, 90

Gárfias, Henry, 61
Gated communities, 54–55
Gateway cities, 83
Gila River, 13, 14, 16
Gila River Indian Community, 113, 117,
    161
Gila River reservation, 16
Gilbert, 78, 172

Gilbert, Dorothy, 129
Glendale, 98, 165, 172, 197, 202
Goddard, Terry, 180–83
Golden Gate Barrio, 63–67
Goodwin Airdome, 173
Goodwin Opera House, 173
Goodyear, 25
Gordon, Phil, 102
Grand Canal, 20
Granite Reef Dam, 42
Green, Mary, 70
Greer Ranch, 36
Groundwater Management Act of 1970,
    116
Growing Smarter Act, 125
Growing Smarter Plus, 126
Growth management, 101, 124–28
Guadalupe, 58–61

Hackett House, 190–91
Hance, Margaret, 181
Hancock, Willam A., 17
Harkins, Dan, 174
Harkins, Dwight "Red," 174
Hayden, Carl, 20, 128
Hayden, Charles Trumbell, 18–20, 75,
    141, 172, 193
Hayden, Dolores, 73, 203
Hayden's Flour Mill, 190
Heard, Dwight Bancroft, 26, 79, 143,
    145, 148, 193
Heard, Maie Bartlett, 143
Heard Museum of Native Cultures and
    Art, 79, 122
Heritage Square, 142, 180
Hillhouse, Reverend Joseph, 27
Hispanics, 29, 66–67, 82, 84, 87
Historical preservation, 151, 188–93

Hohokam, 1, 12, 13–16, 20, 112–13
Homeless, 88, 95–99, 170, 178
Honolulu, 78
Hope, Bob, 37
Hopeville, 42
Hotel Adams, 79
Houston, 102, 153
Hull, Jane Dee, 125–26

Illinois, 81
Immigrants, immigration, 83–87, 157
Indian Bend Wash, 42–45, 84
Indian Gaming Regulatory Act, 116
Indians. See Native Americans; tribes
Ingleside Inn, 25, 27
Inner loop, 151
International Genomics Consortium
    (IGC), 184
International Rescue Committee, 85
Irrigation canals, 14–17, 20–21, 35, 193

Jacobs, Jane, 94
John C. Lincoln Hospital, 27
John F. Long Homes, 33
Jones, Daniel Webster, 75–76

Laird and Dines Building, 174, 190–93
Laird, Hillary and Clara, 191–92
Lake Havasu City, 11
Las Vegas, 13, 78, 83, 104, 116
Lath House, 180
Laveen, 105, 111–12
Leapfrog development, 108–10, 135,
    203
Lehi, 77
Levittown, 33
Light rail, 140, 162–66, 185, 202
Lincoln, Helen, 27

Lincoln, John C., 27
Litchfield Naval Air Facility, 30
Litchfield Park, 25, 31
Litchfield, Paul W., 25
Long, John F., 33–34, 149, 201
Los Angeles, 3, 22, 30, 35, 104, 107,
    140, 153, 155, 160; freeways, 151
Luhrs Building and Tower, 173
Luke Air Force Base, 30, 93

Maricopa Association of Governments
    (MAG), 105, 153
Maricopa Canal, 20
Maricopa County Board of Supervisors,
    4, 23
Maricopa County Flood Control District,
    43
Maricopa Freeway, 150
Maricopa Indians, 113
Marley, Kemper, 135
Maryvale, 33–34, 39, 201
Master-planned communities, 33–34,
    54–55, 93–95, 102, 109, 120–22, 161,
    203, 207
Maxwell, George H., 23–24
Mazatzal Mountains, 13
McArthur, Albert, 7, 79
McArthur, Charles, 79
McArthur, Warren, 79
McDowell Mountain Preserve, 133–35,
    202
McDowell Mountains, 43
Mediterranean architecture, 148
Mercado, 76–78, 87, 183–84
Mesa, 49, 77, 78, 97–98, 115, 164–66,
    172, 174, 198–99
Mesa Canal, 76
Mexican Americans, 61–67

Mexicans, 2, 54, 61–67, 83–85, 157, 202

Miami, 78, 80, 153

Migration, 53, 81–87

Mill Avenue, 19, 174, 188–89

Mill Avenue Merchants Association (MAMA), 188–89

Milwaukee, 177

Minneapolis-St. Paul, 78, 81, 90

Mitchell, Harry, 189, 195

Monti, Leonard, 141–42

Montini, E. J., 1

Monti's La Casa Vieja Restaurant, 141–42, 190

Mormons, See Church of Jesus Christ of Latter Day Saints

Morrison, Howard and Leatha, 118–19

Morrison, Marvin and Kenneth, 119–20

Morrison Ranch, 119–20

Motorola, 32, 79–80

Mumford, Lewis, 94

Murphy, William John, 25

National Reclamation Act of 1902, 23–24

Native Americans, 54, 56–61, 112–17

Naturalization, 84–85

Neoterritorial architecture, 190

New Economy, 188, 196, 203

New River, 105

New Urbanism architecture, 109, 121

New York, 4, 5, 30, 80, 121, 141, 159, 167

North Scottsdale, 74, 107

Norton, W. R., 26

Oklahoma City, 161

Omaha, 78

Open space preservation, 128–35, 206

Orange County, 104

Orpheum Theater, 181

Ortero, Jesús, 62

Ozone, 48–49

Papago Nation, 16

Papago Park, 6, 21, 75

Paradise Valley, 151

Park Central Mall, 174

Particulates, 49–50

Patriot Square, 181

Pedestrian city, 140–41

Peoria, 78, 80, 172

Peoria School District, 90–91

Peplow, Edward H., Jr., 35

Period Revival architecture, 146

Philadelphia, 78, 102, 107

Phoenix Arts Commission, 25

Phoenix Civic Plaza, 96, 178–79, 183, 185

Phoenix Indian School, 56–57, 146

Phoenix Mountain Preserve, 129, 204

Phoenix Mountains, 42–43

Phoenix Mountains Preservation Council, 129

Phoenix Municipal Airport, 28

Phoenix Municipal Courthouse, 182

Phoenix Museum of History, 182

Phoenix Railway Company, 142–43, 146, 148–50

Phoenix Real Estate Board, 72

Phoenix Street Paving Association, 147

Phoenix Symphony Hall, 178

Phoenix War Housing Committee, 31

Piestawa Peak, 6, 13

Pima Indians, 11, 14, 16, 18, 76, 113, 115

Pima Nation, 16

Pima Villages, 113

Pittsburgh, 1, 170

Pizzeria Bianco, 180

Pollution, 48–50

Portland, 81, 101

Prescott, 18, 19

Proposition 101, 127–28

Proposition 202, 125–28

Proposition 300, 152

Pueblo Grande, 15

Puerto Ricans, 59

Pulliam, Eugene, 150–51

Pumpkinville, 17

Queen Creek, 3, 105, 121

Racial succession, 73

Radio Bosnie i Herzegovie, 86

Railroads, 22, 55, 142

Recreational vehicle (RV) resorts,
    122–24

Renaissance Park, 181

Renaissance Square, 181

Reservations, 113–17

Residential segregation, 55–74

Retirement communities, 2, 36–39, 88–
    90, 207

Rimsza, Skip, 184

Rio Salado Project, 195–96

Rio Verde, 74

Roosevelt Dam, 24, 25, 193–94

Roosevelt, Theodore, 23–24, 145

Roserzweig, Newton, 178

Rosson House, 142, 180

Rowan and Martin's Laugh-In, 37

Sacramento, 104

Sacred Heart Church, 64–66

Salt Lake Basin, 75

Salt Lake City, 161

Salt River, 5, 11, 13, 14, 16–18, 20, 23–
    24, 40, 42, 75, 145, 193, 205

Salt River Indian Community, 113–15,
    117

Salt River Project (SRP), 24–25, 29, 35,
    45, 61, 145, 197

Salt River reservation, 16

Salt River Valley Canal, 20

Salt River Valley Water Users Associa-
    tion (SRVWUA), 24, 59

San Antonio, 28, 197

San Carlos Hotel, 174

San Diego, 28, 102, 140, 153

San Francisco, 5, 22, 104, 140, 153, 167

San Marcos Hotel, 27

San Tan Mountains, 13

Sandra Day O'Connor Federal Court-
    house, 182

Scenic Airways, 28

Schleifer, Ben, 36–37

Schnepf Farm, 121–22

Scottsdale, 27, 42–45, 65, 74, 84, 98,
    115, 135–36, 157–60, 172, 197–98,
    202

Scottsdale Airpark, 158–160, 203

Scottsdale Fashion Square, 174, 197

Scottsdale Waterfront South Associates,
    198

Seattle, 5, 30, 81, 102, 104

Senior Citien Overlay District, 89

Sense of place, 8, 53, 109, 137, 140, 161,
    177, 205

Sherman, General Moses Hazeltine,
    142–43, 145, 148–49

Shirley, Frank, 71

Sierra Club, 125

Sierra Estrella Mountains, 13, 111

Silicon Desert, 198

Sioux City, 161

Sirrine, Theodore, 76

Skid row, 9–97, 175–76

Sky Harbor Airport, 28, 35, 51, 65, 66, 79, 123, 157, 159, 164

Smith, Arthur, 71

Smith, John Y. T., 17, 113

Smith, Randolph, 71

Snout house, 104

Snowbirds, 112, 122–24

Social fragmentation, 54, 87–88, 93–94, 99

Social geography, 28, 62, 145

Sonoran Desert, 5–6, 9, 11

South Mountain, 6

South Mountain Park, 6, 128, 161, 204

South Phoenix, 72, 118, 145

Southern Pacific Railroad, 68

Spanish architecture, 148

Spanish Colonial Revival architecture, 146, 193

Sperry Rand, 32

Sports, 80–81

Square One, 181

St. Louis, 5, 17, 90, 177

St. Mary's Basilica, 63, 178

St. Mary's Catholic Church, 62, 63

Starbucks, 177

State trust lands, 130–35

Stegner, Wallace, 53, 118

Stevens, Robert, 71

Street naming, 17–18

Streetcar city, 141, 143

Streetcars, 142–45, 148–50

Sun Cities, 73–74

Sun City, 2, 3, 37–39, 88–90, 201

Sun City Grand, 38, 202

Sun City West, 38, 88, 92, 93

Sun Lakes, 201

Sunnyslope, 26–27, 201

Sunshine, 30

Superstition Mountains, 13

Swilling Irrigating and Canal Company, 17

Swilling, Jack, 17, 19, 61, 68, 113

Swilling, Trinidad Escalante, 61

Symington, Fife, 153, 164, 181–83

Taliesin, 6

Taliesin West, 7

Tanner, L. A., 150

Telephone call centers, 160

Tempe, 5, 17, 18, 19, 60–61, 65, 75, 98, 141–42, 163–66, 169–74, 176, 186–96, 199, 202–3

Tempe Beach Park, 194–95

Tempe Hardware, 190–91

Tempe Normal School, 172

Tempe Town Lake, 170, 193, 195, 204

Thomas Mall, 174

Thompson, Dave, 165

Thunderbird Field, 30

Tohono O'odham Nation, 16

Tolleson, 105

Tolmachoff, Mary, 33

Tonopah, 105

Tower Plaza, 174

Traffic congestion, 152, 154–55, 159–60, 162, 164

Translational Research Institute (TGen), 184–85

Transnational lifestyles, 54, 84

Trent, Jeffrey, 184

Tri City Mall, 174

Trip linking, 166

Tucson, 11, 18, 19, 47, 58–59, 131–32, 172, 206

Tulsa, 78
Turner, E. S., home, 4

United Farmworkers Union, 65
Urban heat island, 50–51, 206
Urban sprawl, 8, 104, 107, 126, 203
Urban village, 112, 155–57, 177, 203
U.S. Environmental Protection Agency
    (EPA), 48
Usury Mountains, 13
Utah Ditch, 76
Utahville, 75–77

Valley Art Theater, 174
Verde River, 11, 16, 24, 205
Vernacular architecture, 141
Verrado, 55, 88, 109–10, 129, 202
Victorian architecture, 142, 193
Vienna Bakery, 190–91

Washington, D.C., 107

Webb, Delbert Eugene, 2, 26, 38, 94
Webb, Lee, 59
Westward Ho Hotel, 174
White Tank Mountains, 13
Wickenburg, 17, 105
Wilcox, Mary Rose, 4
Williams Airfield, 30
Willow Neighborhood, 146
Works Projects Administration (WPA), 28
World War I, 25
World War II, 30
Wright, Frank Lloyd, 6–7, 26, 79
Wright, Frank Lloyd School of Architec-
    ture, 7
Wrigley, William K., 79

Yaqui Indians, 43, 57–61
Yavapai Indians, 113–14
Young, Brigham, 76
Youngtown, 36–38, 88

ACKNOWLEDGMENTS

A great many people read early drafts of this book and helped me to focus the message and refine the prose. Their feedback prevented me from making serious mistakes in logic and presentation. I am forever grateful to Lauren Kuby, Karen Gronberg, and my daughter, Kelly Graf, for their editorial work. Helpful substantive suggestions came from Carol Atkinson-Palombo, Anthony Brazel, Ron Dorn, Andrew Ellis, Gail Fisher, John Keane, Matthew Lord, Nancy Welch, Elizabeth Wentz, and Louis Weschler. I am especially grateful to Judith Martin, the editor of this series, for her careful reading and thorough editing, for keeping me on message, and for helping me to develop a more readable writing style. Barbara Trapido-Lurie translated my ideas for illustrations into maps and figures and lent her eye for design to graphics that convey a geographer's sense of place. Special thanks also go to the National Science Foundation's Decision Center for a Desert City (NSF-0345945) for its insights into the regional climate, water management, and decision making under uncertainty.

This material is based on work supported by the National Science Foundation under Grant No. SES-0345945. Any opinions, findings, and conclusions or recommendations expressed in this material are those of the author and do not necessarily reflect the views of the National Science Foundation.